Camping

Aujourd'hui 34°
Demain 33°
Lendemain 29°

coolcamping

europe

SECOND EDITION

Andrew Day, Sophie Dawson, Keith Didcock, David Jones,
Jonathan Knigh̶ ̶ ̶ ̶ ̶ ̶ ̶ ̶ ̶ ̶ ̶ ̶rner Smith,
R

TELEPHONE CODES	
Portugal 00 351	Switzerland 00 41
Spain 00 34	Italy 00 39
France 00 33	Slovenia 00 386
Luxembourg 00 352	Croatia 00 385
Germany 00 49	Greece 00 30
Austria 00 43	

introduction

We keep hearing that the Eurozone is in crisis. UKIP want out and, as public opinion is stirred up, the rhetoric has reached fever pitch. A Greek exit (a 'Grexit' no less – who makes these words up?) is being talked about, which would signal the slow demise of this grand experiment. In fact, by the time you read this, the Grexit may have already happened. That's the problem with these old-fashioned books, you can't refresh the copy to keep up with the 24-hour news cycle.

Slow down, people. Europe is here to stay. And thank goodness, we say.

Okay, so you're unlikely to see Nigel Farage glamping in Slovenia any time soon, and the chances of the next Tory party conference being held in a giant tipi in the forests of Germany are slim. But that just leaves all the more room for us and our tent pegs!

Europe is superb for camping. The outdoor attractions on offer read like a manifesto for perfect holidays. Sunscorched Mediterranean beaches promise horizontal relaxation and banana-boat fun, while those on the Atlantic Coast offer a comfortable breeze-cooled atmosphere,
with surfers and kite-surfers settling into camping digs for the season. For altitude junkies, the mountains of the Alps and the Pyrénées stand out not only for an abundance of exhilarating spring and summer activities, but also for truly epic views and some of the most scenic camping pitches in the world (turn to p166 if you don't believe the hype). The cooling lakes and rivers of the continent's interior incite activity and adventure at every turn, with some truly spectacular kayaking and swimming opportunities. And let's not forget the walking, climbing, cycling… there's so much on offer, it's difficult to know where to start!

Well, the best place to start is probably with the campsite itself. This book curates what we consider to be a collection of the very best sites across the continent, from humble tent encampments on olive groves in the Mediterranean sun to grand glamping innovations offering a choice of domes, yurts and tipis.

You may notice a trend in that, the further east you travel, the greater the emphasis on the more traditional, smaller sites; while the further west you go in the direction of Spain and Portugal, the more glamping options you encounter. Those more advanced tourist destinations have fully embraced luxury camping, particularly in the hotter climes, where the outdoorsy magic of glamping is enhanced exponentially by the warm air and sunshine. But wherever they are, we have picked the best of both types of camping.

Notable new glamping options include the stunning domed lodges at Glisten Camping in the Basque Country, France (p98), cool tree-house bungalows in a spectacular national park at Lima Escape, Portugal (p40) and glass-fronted glamping 'tubes' made from recycled materials, at O Tamanco, Portugal (p26).

Traditionalists will be keen to explore the simple life at Camping Islas Cíes (p42), located among a group of uninhabited islands off the western coast of Spain, or Camping Chantemerle in Southern France (p140), where shady riverside pitches are the perfect base for wild swimming and exploring the nearby Cévennes mountains. For spectacular alpine views, take your pick from Panorama Camping Sonnenberg (p242) in Austria, or Camping Arolla (p246) and Camping des Glaciers (p250), both in Switzerland. Beach lovers can savour the sand beneath their toes at the bar at Eco Camp Glavotok, Croatia (p294) with an occasional dip in the cool, blue water; or head to Tartaruga, Greece (p302) for ridiculous panoramic views of the Ionian Sea and an opportunity to go swimming with turtles. And if it's idylic waterfront camping you want, then there's also the pitches among the orange trees at Camping Antiparos (p310), where the friendly owners will gladly give you a discount if you turn up clutching a copy of this very book!

This is by no means an exhaustive list – a book that big would be hard to carry! But for one-stop holidays, shorter road trips, or for guaranteeing a backbone of cracking sites on a season-long sojourn, we reckon this collection is pretty hard to beat.

We're voting to stay in Europe. Preferably for the whole summer.

Jonathan Knight
Chief Camper

campsite locator

Hamburg

69

Berlin

GERMANY

Prague

CZECH
REPUBLIC

73

Munich

74

75

6

AUSTRIA

D

80

Innsbruck

Vienna

Maribor

81

91

92

90

SLOVENIA

2

Venice

Zagreb

93

83

94

84

CROATIA

Florence

85

95

86

87

Dubrovnik

88

Rome

ITALY

Naples

89

GREECE

99

96

Palermo

97

Athens

98

100

campsite locator

campsites at a glance

quinta dos carriços

Praia da Salema, 8650-196 Budens, Portugal 00351 282 695 201 www.quintadoscarricos.com

If you're dreaming of guaranteed sunshine, a decent beach, peace, privacy and clean facilities, plus an onsite restaurant so you don't have to move a muscle – oh, and good transport links – then how about this for camping nirvana?

Situated far enough from the Algarve's overdeveloped tourist resorts but within reach of some lively shopping and bar action, this walled, Eden-like campsite is a perfect balance of peace and ease. Marked plots near the entrance are spacious, terraced along tree-lined avenues, and there's a second zone of larger pitches, but wherever you end up you're guaranteed shade – a blessing under the hot Portuguese sun. Hieroglyphs of naked people signal the entrance to the naturist area, but you don't need to worry about *Carry on Camping* antics or wobbly bits at every turn; naturists keep out of sight of clothed campers. It's also a very green site: over the past two decades the owners have planted seeds and cuttings from their travels, creating a botanical mayhem that will make you feel as if you're camping in a garden centre.

If you want to venture further afield, make the 20-minute drive to the lighthouse at Cabo de São Vicente – the most southwesterly tip of Europe (next stop, America) – preferably at a time when you can catch the majestic sunset. Closer to home, a short amble will take you to nearby Salema beach – like many on the Algarve, it's full of pink-skinned Northern Europeans wishing that life could be like this every day.

COOL FACTOR Sunshine, peace and a gorgeous sandy beach.

WHO'S IN Tents, caravans, mobile homes, naturists, well-behaved kids and dogs – yes.

ON SITE Pitches are spread across several different areas, with a specific zone for naturist camping. There are also 13 apartments available (sleeping 2–4). 3 wash-blocks, each with 10 showers, 9 toilets (1 disabled) and 4 urinals, and a unisex block for naturists. Unlimited internet access during your stay is €3, including use of the site computer. A small shop sells food and camping essentials and bikes are available for hire.

OFF SITE Let children run off steam at Albufeira's huge Zoomarine waterpark (289 560 300; www.zoomarine.pt). You can also spot dolphins on a specially designed boat with Algarve Dolphins (282 087 587; algarve-dolphins.com). Water sports a-plenty can be found all along this part of the coast (paddling, surfing, boat rental) and diving is also hugely popular. Much of the area also falls within the Parque Natural do Sudoeste Alentejano, making it a real gem for cycling and walking trails.

FOOD & DRINK If you fancy a change from the onsite restaurant, try O Lourenço (282 698 622) in Salema, which serves a fantastic fish supper.

GETTING THERE From the A22 east-west motorway, take the second exit to Lagos ('Lagos Oeste') and then the N125 towards Sagres until you find the roundabout to Praia da Salema.

PUBLIC TRANSPORT From Faro take the train to Lagos, from where regular buses make the 16km journey, and stop right outside the campsite.

OPEN All year.

THE DAMAGE Tents €6–€9.90, campervans €9–€12.80, caravans €8.40–€12.60 (depending on season). Adults €6, children €3, cars €6, dogs €2.50, electrical hook-up €4.

tipi algarve

Rasmalho, Monte Joao Afonso 8500-069, Portugal 00351 935 271 818 www.tipialgarve.com

Did you know that the Algarve is Europe's sunniest region? With an annual average of 3,000 sunshine hours, it's even sunnier than California. And as for rain, the *Algarvios* don't even have a word for it... well that's not strictly true (it's "chuva" in case you're interested), but it almost never rains between July and September. Little wonder, then, what attracted Hertfordshire couple Calvin and Samantha Newport to the southwestern tip of the Iberian Peninsula.

As you navigate the serpentine roads, high into the hills of Serra de Monchique, the views of the Algarve coastline are as spectacular as you would expect. Monchique and the neighbouring spa town of Caldas boast steep cobbled streets, whitewashed houses and fragrant eucalyptus trees. Happening upon a secluded valley between Silves and Monchique, the Newports were one of the pioneers of eco-friendly Portuguese glamping, opening Tipi Algarve in 2008. Their ambitious project was a true labour of love. Jack-of-all-trades Calvin is no stranger to the sustainable life, having built his own barn-style dwellings in the UK and Spain. Surrey girl Sam left her high-flying job in the city of London to travel the world learning holistic therapies. She's now a fully-qualified therapist and yoga teacher and brings her hands-on healing to guests at the Tipi Algarve. The Newports are also mad VW-campervanners (not to mention keen organic gardeners), and we reckon that they know a thing or two about what eco-conscious campers want.

Visitors to this secluded, sunny retreat really couldn't want for much else. There's a choice of quirky abodes, including Native American-style tipis, yurts or comfy safari tents. All include a double bed with fluffy bedding, cushions and towels, plus storage for clothes and other things as well as electrical power outlets. There are shaded private cooking facilities outside each tent, plus a sheltered dining area with tables and chairs and a hammock. All kitchen essentials are available, so you don't need to bring anything of that kind, which should help to keep your luggage down.

At night the communal area 'chill-out lounge' and terrace hosts barbecue evenings under starry, light pollution-free skies. The eco-friendly communal wash block features solar-heated showers and toilets, which flush on to the nearby reed beds. There is an outdoor yoga temple with fantastic views of the protected forest and valley, a swimming pool and a 'Zen pond' with Koi carp, chickens and ducks. There's also an exceptionally friendly labrador, Sunny, who is a big hit when playing fetch with the kids. Supporting the eco-friendly ideal of traditional camping, glampers can also pick their own organically grown goodies from the site's vegetable patch. And if on the off-chance you grow bored of life on site, the nearby beaches and the easily driveable historic towns of Silves and Lagos are well worth a visit.

Could a glamping enthusiast keen to spend time in southern Portugal ask for much more? We think not!

COOL FACTOR A quirky, eco-friendly hillside hideaway in Europe's sunniest region.

WHO'S IN Glamping couples, families and small groups – yes. Dogs – no.

ON SITE 4 Native American-style tipis (2 x 7.5m and 2 x 5m); 1 yurt (6m); 3 regular safari tents (6m); and 1 large family safari tent (7m). 6 individual private kitchens with crockery, cutlery, pots and pans. Shower block and toilets. Chill-out lounge and sun terrace. Vegetables available from the organic garden. Well-being therapies on request and yoga temple. Koi carp pond, ducks, chickens, cats and a dog. Outdoor playground with swings, slide and a sandpit and a small games room with pool table, table football, board games, cards and books. Swimming pool.

OFF SITE Your hosts can arrange any number of activities from the site, including boat excursions, surf lessons, horseriding, and parent-and-child fishing packages. It's really all about the beaches here, though, and there are some absolutely cracking seaside spots all within easy reach, including Portimão, Alvor, and Meia Praia. The nearest large town, Lagos, is a living monument to Portugal's maritime past, with old city walls and the stunning Igreja de Santo António (282 762 301) among the town's historic wonders.

FOOD & DRINK Calvin and Sam recommend Restaurante Zavial (282 639 282) near Sagres, where you can enjoy delicious, home-cooked favourites on the terrace – the views, overlooking one of the Algarve's best surfing spots, are outstanding and the piri-piri chicken (€8.50) is a particularly popular dish.

GETTING THERE Directions are only given upon booking.

PUBLIC TRANSPORT ATS airport transfer can pick you up from Faro airport and drop you at the door. They are based in Portimão and also provide a local taxi service to Portimão and the local area.

OPEN April–September.

THE DAMAGE Double tipis €325–€360 for 7 nights; family tipis €520–€575 for 7 nights; yurt €520–€575 for 7 nights; safari tents €430–€475 for 7 nights.

quinta de odelouca

Vale Grande, Monte das Pitas, CxP 644-S, 8375-215 São Marcos da Serra, Portugal 00351 282 361 718
www.quintaodelouca.com

Let's get the Algarve elephant out of the room: Portugal's popular holiday destination sold its soul to the tourist devil 50 years ago and never looked back. Brash resorts clutter parts of the sandy south coast, attracting swarms of bucket and spade-wielding Brits every summer. However, the forested Serra de Monchique, the Algarve's mountain range, is a totally different story – more about charming castle towns and chestnut woods than beach bars and holiday villas. High above the coastal crowds, Quinta de Odelouca overlooks a tranquil river basin and is a serene base for exploring the unspoiled Algarvian countryside.

Almost all of the 25 pitches come shaded by olive trees, but from May to September campers are advised to pack some extra gear to ensure a spot of shadow (tarpaulin will do). The basic-but-clean sanitary facilities offer something for everyone – there's a baby-changing room, disabled friendly showers and a chemical disposal point for the caravanning community. There's even a saltwater swimming pool, perfect for cooling off on those scorching summer afternoons.

But those are the details. The big picture is that Quinta de Odelouca has an outstanding mountain vista, with high peaks puncturing the blue skies all around. Given this rural location, the site is a perfect base from which to do some serious hiking, mountain biking or canoeing. The sloping mountains of the Serra de Monchique are made up of chestnut woods and fleeting oaks, and it's one of the few areas of Portugal that displays dazzling colours in autumn. However, if operating an accelerator pedal is more your idea of a workout, then the winding mountain roads are a tempting prospect too.

With so many interesting pursuits on your doorstep, it might be a struggle to stand still long enough to achieve some all-important rest and relaxation. But as the sun sinks behind distant hills, zip up those tent-flaps, snuggle into your sleeping bag and join Quinta de Odelouca's version of the Mile-High Club – snoozing above sea level in the freshest of mountain air. After spending a few days camping in this lofty spot, most outdoor enthusiasts will find it difficult to say goodbye. But don't worry, you're welcome back any time.

Quinta de Odelouca

2000

COOL FACTOR Low-key camping in the Algarve mountains with excellent options for walking, biking and canoeing.

WHO'S IN Tents, caravans, campervans and well-behaved dogs – yes. Large groups – no.

ON SITE 25 pitches (all with electric hook-ups), showers, washbasins, saltwater pool, Wi-Fi, disabled facilities, baby-changing, washing machine, chemical toilet disposal and BBQ for use.

OFF SITE Silves makes for a pleasant day-trip. It's a sleepy town of winding backstreets that has one of the best-preserved castles in the region. Head for Monchique in early March for the town's famous sausage festival. In Marina de Vilamoura, Algarve Seafaris (289 302 318; algarve-seafaris.com) offer fishing trips, and there's also the spa town of Caldas de Monchique, situated by a narrow gorge with dramatic rocky cliffs.

FOOD & DRINK The site serves twice-weekly meals for its guests February–June; there are also several authentic Portuguese restaurants within walking distance. Further afield in Monchique, O Luar da Foia (282 911 149) serves fresh, well-presented food with a spectacular hillside view, and the same town's O Parque (282 912 022) is a cosy place serving down-to-earth dishes.

GETTING THERE From the north, pass São Marcos da Serra and the viaduct over the IC1. After 200m follow the small road on your right and the campsite signs. From the south, don not stop on the IC1; drive 200m further to the São Marcos da Serra exit. Cross to the other side of the IC1, then take the right (sign posted Portimão/Albufeira) and, after 200m, follow the small road on your right.

PUBLIC TRANSPORT Either take a train to São Bartolomeus de Messines, 15km away, or a bus to a stop 2km away on the IC1.

OPEN Early January–early November.

THE DAMAGE Car/caravan/campervan, 2 persons and electricity €17.85, plus 2 children €22.25. Wi-Fi €1 per day.

o tamanco

Rua do Louriçal 11, Casas Brancas, 3108-158 Louriçal, Portugal 00351 236 952 551 www.campismo-o-tamanco.com

Back in the spring of 1998, armed with little more than a rusty VW campervan and a rough plan to open a beach bar, Hans and Irene drove down Portugal's glorious west coast in search of a simple, less hectic life. Months passed before the Dutch duo locked eyes on a delightful campsite in the heart of Costa da Prata, a region known for its bounty of traditional villages, glacial lakes and pristine beaches. That campsite was Campismo O Tamanco and, while many of its competitors are content to create a few touring pitches and hope for the best, Hans and Irene decided to offer an altogether more distinctive camping experience. And we think you'll love it…

Campismo O Tamanco buzzes in the way a campsite should. Like the region, the site has plenty of rustic charm yet provides contemporary accommodation that's in keeping with its natural surroundings. As well as tents, you'll notice eight innovative glamping 'tubes' made out of reclaimed materials, two stylishly furnished yurts, two wooden bungalows and a (very cool) converted Bedford truck, fully loaded with snug beds, a wood-burning stove, gas cooker and BBQ – perfect for a spot of al fresco dining.

Beyond the campsite grounds, the Costa da Prata (the 'Silver Coast') boasts fishing villages, castles and monasteries. Chief among the region's most popular sites is the 12th-century Abbey of Santa Maria (60km), where the tragic love story of King Pedro I and his beloved Inês de Castro unravelled – a harrowing tale that makes Romeo and Juliet look more like Wayne and Waynetta. Adding to the region's appeal is Portugal's recent surf boom (now only second to football in terms of popularity) and, in winter, when the waves are at their most colossal, the coast here attracts the surfing elite (the Guinness World Record for the biggest wave ever surfed was recently recorded here). Luckily, between May and October the waves are suitable for mere mortals.

It's easy being a happy camper when you pitch up at Campismo O Tamanco. 'Down to earth, yet up with style' is how Hans and Irene describe it and, frankly, we couldn't put it better ourselves. With its unequalled coastline, magical forests and exceptionally welcoming locals, it's easy to see why the Costa da Prata was the couple's preferred destination. So why not join them?

COOL FACTOR Owners who know a thing or two about camping – and a location that's easy to fall in love with.

WHO'S IN Tents, glampers, caravans, motorhomes, kids and dogs (if they are friendly to the chickens!) – yes.

ON SITE In addition to 50+ camping pitches, O Tamanco has 2 yurts (sleeping 4), stylishly furnished with a double bed, table, kitchen, wood-burning stove, cool-box and radio. Outside there's a private bucket shower, eco-toilet, chairs and a picnic table. They will also supply an additional 'Yurpi', which sleeps 2 children. There's also a converted, vintage Bedford truck (sleeping 2) with wood-burning stove, gas cooker, crockery, BBQ and picnic table; 2 wooden bungalows (sleeping 4); and their brand new 'tube' accomodation (sleeping 2) with electrical charging points and beds (bring your own sleeping bag). Communal kitchen, toilet block, laundry service, Wi-Fi and games shack, fridges, books and magazines – and a spacious swimming pool hidden among the rich vegetation.

OFF SITE On a hill behind the site, goats, potbelly pigs, chicks and guinea pigs potter in a children's farm. Nearby Germanelo Castle (239 561 132) sits perched 367m high on a rugged hilltop, and the panoramic views over the Rabaçal Valley are worth the trip alone. The small town of Louriçal (6km) makes for a great day out; it's a sleepy town with a weekly market, a Convento of the silent order and a view over the rice fields. Further afield are the epic sands of Figueira da Foz (33km), which are popular with both sun tan-fans and surfers.

FOOD & DRINK The onsite 'Cantina' offers delicious homemade meals made with fresh local produce, and a baker pays a daily visit to the site with fresh bread and croissants. There is a handful of decent restaurants in Louriçal, including Restaurante O Ze (236 962 172; restauranteoze.net) and Pizzaria Ratolas (965 600 824).

GETTING THERE From the A1 highway, take the Pombal exit, followed by the IC8 (direction Figueira da Foz), then turn off at the last exit, Outeiro do Louriçal. From the A17, follow the highway before taking the Carriço exit.

PUBLIC TRANSPORT Pombal (15km) and Louriçal (5km) train stations are the closest to the site and there's a pick-up service available. The nearest bus stop is 1km away.

OPEN March–October.

THE DAMAGE July/August pitches from €25 (for 2 people), including camping equipment, car and electricity; children 0–3 years €2, 3–12 years €3.50. Tubes from €25 per night. Yurts from €65 per night; Bedford truck €60 per night.

termas da azenha

Rua João Henriques Foja Oliveira, 3130-433 Vinha da Rainha, Soure, Portugal 00351 916 589 145
www.termas-da-azenha.com

In ancient Greece the god of medicine, Asclepius, inspired the construction of many temples built next to 'healing' water springs. About 3,000 kilometres away, and some 3,000 years later, Asclepius is a little-known character among the villagers of present-day Soure in western Portugal. Nevertheless, any lack of knowledge of Greek mythology doesn't detract from the locals' appreciation of their own self-proclaimed healing waters. Their luscious landscape is literally bubbling over with springs, and the temple, where you can experience their curative powers for yourself, is called Termas da Azenha.

More than just a place to set up camp, this Atlantic-meets-Mediterranean complex (incorporating hotel rooms, reception, holiday rentals for couples and families and a café) is a fascinating find. The exteriors are all curvy, white-washed walls and spring-yellow columns, while the inside is decorated with a wall-to-wall underwater theme. Mosaics are a big visual attraction, with more than 16,000 tiles used to create various mermaids, dolphins, urchins and other mystical creatures in a stunning walk-through aquarium. Any spot that isn't covered in ceramic tesserae is occupied by a sculpture, picture or poem. It's a gallery that is being added to constantly – by guests, too, who can join weekly craft sessions.

The fabulous-looking spa is built around a water spring that the owners believe dates back to Roman times and is said to cure eczema.

A few soothing hours in the large hall with the original treatment rooms on each side will do a lot to de-stress your burnt-out soul. Whether you opt for a sunken bath or a relaxing massage, you'll end each day feeling thoroughly refreshed and ready to explore the rest of Termas da Azenha.

Outside, the camping area is not the biggest campsite you've ever clapped eyes on – in fact the space is maxed out with just four families – but it has a fresh, open feel, with springy grass and large pitches. The site is also slightly tiered so you can camp down or up the hill, depending on the view you're after. In both the lower and upper levels you'll find a devoted shower, sink and toilet but you may prefer to use the spa's facilities. When you've had your fill of massages and enjoyed your bath(s), you might want to try to burn off some energy elsewhere. The surrounding area is great for walking, and of course the Atlantic coast is great for surfing, while nearby Figueira da Foz is a nice resort and offers some of the best diving in the country. After a heavy day's activity, head to Lavos for a sunset drink before checking out one of the beach restaurants there, such as A Pérola do Oceano, a well-known seafood haunt that's very popular hereabouts.

However, as you breathe in the view of the wetlands from your tent and soak up the calm atmosphere, it's hard to imagine doing anything more strenuous than dropping by the spa for yet another massage. And what on earth would be wrong with that?

COOL FACTOR Camping meets spa treatments – with wonderful results.

WHO'S IN Tents, campervans, caravans – yes. Dogs – no.

ON SITE A shower, a sink and WC. When these become too busy, you can use the 3 spa showers. The spa has steam rooms, sunken baths and 3 massage rooms (warm water, shiatsu and sports massages). There are two small pools, a library and a music area with a piano and a few string instruments. There is Wi-Fi (€4 per hour), a washing machine (€5), an outdoor solar kitchen – and the owners' beloved donkey, Esmé, who the kids can ride on for €5.

OFF SITE Surf at Praia do Cabadelo, south of the River Mondego, or just stay put to make mosaics.

FOOD & DRINK A baker visits the site daily; you can pre-order a 3-course vegetarian evening meal (€12), and lunches can be arranged for a minimum of 5 people. Book a table for a beach meal at Pérola do Oceano in Lavos (233 946 127). The nearest supermarket is 4km away in Vinha da Rainha.

GETTING THERE From Porto take the A1 towards Porto/ Coimbra. Leave the highway at Condeixa and follow the N1 towards Lisbon and the signs to Soure. Cross 2 roundabouts, a railway line, and then turn left at the T-junction and right at the next junction. After 4km you'll see signposts for Vinha da Rainha. Follow the road for just over a mile (2km) until you get to a T-junction. Facing O Choupal cafe, turn right and follow this road until you arrive at Termas da Azenha.

PUBLIC TRANSPORT Catch a train from Porto or Lisbon to Soure, from where the owners will pick you up for €10.

OPEN All year; but during winter you'll probably feel warmer in one of the hotel rooms.

THE DAMAGE 2 people with a tent and car cost €13.75–€15. Electricity €3 per day. There are 5 rentable caravans: €12.50 per day; €85 per week. The owners also have hotel and B&B rooms as well as rooms in 4 family houses and 2 studios.

yurt holiday portugal

Lugar Várzeas, Pracerias, Celavisa, 3300-207 Arganil, Portugal 00351 235 208 562 www.yurtholidayportugal.com

At the turn of the century, Hannah McDonnell and Derrick McLean packed their new-born baby and a few belongings into their campervan and, eschewing the urban sprawl of south London, drove towards the hills and valleys of rural Portugal. In the mountainous village of Pracerias, an hour's drive from Coimbra, they bought an abandoned roadside goat shed and then spent two years transforming it into a traditional slate *xisto* house. After the birth of their second child, they began planning their unique eco-tourism venture.

Taking supreme care to nurture their smallholding, they carved zig-zagged rows of steps down the hillside and positioned the first of their two locally crafted yurts on the valley floor. Opulent and decadent, this beauty – known as Chestnut Tree Yurt – is perched on top of a raised platform to level with the natural slope of the land, sheltered by the branches of a sprawling chestnut tree. Inside, it's a riot of colour with vibrant orange, purple and red covers swathing an old-fashioned, brass-knobbed bed, and an array of collectible, retro furnishings, with the turquoise canvas setting off an imposing Egyptian Ankh 'symbol of life' design on the roof. Their second yurt, Apple Tree Yurt, is home to lighter tones of white and blue, and there is plenty of space to walk around and stand tall in both. When the weather is hot you can open up the roof altogether before lying back on the bed to gaze at the stars – though it's worth knowing that the site also now has handy heaters for colder spring nights. Each yurt can sleep either a couple or a family of four, plus they also have a bell tent to absorb extra folk or for the kids to have their own space.

Vines, olives, figs, lettuces, watercress, broccoli, courgettes, basil – and a lot more – grow on the site's organic allotments; the family's chickens lay

your breakfast eggs, and the site serves up tasty meals on the verandah (next to the house), where you can mingle with other guests. At special request, Hannah and Derrick will also serve breakfast down at the yurts – if you're planning a busy (or lazy) day then you can pre-book dinner as well. Derrick's home-cooked three-course meals washed down with a bottle of local Dão wine in your own secluded sanctuary are hard to refuse.

The site's green credential's are strong. The yurts' electricity is solar powered, while the shower runs on gas heaters, providing reliable, hot water. The fridges are 'pot-in-pot' eco fridges, and there's also a composting loo with a cleverly modern, odour-free design. It's the feeling of isolation, though, that is the main attraction here. Private and hidden from the road, the garden is at your disposal (yours and that of the family's two Labradors, Balu and Asha) so you can really relax

among the fresh scents of pine, eucalyptus, jasmine and orange blossom, without ever having to rejoin civilisation. When you do fancy some company, seek out nearby Arganil's vibrant Thursday morning market, where some of the region's finest farmers and local artisans ply their produce. But otherwise there's blissfully little to do apart from walking, swimming or just idly contemplating your navel.

Anyone who's seeking the ultimate escapist retreat or simply looking for a stop-gap on a longer trip would do well to hole up at Lugar Várzeas for a while. This serene spot makes an ideal destination for honeymooners or small groups who are looking to use the two yurts at once. Those who linger longer reap the true rewards – adventures with wild swimming, and hiking trails or alpaca treks through the beautiful and remote Portuguese countryside.

COOL FACTOR Luxurious and bohemian; perfect for those seeking secluded relaxation.

WHO'S IN Glampers, families, groups, honeymooners and retreaters – yes. Tents, caravans, campervans and dogs – no.

ON SITE 2 yurts. The Apple Tree Yurt has a pod attached with twin beds, making it perfect for larger families. 1 bell tent is also available for families. Inside each yurt there is a double bed, 2 children's beds on request, power points, a wardrobe, games, books and eco 'pot-in-pot' fridge (2 differently sized terracotta pots sandwiched with coarse sand and saturated with water). Each yurt has its own private bathroom with hot and cold water, shower, sink and a modern, Swedish-made compost toilet, garden table and chairs, ping-pong table, badminton nets, swings and hammocks. Hannah and Derrick also offer visitors a popular honeymoon package, including massages and local excursions.

OFF SITE Local sights include the spectacular Convento do Cristo at Tomar and the Pegos Aqueduct just outside Tomar. There's also the ancient university city of Coimbra, where there's loads to see, or you can just enjoy the more bucolic pleasures of a canoe trip along the River Douro (235 778 938).

FOOD & DRINK A fabulous breakfast is included in your booking and tasty verandah suppers are available on site, with cocktails served at 6pm. There is also a handy honesty bar so that you can enjoy a sundowner at your own convenience.

GETTING THERE From Porto airport it is a 1½ hour drive. Book in advance and exact directions are provided by Hannah and Derrick.

PUBLIC TRANSPORT The nearest train station is Coimbra and the nearest bus station is Moita de Serra in Arganil. Hannah and Derrick recommend car hire, as the site is very remote and public transport is limited.

OPEN April–October.

THE DAMAGE Yurts: two adults B&B £65/€75 per night including tax; €450 per week. Under-3s go free; 3–12s are €10 each per night. Yurt pod or bell tent €55 per week. Minimum stay 2 nights. Guests pay a 50% non-refundable deposit on booking. Cash only on site.

senses camping

Quinta do Rio, Faia Guarda, 6300-095, Portugal 00351 910 488 800 www.sensescamping.com

Captivating due to both its cultural and natural history, the Serra da Estrela (meaning 'mountain range of the stars') was one of Portugal's first designated nature reserves, and it remains the country's largest protected natural area. The craggy, boulder-scattered pastures, rushing rivers and bizarrely shaped gorges form one of Portugal's most unique and spectacular landscapes. With the Serra's vast network of hiking trails covering fertile valleys, vibrant orange groves and Portugal's tallest peaks, it's astonishing to think that only a relative few take on these awe-inspiring paths. Oh well... their loss is most definitely your gain.

Bordering the twisting Mondego River, Senses Camping is a perfectly positioned base from which to explore this beautiful region. A family-run business, hosted by welcoming couple Natasha and Michel, Senses offers a wide choice of camping accommodation, from traditional, spacious tent pitches, spread out among fruit trees and three hectares of peaceful, private land, to cosy safari tents, bell tents and other pre-pitched alternatives (sleeping up to six people) that are perfect for families or for those who just want to spread out a bit. Accommodation is furnished with plenty of creature comforts, including rugs, fridge, cooker and an outdoor terrace.

One thing that sets this place apart is the amount of activities on offer. After visiting the region on a holiday, Natasha and Michel felt compelled to set up a campsite inspired by their personal passions in yoga, health and art. Michel is a professional sculptor and his creative workshops allow kids and adults alike to create their very own masterpieces in the media of clay, wood or stone. Or, if you're seeking some stress relief, then take a deep breath and sign up for one of the yoga classes, held twice a day by fully qualified instructors.

The rest of the time you're more likely to be disturbed by the light thud of an apple dropping from one of the trees than anything else. When morning comes, the chances are you'll be roused by the sound of birdsong and trickling water from the Mondego River – a truly idyllic way to start your day. So, if you're dreaming of a relaxing European retreat and are still undecided where to go, we suggest you come to your senses and... well... come to Senses.

COOL FACTOR Relaxed camping in Portugal's most beautiful national park.

WHO'S IN Glampers, campers, tents, campervans, dogs – yes. Large motorhomes, caravans – no.

ON SITE Several traditional camping pitches are available (some with electricity) with plenty of space, along with more luxury options: safari tents (sleeping 4–6) with fridge, BBQ, beds and bed linen, sink and electricity; bell tents (sleeping 2–4) with floor beds and linen; and basic pre-pitched tents with sleeping mats and pillows. There are 4 showers, 3 toilets, in separate female and male facilities. There's also a laundry, a restaurant, a lovely pool area (including a kids' pool), free Wi-Fi and badminton, while the river offers lots of scope for fishing. Onsite workshops include sculpting, yoga, horseriding and other creative activities.

OFF SITE Senses' guided horseriding experience is a wonderful way to explore the stunning surroundings and pretty towns; treks last around 4 hours and cost €15 per hour (lunch included). Shorter rides can be arranged. Visit the Dominio Vale do Mondego, in the Serra da Estrela, known for its artwork and colourful culture. Further afield, the medieval capital of Portugal, Coimbra makes for an interesting day-trip. The city's university is Portugal's oldest and most distinguished, and a third of the Coimbra's population are students. Many tourists make Coimbra their base for visits to the medieval fortress of Montemor-o-Velho (239 687 300) and the Roman ruins located at Conimbriga.

FOOD & DRINK There's an onsite restaurant, set in a mature English-style garden, which matches free-range, organic meat with vegetables grown in the site's garden on a menu that changes every day. There's also a bar, cradled by a large oak tree that offers both shade and atmosphere. There are plenty of dining options in the nearby city of Guarda (a 15-min drive away), including the excellent Restaurante Belo Horizonte (271 211 454), Restaurante Robalo (271 754 189) and Sardinha (271 215 448; marisqueirasardinha.com), which does fabulous seafood.

GETTING THERE From Porto airport, follow the A44 or A4 to Porto and the A1 toll road. Head towards Lisbon and take the Aveiro/Viseu exit on to the A25. After Viseu, leave at exit 28 and follow signs for the IP5/Porto de Carne. Take the Transito/Porto de Carne exit to the N16 and follow this for 12 miles, then turn right to Faia. Drive down the valley and, at the roundabout, turn into the village of Faia (3rd exit). Continue straight through the village and follow the new road to the top of the hill; take a right turn at the T-junction, and the road will take a left turn where the tarmac road ends. Keep going down the hill and you will see the site's olive orchard on the right-hand side; drive around it and the campsite is on the left.

PUBLIC TRANSPORT There are good bus connections from Porto, Lisbon and Madrid to Guarda. You can also take the train from Porto or Lisbon to Guarda, and an international night train to Lisbon from Paris stops in Guarda too. From Guarda station take a taxi (€15) in the direction of Chaos, then Pero Soares, and finally Dominio Vale do Mondego. The site can also arrange a pick-up service.

OPEN Beginning of May–end of September.

THE DAMAGE Pitching your own small/large tent costs €3/€6. Safari tents are €65 per night, every extra person €10, children under 3 years old free. Bell tents €35 a night, every extra person €7.50, children under 3 years old free. Basic tents €17.50 a night.

lima escape

Parque de Campismo de Entre Ambos-os-Rios, Lugar de Igreja, 4980-312 Entre Ambos-os-Rios, Ponte da Barca – Viana do Castelo, Portugal 00351 258 588 361 www.lima-escape.pt

Lima Escape is what estate agents would call 'wonderfully appointed' – nestled on the western-edge of the Peneda-Gerês National Park (also known simply as 'Gerês'), where 70,000 hectares of vast, amphitheatre-shaped space wows visitors each year with deep river valleys, colossal peaks and magical forests of oak and sweet-scented pine. With so much exploring to be done, you'll need a campsite closeby where you can sleep off that sweet hiker's fatigue. Thankfully, Lima Escape ticks that box and many others.

The site is huge (there's capacity for 400 campers), yet it maintains an intimate atmosphere while at the same time showing off the vast, spectacular natural beauty of its position. Pitching up in lush woodlands, surrounded by oak and pine trees, while the River Lima snakes its way nearby, is a real pleasure for even the most seasoned camper. When the torches are switched off and all you can hear is the wind in the trees and the soft ripple of water, you realise that you have arrived in bona-fide camping heaven.

One thing's for sure, you won't get bored. If you're an enthusiastic rambler, you'll love the surrounding mountains, which offer a multitude of high-elevation paths and mountain-biking treks, with views to knock your socks off. Gerês is Portugal's first and only national park and is spread across four dramatic granite peaks. It's especially popular with hikers in April and May when its twisting trails bloom with wildflowers. The park is also home to over 140 bird species, including the eagle owl, honey buzzard and the whinchat, all

of which are seldom seen elsewhere in Portugal. Animal lovers are also in luck, with ibex, wolf (don't get too close!), pine martin, stoat and wild Garrano ponies all roaming the park's many moorlands.

Back at Lima Escape, your time is very much your own. In the evenings many choose to rendezvous by the snack bar, taking advantage of the full-flavoured food (homemade pies, sausages and hamburgers) or sipping a cold beer on the terrace. However, if you'd prefer some 'me time', Lima is also the kind of peaceful, unspoiled patch where you can unwind without fear of being disturbed.

COOL FACTOR Perfect for explorers and snorers alike.

WHO'S IN Tents, glampers, caravans, small groups, dogs – yes.

ON SITE Space for up to 400 campers. 2 tipis, 2 bell tents, 2 tree-house bungalows, a camping van and an apartment (for 4 people) with a fully equipped kitchen, bedroom, living room, toilet and shower. Tipis, bell tents and tree-houses are each fully furnished and have private showers and toilets. 2 stone buildings have showers and toilets, a washing machine, a snack bar with 2 shady terraces and free Wi-Fi. 2 covered BBQs with tables and electric plugs for cooking and eating.

OFF SITE Across the valley lies the authentically Portuguese town of Lindoso, whose highlights include a hilltop fortress and recently restored castle, which houses a small exhibition on the surrounding region. Tranquil Ponte da Barca (a 12-minute drive away) has a romantic riverfront park, enchanting 16th-century bridge and tiny old centre.

FOOD & DRINK An onsite snack bar serves a variety of grub on a shaded terrace, a shop in reception sells essential groceries and the onsite restaurant 'Ageda do Artur' serves Minho dishes and local wine. In Lindoso (15 minutes away) Lindo Verde (258 578 010) serves standard Portuguese fare.

GETTING THERE From Porto airport, join the A3 travelling 75km in the direction of Valença. After passing Vila Verde, drive 10km and take the 2nd exit to Ponte de Lima. Beyond the toll, pass the ring road and take the 2nd exit (Ponte da Barca) on to IC28. After 15km you cross the River Lima then take the 2nd exit to Lindoso. After 10km you will see the sign 'Ambos-os-Rios', after which turn left on the crossroad and follow signs.

PUBLIC TRANSPORT A daily shuttle bus runs from Porto airport to Ponte da Barca, where you can take a bus to Lindoso that stops 20m from the site. The nearest train station is Braga, from where you can take a bus to Ponte da Barca. From Ponte da Barca there are 2 buses per day to Lindoso.

OPEN All year, except 2 weeks in the 2nd part of November.

THE DAMAGE Tent pitches €3.35–€5 per night for 2 people; caravans €4.40–€6; children (5–10 yrs) €2.50–€2.90; children up to 4 free. Tipis €50 per night; bell tents €60 (both based on 2 sharing, including breakfast); cars €4–€6.50; electricity €2.30–€3.00 and dogs €1.

camping islas cíes

Ria de Vigo, Pontevedra, Spain 0034 986 687 630 www.campingislascies.com

Mmmm. Let's see. A group of uninhabited islands off the western coast of Spain, turned into a national park in 1980, and with limited access by ferry. No roads, so no cars, campervans or caravans. But there is a campsite. Interested? You should be.

Las Islas Cíes – made up of Isla del Norte, Isla do Faro and Isla de San Martín (though each are known by endless different names) – are just off the Galician coast, across the bay from the city of Vigo, and only accessible by a special ferry service. This naturally has the effect of limiting the numbers of visitors each day and, to prevent keen campers from pitching up for the whole summer, stays are limited to 15 days at a time; you need to get a *tarjeta de acampado* (camping ticket) at the camping office at the Estación Marítima de Ría in Vigo before you head over. Once you've arrived, there are handy barrows to help you wheel your gear across from the jetty and, once your tent's up and your kit stowed, or you have found your pre-pitched tent, you're free to explore your surroundings, just like proper Famous Fivers.

Some areas – like the cliffs – are closed off to the public and accessible only to guillemot or gull. But you're more likely to emerge from the campsite's trees and head for the curving sand of the Playa de Rodas, where the locals often come to sun themselves. They like to think of this as their little slice of the Caribbean and, on a fine day, who are we to argue?

COOL FACTOR Island camping with nothing but mountains, sea and sand.

WHO'S IN Tents – yes. Campervans, caravans, cars and motorhomes – no.

ON SITE Provisions are decent enough, with hot showers and washing facilities. Otherwise this not a campsite with too many thrills and spills, although there is a handy supermarket and café on site.

OFF SITE There are plenty of lovely beaches on the island. Bring some binoculars and a Bill Oddie book and enjoy the abundance of birds. Snorkelling and kayaking can also be arranged from the site office.

FOOD & DRINK For the real experience bring your own food and cook it yourself (though, sadly, campfires are not allowed). You also need to take all your rubbish back to the mainland with you when you leave. Back on the mainland there's a lovely *parador* on a rocky promontory at Baiona (986 355 000), due south of the islands, where you can enjoy a meal of local Galician cuisine in its restaurant. There's a special *menú degustación* at €33.

GETTING THERE The ferry company, Mar de Ons (986 225 272; mardeons.com), sails boats from the Estación Marítima de Ría in Vigo several times a day between May and October; there are also services from Baiona; check in advance for sailing times. Outside these months there are only boats on Saturdays and Sundays. The fare is €18.50 return per person.

OPEN Mid May–mid Sept, plus the Easter holidays.

THE DAMAGE Reservations required. Pitches €7.50–€8.50; adults €7–€8.25; children (3–12 yrs) €5.50–€6.20. Pre-pitched tents €45–€75 per night.

camping sisargas

w / Filgueira, 12 15113 Malpica de Bergantiños, A Coruña, Spain 0034 981 721 702 www.campingsisargas.com

Rocky peaks, winding inlets and dozens of deserted beaches – welcome to the eerily beautiful Costa da Morte. Its rather fearsome name ('Coast of Death') stems from the constant clobbering the shoreline receives from the Atlantic and the countless shipwrecks that litter the seabed. Wild, windy and often foggy, this unspoiled part of Galicia, on the far west of Spain's northern coast, is not nearly as busy as the neighbouring regions to the south, yet it boasts similarly beautiful coves, wide sweeping bays and tiny fishing villages huddled against dramatic headlands. Being off the beaten track won't appeal to everyone but the sense of isolation and lack of large-scale tourism is all part of the attraction of this low-key but well-equipped campsite.

Located between the villages of Carballo and Malpica in a lush forest of pine and eucalyptus trees, Camping Sisargas is the ideal base for exploring the Costa da Morte and beyond. This peaceful, family-run campsite offers 145 spacious plots with shade and shelter on a comfortable flower-fringed lawn. You will never see tents side by side here. 'We like the fact that people have their space' says Gema, one of the site's approachable employees. In fact, being off the tourist trail means that Sisargas rarely gets full, so campers have the luxury of choosing their own pitch. Besides the campsite pitches, there are six modern bungalows, five cosy Canadian huts and a plethora of first-rate facilities, including a café, restaurant, free Wi-Fi, a swimming pool, barbecues, a tennis court and a playroom for rainy afternoons – which aren't as infrequent as you might think

in this relatively wet part of the country (the rain that's supposed to fall mainly on the Spanish plain actually mainly drops on hilly Galicia). Even when the sun is shining and the days are bright and sunny with a light you won't find anywhere else, the nights can be chilly.

The local area is surrounded by woodland paths (some paved, some not), which are great for walking, cycling or just getting lost. This is a very tranquil site, so the owners politely request peace and quiet from midnight untill 9am, ensuring that the only sounds to be heard are birds chirping above, the wind whistling through the tall trees and, if you're lucky, the squeak of a black squirrel. The atmosphere is unbeatable: secluded, inviting and wonderfully natural. Isn't that what camping is all about?

COOL FACTOR 5 beaches within 5km of the site, most of them wonderfully secluded.

WHO'S IN Anyone who wants to be in contact with nature and have a relaxed holiday! Tents, caravans, kids, groups and pets – yes.

ON SITE 145 spacious and shaded plots (52 with electrical hook-ups), 5 Canadian huts, 6 mobile homes and an area that is not divided in to pitches for larger groups (up to 15 tents or so). 1 sanitary block (separate entrances for men and women) with 18 showers, individual heaters, free hot water, 20 toilets and 20 sinks. On the outside of the sanitary block there are another 10 sinks for washing dishes, 10 sinks for washing clothes and 2 areas for hanging clothes to dry. Sisargas also has toilet facilities for the disabled and baby-changing, and the site has washing machines and dryers for use at an extra cost. Free Wi-Fi (in the common areas), BBQs for common use, swimming pool, tennis court, basketball, table tennis, a library with books and magazines in several languages and a playground for younger children.

OFF SITE Celtic Galicia offers campers an alternative Spanish experience. Despite its natural beaches and some of the best seafood in Europe, the region remains largely unexplored by tourists. The Refugio de Verdes makes for a nice trip; a series of ruined watermills and bridges on a fast-rushing, picturesque stretch of river. The port city of La Coruña and the medieval pilgrimage city of Santiago de Compostela are both less than an hour away by car. The Costa da Morte also has many secluded beaches and craggy cliffs, including – 20 mins away by car – Razo beach,

one of the best surfing spots in Spain, with surf schools and board rentals for all abilities.

FOOD & DRINK The site has a restaurant and coffee shop, serving breakfast, lunch and dinner; a selection of beers and local wines; and fresh, homemade pizzas. There's a small shop selling freshly baked bread and croissants and basic food supplies. Off site, there is a good restaurant at walking distance from the campsite – 250m away – and you can eat excellent seafood in the town of Malpica de Bergantiños, just over 2km away. Try the Marisqueria Casa Rosa; (981 721 015; restaurantecasarosa.com) or the fantastic high-end eatery, As Garzas (981 721 765; asgarzas.com), with one Michelin-star, in Porto Barizo, 5km away.

GETTING THERE The campsite is 47km from La Coruña and 59km from Santiago de Compostela. In both cases, take the highway A9 towards Carballo, from where you should head towards Malpica de Bergantiños. Camping Sisargas is on this road, about 2km before reaching Malpica.

PUBLIC TRANSPORT There is a bus stop 100m from the site and several buses a day run between here and Carballo, which has good links with many other destinations, including La Coruña 3 times a day.

OPEN Mid June–mid September (bookings recommended July–August).

THE DAMAGE Sisargas doesn't charge per pitch, prices depend on the number of people and tents – 2 adults plus tent and car will set you back €23.50 per night. Caravans €6.60 a night, campervans €10 a night. Pets cost €3.50, electricity €4.50. Canadian huts €38.50 a night, mobile homes €60 a night.

SISARGAS
CAMPING

Tfno: 981 721 702
reservas@campingsisargas.com
www.campingsisargas.com

camping playa de taurán

Playa de Taurán, 33700 Luarca Valdés, Spain 0034 985 641 272 www.campingtauran.com

The Asturian coastline of northern Spain is arguably the most unique pocket of the vast Iberian peninsula. This verdant landscape has such wildly diverse topography; it's a brilliantly bucolic contrast to what can seem like the endless aridity of Spain's southern steppes. There are some 24 nature reserves in this region, including the sprawling Picos de Europa Parque Nacional. Cut off from the rest of the country by these snow-capped Alpine peaks to the south, Asturias retains a character unique from the rest of Spain. No campsite in the region better typifies this quality than the wonderful Camping Playa de Taurán.

Arriving for the first time at this clifftop hideaway is a pretty special experience for anyone. So when amiable Dutch host Sander first arrived, from a land not blessed with quite such dramatic contours, the wow factor was well and truly off the scale. Perched on a steep cliff with panoramic vistas of the Cantabrian Sea, Camping Playa de Taurán is perhaps the region's best located campsite. With the titular beach to its west and the boundless meadows of San Martín de Santiago to the south, this family-run, family-friendly site is the ideal base for those wishing to discover the treasures of this largely overlooked destination.

There is ample space for 100 tents, campervans and caravans. Many pitches are equipped with electricity and Sander will happily get the long cables out for those brave souls pitching nearer the cliff edge. Nearly all these shady pitches boast sea views and a cooling Atlantic breeze. Conscientious as ever, Sander has also set aside a zone for larger groups, so they don't infringe upon their neighbours. There's a wealth of pleasingly small-scale activities for children: a supervised swimming pool, afternoon kid's club, handicrafts and traditional games. The site also has a small farm with veg patch and all manner of native Asturian animals, including *asturcón* ponies, *bermeya* goats, *xalda* sheep, and *pita pinta* chickens. Taurán beach is also just a 200-metre stroll downhill.

Known locally as 'The White Town on the Green Coast', the gorgeous nearby harbour town of Luarca offers plenty in the way of offsite distractions, not least those of the gastronomic kind. Asturias is the home of Spanish cheese, so be sure to sample the famous *Cabrales, Gamoneu, Afuega'l Pitu,* and *Los Beyos* varieties in one of the town's little waterfont *chigres,* along with *fritos de pixín* (deep-fried monkfish pieces) and a glass or two of the region's famous tipple, Asturian cider.

With its stunning, wind-swept beaches, dramatic clifftops and imposing mountains, this verdant land doesn't feel like Spain. The fiercely proud locals have a saying round these parts: 'Asturias is Spain - the rest is conquered territory'. We're inclined to agree; perhaps this region is the true essence of Spain.

COOL FACTOR Stunning views of the Cantabrian Sea from this family-friendly, clifftop campsite.

WHO'S IN Tents, caravans, motorhomes, groups, well-behaved dogs – yes.

ON SITE 100 pitches. Caravan and motorhome pitches all have electricity; some tent pitches also have electricity. Well-kept facilities block with free hot-water showers. Bar (with meals available). Small onsite shop selling camping essentials and some groceries. Library. Games room. Internet access. Laundry. BBQs and picnic spot. Free swimming pool. Children's playground. Table tennis, table football, billiards and basketball. Scuba-diving gear hire and courses are available; just ask at reception. There is also mooring for boats. Campfires not permitted.

OFF SITE The pretty fishermen's town of Luarca lies just 2.5km from the campsite and has a charming old lighthouse – well worth a visit if you're looking to capture snaps of the rustic side of this coastline. Luarca's beach is a short 1,500m stroll downhill from the site. There are showers and a bar that serves lunchtime meals. It's a great spot for surfing, canoeing and snorkelling.

FOOD & DRINK Don't be misled by the name; Sport (985 641 078) is Luarca's loveliest restaurant (though one of the more pricey), with good wine, wonderful locally caught seafood and live music on the terrace. No visit to this region would be complete without sampling some of the local cider. Whet your whistle at one of Luarca's atmospheric old taverns, or *chigres*. The zingy *sidra* is served *escanciada* – flamboyantly poured from a great height – and goes perfectly with a steaming bowl of *fabada asturiana* or *boroña* and *queso de Cabrales*.

GETTING THERE Coming from motorway E-70 (A-8), take exit 465 (Luarca/El Chano) and follow the signs towards Luarca. Once in Luarca, head 2.5km up 'la Peña' and the campsite will come into view.

OPEN April–October.

THE DAMAGE Adults €4.50; children €4; tents €4.50–€5; caravans €5.50; car €4; electricity €4.50.

lagos de somiedo

Valle Lago, Somiedo 33840, Asturias, Spain 0034 985 763 776 www.campinglagosdesomiedo.com

Everywhere with a bit of spare countryside seems to claim that it's one of Europe's last pristine wilderness. But in the case of the Parque Natural de Somiedo in the Cordillera Cantábrica mountains of northern Spain, it's probably true. Why? Because there be bears up here. And not your cuddly Paddington sort either. These guys are the real deal – the kind of sharp-toothed teddies that fancy something a bit meatier than a marmalade sandwich when it's time for dinner. Mind you, they're only little, even on their hind legs, so they're nothing to worry about. The wolves, on the other hand...

These furry friends have stuck around in these mountains because there's honestly very little to vex them here. The area was made a national park in 1988 and in 2000 was declared a UNESCO Biosphere Reserve. The result is a carefully preserved wilderness that is ideal for wildlife; and just perfect, too, for wandering the *brañas* – high-mountain meadows – with only a Gandalf staff and a half-eaten pack of biscuits to sustain you.

Camping Lagos de Somiedo is up such steep and twisty roads that not that many campers (and even fewer caravanners) make it up here. If you do the journey by car you'll be clutching for first gear on a couple of the hairpins. The winding roads cling to the sides of these deep limestone valleys and the resulting rock crumble means you'll have to keep an eye out for rock falls. Sometimes it's just a slip of pebbledash, but occasionally you'll find a chunk the size of a half-decent watermelon sitting in the middle of the road.

Luckily you leave the rocks far behind when you arrive at the site, high up in the unspoilt village of Lago. It's a fairly compact campsite by the side of a small stream which runs down from a nearby lake. Cars are confined to an entrance car park, so the camping area is blissfully free of clutter and there's plenty of room to spread out and make yourself at home. There's even a discreet little hideaway patch of ground on its own across the stream, accessed by a rather charming rickety old wooden bridge.

Lago itself is a throwback to an earlier era, the only real signs of modernity being the telephone wires strung from house to house. Spring comes late in these mountains – the trees can still be budding in May and there can even be flurries of snow – but once summer arrives there's everything that you require for that supreme high-mountain feel: birds of prey wheeling through the skies, cow bells clanking on the hills, lazy dogs and horses blocking the road.

The locals are enthusiastic bee-keepers, so there are plenty of stripy stingers swigging nectar from the flowers and bumbling around drunkenly looking for a dust-up. And then, of course, there are the bears. And the odd wolf. But at least you can console yourself with the thought that they're likely to be more scared of you than you are of them. Yeah, right.

COOL FACTOR Pristine, remote mountain camping in a village so quiet you could safely take a siesta in the middle of the main street.

WHO'S IN Tents, caravans, campervans – yes.

ON SITE Plenty of room for tents in informal pitches. Facilities are basic but clean. There's a rustic wash-block with hot showers and a couple of WCs, and a few outside washing-up sinks. Elsewhere, there's a restaurant/bar, supermarket, launderette, BBQ, children's playground, pétanque, bowling and mini golf.

OFF SITE Make the 7km walk from the site up to the lake or, if that seems a bit too strenuous take the more relaxing option and see the lake on horseback. El Chugarín (985 763 678) run various rides lasting between 2 and 6 hours in duration. The ride up to the lake is the 4-hour option and costs a reasonable €25 per person.

FOOD & DRINK There's a dinky little bar on the site, a sort of mountain refuge hut-cum-wine bar, but if you fancy something posher then head down to Pola and enjoy an evening in the restaurant at the Hotel Castillo del Alba (985 763 996; hotelcastillodelalba.es), where the food is excellent. For fresh food supplies, there's always Guillermo's Supermercado in the village.

GETTING THERE From the A8 coastal road, take the A16 from Riberas and follow the signs for Belmonte on the AS227 and on to Pola de Somiedo. Once there, turn left down the hill and carry on through the town, following the signs for Valle de Lago. Past the church the road starts to climb the 7km up to the village, where the campsite is on your right.

OPEN Start of June–end of September.

THE DAMAGE Adults €5, children (3–10 yrs) €4, tents €7, campervans €10, cars €4, electricity €4.

cloud house farm

Finca Casa Nube, Genalguacil 29492, Malaga, Spain 0034 645 238 742 www.cloudhouse.es

There are yurts and there are yurts – and as experienced glampers we reckon that Cloud House is in the 'truly exceptional' bracket, paving the way for the new generation of UK glampers heading to warmer climes.

This author's kids have grown up cool camping and are as accustomed to staying in tipis and yurts as they are under the more traditional forms of canvas, so it was with high expectations that we arrived at our handcrafted Mongolian yurt here in southern Spain. There are two yurts at Cloud House Farm: the Woodland Yurt, which has great views of the valley, and Orange Grove Yurt which, at the right time of year, offers the chance to pick your breakfast right off the surrounding trees. Each one is 5 metres in diameter and has space for a double bed and futons for the kids; there is solar-power electricity, which fires up your own iPod dock, a wooden deck and shaded seating area, plus a private outdoor bathroom and shower. You get a generous welcome pack on arrival and there is a fantastically old-fashioned *supermercado* in the (typically) whitewashed nearby village of Algatocin where, as well as the fresh melons, tomatoes, bread, wine and ice for your cool-box, they sell fantastic terracotta pottery.

As for the location, it's amazing – and feels incredibly remote. The views are outstanding and there are acres of space to explore and play games in; there's a hammock, rope swings, swingball, ancient cork oaks, and orange and lemon groves for shade. Not surprisingly, the hiking opportunities are endless, but you can also swim in the river or just sit outside your yurt and soak

up the peace and quiet. The swimming in the river is great too, but it's also worth knowing that there are great eating experiences only 20 minutes' drive away.

And, in the morning, you can wake up to the sound of bird-song so piercing it seems otherworldly. This is luxurious, boutique glamping at its glorious, bucolic best.

COOL FACTOR Chic Mediterranean glamping complete with stunning views.

WHO'S IN Families, couples, honeymooners – yes. Large groups – no.

ON SITE The yurts have wooden floors, a double bed, large chest of drawers, 2 single futons, a wood-burning stove, solar-powered electrical sockets, bedside lamps and an iPod dock. Outside is a dining area shaded by a grapevine and bougainvillea. The wooden outdoor kitchen has running water (not for drinking), a gas hob, fridge, cool-box and all the utensils required – and there are fresh herbs a-plenty growing nearby. A little track leads to your private wooden washroom, which has a traditionally tiled shower fed by a mountain spring – and a compost loo with a view to die for.

OFF SITE The local village of Genalguacil (20 minutes' drive away, or a steep 45-minute walk) is home to an arts festival every 2 years, and its tiny alleyways are full of pieces of sculpture and white washed walls painted with ultra-modern graffiti. The local rivers Rio Genal and Rio Almarchal have several natural pools, which are perfect for swimming, especially in the heat of the day. The historic town of Ronda is just over an hour's drive away, and a mountain road leads down to the coastal resort of Estepona, about an hour away.

FOOD & DRINK Don't miss an evening at Galleria El Visir (636 107 374), Genalguacil's premier restaurant and bar, both for its contemporary take on the region's traditional food and the exceptional and friendly service.

GETTING THERE Situated between the 3 white towns of the Serranía de Ronda (Genalguacil, Benarraba and Algatocin), Cloud House Farm is found at the end of a 2km-long dirt track deep in the Sierra Bermeja foothills, a 2 hour+ drive from Malaga airport. The most obvious way to reach it is to follow the A7 coast road and then take the road up into the hills from just outside Estepona.

OPEN Mid May–mid October.

THE DAMAGE From £70 per night for 2 adults. Children aged 2 and under go free; those aged 3–12 years; an extra £10 per night. Minimum stay 4 nights/7 nights in July/August.

eco camel

Finca Andijar, Igualejar, 29440 Málaga, Spain 0034 784 093 3113 www.ecocamel.co

The ancient *pueblos blancos* ('white towns') of the Serranía de Ronda clamber up hillsides amid some of Europe's most dramatic mountain scenery. You only need to walk a few minutes beyond the steep lanes of these towns to find yourself alone in the Andalucian countryside, with only the occasional ibex or griffon vulture for company. The region's wildlife and fascinating history are reasons enough to visit, but now we're pleased to say that we have found another – a brand new, off-grid hideaway, with chestnut forest views that will truly knock your socks off.

'It's a bit like landing on the moon!' says Eco Camel's creator and welcoming host, Roger; and as you take in the remote, untouched landscape from your private decked terrace, you can't help but agree. The site's only 5-metre bell tent sleeps two and comes furnished with a cosy king-size bed, soft white cotton sheets and plenty of creature comforts. This homely abode is clearly well loved, and has ample storage room to tuck away those walking boots after a good day's rambling in the mountains. Just outside your tent you will find an en suite wetroom with hot and cold running spring water, a flushing toilet and sink; it's lit by LED energy-efficient lighting and fresh towels are provided daily. Energy is provided by wind turbines and water is harvested from a spring located 700 metres up the mountain.

Off site, a visit to nearby Ronda is a must: it's an ancient place, built across a famously deep gorge and overlooking the white villages that dot the region's rich valley slopes. There's lots to see, including the town's Arab city gates, its palace,

convent, bullring and busy Sunday market, which overflows with fine food, local ceramics, flowers... you get the picture. Birdwatchers should look out for the Lesser kestrels nesting in the cliffs beneath the Alameda while, lower down, crag martins can be spotted. A favourite with the Romantics of the late 19th century, Ronda has a number of museums and retains quite a bit of low-key charm, despite the regular flow of Costa del Sol day-trippers.

There's glamping, and then there's off-grid glamping. Eco Camel is most definitely the latter. All this was only made possible by Roger's desire to create a truly eco-friendly experience. Despite its impressive eco credentials, the site doesn't lack in the comfort stakes, either, with the sort of facilities you would expect in a boutique hotel. So why not switch off your phone and start roaming this wonderfully unspoilt corner of southern Spain?

COOL FACTOR A luxurious mountain hideaway in southern Spain's remote Serranía de Ronda.

WHO'S IN Glamping only. No tents, caravans, campervans or pets.

ON SITE A 5m bell tent with king-size bed (including bedding and linen), carpet, chairs, chests, clothes stand and bronze lamps, UK-standard sockets, TV and speakers. Outside there is a fridge for chilling water. Everything is powered by wind and sun. There's a terrace, secluded by trees, with views over the surrounding mountains, an en suite bathroom with energy-efficient lighting, hot and cold running water, flushing toilet and sink. Fresh towels are provided daily. Mountain bikes available to hire.

OFF SITE Separating the old and new towns, the Puente Nuevo bridge is Ronda's most recognisable sight, straddling the dramatic gorge. The Plaza de Toros is a mecca for bullfighting aficionados; more than 200 years old, it is one of the most revered bullrings in Spain. The Museo Lara (952 871 263) is a lovely private museum, with a priceless collection of gramophones, clocks, weapons, opera glasses, fans and more.

FOOD & DRINK Breakfast is included and comes with freshly squeezed orange juice, tea, coffee, fresh fruit, homemade yoghurt, freshly baked croissants and toast. If you want you can have a cooked breakfast. Packed lunches can also be provided, as can lunch or 3-course meals. When booking, remember to indicate if you would like a meal on arrival.

OPEN Early May–late September.

GETTING THERE Take the AP-7 (N-340) to San Pedro de Alcantara, then the A-376 towards Ronda. After 15 minutes you will see a lay-by on the right; use this to turn and cross the road, where you should follow the sign to Igualejar. Follow the road to the bottom and the village is on the right. Take the road to the left and after that follow Roger's directions (which he'll give you when you book).

PUBLIC TRANSPORT Eco Camel can be reached by bus from Malaga in 1 hour 45 minutes.

THE DAMAGE €65 per night for 2, including breakfast.

chaparra eco lodge

Chaparra Eco Lodge, Lanjarón, Spain 0034 674 154 176 www.chaparraecolodge.com

In the interests of health and safety, we at Cool Camping strongly suggest that you pack a jaw-sling when visiting Chaparra Eco Lodge. While making your way up the winding A-348, don't allow the lower half of your face to succumb to the force of awe-inspired gravity. But be warned – this might be easier said than done. Nestled into the hillside of the spectacular Sierra Nevada (home to Spain's tallest peaks) is Chaparra Eco Lodge, a fabulous glamping site in an extraordinary mountain location.

Having taken in the epic view, prepare yourself for more delights as you navigate past the fruit and nut trees on your way to your gorgeously authentic yurt. Each surprisingly spacious and fully insulated abode comes lovingly furnished with a king-size bed, bedding and furnishings, making any stay more than comfortable. But what sets these yurts apart are the astonishing views towards the Mediterranean, and all from the privacy of your own terrace. A glass of local wine + that view at sunset = sheer bliss!

When you finally decide to venture out, the lovably traditional spa town of Lanjarón is right on your doorstep. Lanjarón is a 'real-deal' Spanish town and a breath of fresh air compared to some of its neighbours, which resemble jam-pots to the waspy swarms of tourists that gather every summer. Interestingly, the World Health Organization recognised friendly Lanjarón as a place of 'Great Longevity' as many of its citizens live well into their hundreds. Given the quality of its water, climate, fresh mountain air and Mediterranean diet, it's not hard to see why the locals are some of the healthiest on the planet. In June the town celebrates its annual fiesta of San Juan, known as Spain's biggest water fight. People from far and wide come to celebrate, with streets packed with crowds of people whose buckets, water pistols, fire hoses and even lorries are filled with water!

Whether you're here for mountain horseriding, hiking or to do a spot of bird watching (birds of prey are regularly spotted), all these activities are quite literally on your doorstep. Or, you could always just relax by the pool. With a view like that, who could blame you?

COOL FACTOR In the heart of the spectacular Sierra Nevada (home to Spain's tallest peaks) and boasting its very own natural springs.

WHO'S IN Glampers, couples, groups and dogs (by arrangement) – yes. Tents and caravans – no. Children age 7 and over welcome. For younger children, please contact the site.

ON SITE 2 fully-insulated yurts, each with a king-size bed and room to fit a bunk for 2 younger children or one single mattress for an older child. One 5m bell tent with a proper double bed and plenty of room for up to two children. Shared hot shower and toilet. Other shared facilities include a swimming pool filled with natural spring water, an outdoor lounge with plenty of places to relax in hammocks and deckchairs and a hot tub on its own private deck. There's also a BBQ, simple cooking facilities, a fridge, free Wi-Fi, phone and laptop charging facilities and pétanque set. Mats, umbrellas, bat and ball games and cutlery for picnics can all be borrowed to take to the beach.

OFF SITE Next door, Caballo Blanco (627 794 891; caballoblancotrekking.com) offer wonderful horseriding treks across the mountains. It's a great way to discover the region and directs you to some of the most spectacular views around – on a clear day you can even see the coastline of Africa. Riding lessons are available by the hour and there's a wide choice of horses to suit beginners, intermediate or advanced riders. Further afield lies the magnificent city of Granada, boasting the remarkable Alhambra Palace, (902 441 221; alhambradegranada.org). The palace's complex of various buildings and fortifications was constructed over many years and this resulted in contrasting architectural styles. Given its popularity, it's worth booking tickets in advance. The beaches of the Costa Tropical (also known as Costa de Granada) arguably provide a more authentic Spanish experience than those of the Costa del Sol. With its long, wide beach and lovely promenade, Torrenueva is a particularly nice resort.

FOOD & DRINK A full cooked breakfast is included in your booking and there's also an honesty bar with soft drinks, beers and wines. Guests are free to help themselves to tea and coffee. Plates and cutlery can be used to make your own lunch and picnics can be provided for days at the beach. The town of Lanjarón (6km down the track) has a decent selection of restaurants and bars serving an array of delicious Mediterranean seafood. Try Casita de Papel (958 770 028; lacasitadepapel.es), with its tasty tapas, or Bistro 31 (958 771 381). The ambient and ever-busy Baraka (958 785 894; teteria-baraka.com) in central Orgiva specialises in traditional Arabic dishes as well as Spanish classics and does great juice (but serves no alcohol). Not far away on Avenida Gonzales Robles, Almazara El Jardin (958 784 628) is a great place to enjoy freshly-made pizza, sit in its garden and listen to live music.

GETTING THERE Chaparra is situated 6km from Lanjarón (via a very scenic road). From Lanjarón, leave on the Orgiva road. Just 200m after the town limit, turn left up the hill following the prominent signs to Caballo Blanco. As you pass the entrance, the site is the next left down a concrete track.

PUBLIC TRANSPORT From Málaga, buses run to Lanjarón, via Granada, several times daily and take just over 3 hours.

OPEN Easter–end of October.

THE DAMAGE €75 per yurt per night; bell tent €60 per night with a small supplement for children aged 10 and under (€12). For a week's booking a 5% discount is offered.

green mountain yurt

Cortijo Opazo, 18415 Pórtugos, Andalucia, Spain 0034 646 430 656 www.greenmountainyurt.com

When Robert King and William Read first moved to the Sierra Nevada mountains they had a fair task ahead of them, with the early days devoted to renovating a farmhouse to create both their home and an accommodation business. Once they had done that they were able to turn their hands to the true purpose of this hillside haven: establishing a stunning garden to fill the 8,000 square metres that surround the main building. A patchwork of formal gardens, untended wildflowers and climbing wall plants, the garden holds, in a quiet private corner, amid blossoming trees and sun-scorched grasses, the glorious Green Mountain Yurt. A secluded off-grid abode set against a backdrop of steep mountain valleys peppered with quaint Andalucian villages and with every comfort required for a luxury Spanish getaway, this is no ordinary glamping experience. The structure itself matches the beautiful setting: following a traditional Mongolian design, the canvas is lined with a thick wool felt interior, providing warmth in the winter while also reflecting away the infamous summer heat. The steam-bent, chestnut wood is sourced locally and the yurt is built in the nearby town of Cadiar. Inside, the decor continues the natural feel, with white wooden furniture, a wood-burning stove, Moroccan rugs and a light, full-sized double bed.

Outside, on a raised wooden deck, the Green Mountain Yurt Shack provides a shaded outdoor area for cooking, accompanied by a private bathroom with an incredibly well-equipped modern shower, washbasin and cleverly designed composting toilet. The kitchen area has everything you need for a self-catered holiday – all the utensils, along with twin gas hobs, a fridge and ample preparation and storage space. Guests can use vegetables from the garden and eggs from the hens that scratch around or, for those fancying a night off, a home-cooked meal can be ordered and will be freshly prepared by Robert and William, back in the main house.

Despite all the comforts you'd expect from hosts who already run a successful self-catering business, the Green Mountain Yurt also boasts top eco credentials and is an entirely off-grid hideaway. There's solar-powered lighting throughout, working alongside a separate solar panel that heats the shower and hot water. A gas supply runs the kitchen hobs and the small fridge, while those still desperate to charge a phone or use the Wi-Fi can meander back through the garden and use the facilities in the main house. It is from there that you can also jump in the car to go to the coast or to historic Granada, which is just over an hour's drive away. Happily for most visitors, the setting provides holiday enough, without the humdrum of driving around. An exploration of the mountains can be done right from your doorstep: horseriding, canyoning and natural bathing in the mountain streams always prove popular, while such distinctly rural activities shouldn't take away from the fact that a host of quaint towns and villages are within easy walking distance.

COOL FACTOR A beautifully located, eco-friendly yurt with every comfort required, despite its secluded off-grid, mountainside setting.

WHO'S IN Glamping only. No tents, caravans or campervans. Though the yurt is well suited to couples, families can have a separate 'pups' tent' erected if needed, adding space for up to 2 extra children. Pets by prior arrangement.

ON SITE The Green Mountain Yurt is furnished with a full-sized double bed, dining table with chairs, sofa, a wood-burning stove, solar-powered lighting and assorted rugs, cushions and soft furnishings. It has a glazed front door and 2 large double-glazed windows to let the light in and keep the weather out, along with mosquito netting screens. Outside, guests have a large area of garden plus a vegetable patch, with outdoor furniture and sun loungers. 'The Shack', a timber construction, provides you with a shaded outdoor kitchen raised on a wooden deck, and all the equipment you need for cooking: crockery, plates, cups, glasses, cutlery, pots and pans for up to 4 people. There is a sink with hot and cold running water, a twin gas ring stove and a gas-powered fridge and food storage containers. At one end of the shack you will find the 'eco' bathroom – an enclosed room that has a shower, washbasin and a dry compost toilet. Hot water is provided in the kitchen and bathroom via a dedicated solar panel and there is a basic solar lighting system in the bathroom, kitchen and yurt interior. Facilities for charging phones, laptops and so on are available at the main house, as is a Wi-Fi connection.

OFF SITE From the site there are lots of possible walking routes through the Parque Nacional Sierra Nevada and the area is a paradise for outdoor enthusiasts. Horseriding, canyoning and trail-running are all popular, while swimmers can enjoy natural bathing in mountain streams and waterfalls. There is also a local public open-air swimming pool within walking distance. Exploring the old villages of the Alpujarras is

another obvious pastime, and these rural spots still house some excellent rustic eateries. The coast of the Costa Tropical is a 1-hour drive away, while Granada and its famous Alhambra (902 441 221; alhambradegranada.org) is a 75-minute drive.

FOOD & DRINK Drinks and tapas await your arrival and home-cooked meals can be ordered up to 24 hours in advance. Traditional Spanish, Moroccan and oriental dishes are available. Those who prefer to use the onsite cooking shack can use produce from the vegetable garden and eggs courtesy of the free-range hens, or head into Pitres, 1.5km away, which is the nearest place for shops. Robert and William also supply a list of the best local eateries, which include – within walking distance in the the villages of La Taha – a bar selling tasty homemade pizzas, a French owned vegetarian restaurant, L'Atelier (958 857 501), the Mecina Fondales hotel (958 766 254), which serves a full restaurant menu, and a traditional Spanish restaurant, El Aljibe (958 857 312).

GETTING THERE The nearest airports are Málaga, Granada and Almería and the best way to get to the property is to hire a car or catch the bus (see below). Driving directions will be sent upon booking.

PUBLIC TRANSPORT The nearest train station is Granada, 80km away, from where buses run 3 times a day. The nearest bus stop is in Pitres, 1.5km away, from where Robert or William wll pick you up, or you can asked to be dropped off at the top of the road to Atalbéitar, just 200m from Green Mountain Yurt. Robert and William can also arrange transport for you from as far away as Málaga.

OPEN April–October.

THE DAMAGE The yurt costs from €60 per night for 2 people. Minimum stay 4 nights. Extra people cost €8 per night in an additional tent (supplied with sleeping bags and a mattress).

camping & bungalows vall de laguar

Sant Antoni, nr.24, 03791 La Vall de Laguar, Campell, Alicante, Spain 0034 965 584 590 www.campinglaguar.com

Think Costa Blanca and images of Benidorm, packed pools, loud bars and tourist-infested promenades spring to mind. But the Marina Alta, the northernmost stretch of Spain's much-visited southeast coast, is another world entirely. Though it is part of the region of Alicante (and, more broadly speaking, the autonomous community of Valencia), this lush, mountainous region remains remarkably unspoilt. High in these hills that wild boar call home lies the Vall de Laguar, a breathtaking valley dubbed 'the pearl of Valencia'. Rising over 800 metres above sea level, this region hosts some pretty spectacular views, with unparalleled vistas stretching as far as the azure waters of the Med. And from the pitches at the suitably sky-scraping Càmping Bungalows Vall de Laguar you can really contemplate the stunning scene before you.

Nestled in the village of Campell which, along with Fleix and Benimaurell, comprises the three villages of *La Vall*, this refreshingly low-key campsite is one of the region's true gems. There is space for 65 pitches but it never feels crowded, thanks in large part to its ingenious terrace design. A nod to ancient Mediterranean farming tradition, the dry-stone terraces blend seamlessly into the surrounding landscape. The site is family-run and family-friendly, though without the need for day-glo distractions for the kids. Unless, of course, you count the open-air swimming pool – a refreshing godsend under the cloudless summer skies. The cute little onsite café/bar, 'La Bruixa de Laguar' (named

after the village's legendary witch) serves lovely local treats, while the spacious terrace hosts cinema nights on summer evenings.

It's no surprise that the Vall de Laguar is known as the 'trekking capital' of Valencia, blessed as it is with stunning natural eye candy. From the *Barranco del Infierno* ('Hell Canyon') to the prehistoric cave paintings of Pla de Petracos – a UNESCO World Heritage Site – there's no shortage of places to explore and you'll inevitably cross paths with more than a few determined folk following in the footsteps of the marauding Moors. Your hosts will kindly provide maps and other tourist information to make sure you don't get lost. The historic coastal city of Dénia is also just a short drive away, and its golden sands and traditional white houses, plus the attractions of the nearby Montgó Nature Reserve, make it a great area to spend the day, safe in the knowledge that you can beat the heat with a hasty retreat to your campsite in the hills.

COOL FACTOR A walkers' dream in a beautiful mountain valley that has been dubbed 'the Pearl of Valencia'.

WHO'S IN Tents, caravans, large groups, well-behaved pets (not permitted in the bungalows) – yes.

ON SITE 65 plots, all with electrical and water hook-ups. 2 heated buildings have warm water showers, toilets and sinks. Laundry with tumble dryer. Small library. Small café/ bar. Open-air pool with *chiringuito* bar and terrace. Free Wi-Fi throughout. BBQs provided.

OFF SITE The beaches of Dénia are only a half hour drive away (19km). Sample the seafood, splash in the surf or head further down the coast to the secluded coves of Xàbia and Calpe. In July the famous week-long 'Bous a la Mar' ('Bulls at the Sea') festival takes place in Dénia, when daring revellers provoke the animals to chase them down the town's main street *Marqués de Campo*, straight into the sea. Spain's third city, Valencia, is around 100km away. It's a vibrant city which boasts impressive contemporary architecture, a charming old quarter and buzzing nightlife. If you're visiting in March, be sure to attend the city's massive *Fallas* festival, when huge papier mâché effigies are set ablaze throughout the town.

FOOD & DRINK The onsite cafe/bar serves a decent if small selection of tapas, baguettes, salads and mixed plates. There are great restaurants in the nearby villages offering typical Alicantean cuisine such as *arròs a banda* (not to be confused with *paella*). In the closest village, Campell, you'll find a baker and butcher and there's a market every Thursday morning selling fresh veg and other supplies.

GETTING THERE Leave the Motorway AP7 at exit 62 (in Ondara-Dénia) and follow signs to Oliva and then Orba. Once in Orba keep on the new bypass and then follow directions to "Fontilles" or "Vall de Laguar". After 7 minutes, you'll be in the village of Campell, beyond which you should follow the signs to the Càmping Vall de Laguar.

OPEN All year.

THE DAMAGE Adults €5.25–€5.90, caravans €6.50–€7.50, campervans €8–€8.90, tents €5.25–€5.90, electricity €3.60–€3.90. Reductions available for multiple nights.

camping villa de viver

Partida de las Quinchas, 12460 Viver, Castellón, Spain 0034 964 141 334 www.campingviver.com

Spain is a vast country of contrasting regions and provinces. You'd be hard pressed to explore it all in a year's worth of camping breaks, but we know of a spot that conveniently straddles some of the country's most vibrant, diverse and unspoilt areas. High up on the lush lower steppes of the Alto Palancia, the charming Castellón village of Viver plays host to the equally lovely Ana and Eduardo, whose blissfully chilled-out campsite, Villa de Viver, is one of the region's hidden hotspots.

The site boasts 65 pitches, with ample shade provided by the many fragrant pines towering overhead. The views from here are spectacular, with expansive vistas overlooking the Rio Palancia and Las Penas Rubias. Despite its size, there's a real sense of silence and seclusion here. But this isolated rustic charm doesn't mean Villa de Viver skimps on facilities. Besides the pristine wash-block and well-stocked shop, campers can cool off in the spacious swimming pool or unwind with a *cerveza* or two courtesy of the onsite *chiringuito*. There's a relaxed, inclusive air to life at Villa de Viver. It's very much a family-friendly site and it also welcomes groups (be sure to ask about the camping bungalows, bungalow tents and dormitories). 'We do not organise things to keep the kids buzzy', as Eduardo puts it, with that inimitable Dutch breeziness. And why would they need to in a spot as enviably located as this?

Location-wise, Villa de Viver takes some topping, offering the very best of Castellón and neighbouring Aragón. It's a region known as the 'route of the springs', with snaking rivulets and a verdant mountainous landscape. There are trails to be hiked (the Serra Calderona and Montes Universales), a national park to explore (Serra d'Espada) and the famous beaches of the east coast are but a short drive away. But the real finds here are the traditional mountain villages, untouched by mass tourism. To walk the quaint cobbled streets and marvel at the medieval architecture of Navajas, Segorbe and Toro is a real pleasure. As Eduardo puts it, from strolling the streets, 'in about 30 minutes you can be at the beach and in about one hour you could be skiing in Valdelinares and Javalambrel!' A country of contrasts, indeed.

COOL FACTOR Blissfully chilled-out, family-friendly camping in a beautiful location.

WHO'S IN Tents, caravans, campervans, dogs – yes. Groups are also permitted by pre-arrangement.

ON SITE 65 pitches with electric hook-ups and plenty of shade. The facilities block houses showers and toilets, and there is a smaller room with 4 private bathrooms. Laundry facilities are available. Free hot water and drinking water. Grey water disposal. Swimming pool with terrace and views over the valley. Restaurant and bar.

OFF SITE The site is situated equidistant between the ancient city of Castellón de la Plana and the port of Valencia – Spain's third largest city. The historic medieval town of Teruel is just 45 minutes away; here you should be sure to visit the town's famous 14th-century towers and the Mausoleo de los Amantes (978 618 398; amantesdeteruel.es), the final resting place of Teruel's iconic star-crossed lovers, Isabel de Segura and Diego de Marcilla. Also in Teruel, for young and old alike, Dinópolis (978 617 715; dinopolis.com) is a 3D multimedia extravaganza, bringing prehistoric monsters to life. The spa town of Montanejos boasts the famous hot thermal springs of Fuente de Baños and there are lots of lovely authentic villages to explore, including Albarracín, which is often acclaimed as the most beautiful village in Spain. See it before UNESCO declares its gorgeous cobbled streets a world heritage site and the crowds descend.

FOOD & DRINK Your kindly hosts serve a daily *table d'hôte* menu in summer. You can also order freshly baked bread for the morning. In Viver you'll find a decent – if pricey – restaurant in Thalassa (964 141 258; restaurantethalassa.com). The Castellón region also boasts some of Spain's most famous cuisine, including *mariscadas* and, of course, paella. The region is noted for some tasty sweet treats too, including delicious nougaty turrón. You could also take a day-trip to Alboraya, which is home of a sweet, sticky confectionery known as *fartons* (stop sniggering!).

GETTING THERE From Zaragoza, follow the A23, coming off at the exit for Jerica. From here, follow the signs to Viver. Once you get to the village, follow the camping signs.

PUBLIC TRANSPORT There's a bus stop in Viver, 4km from the site, where buses from Teruel and Valencia stop. The train station, Jerica-Viver, has services to Valencia and Teruel.

OPEN March–November.

THE DAMAGE 2 adults, tent or caravan with car, or campervan, with electricity: €23–€27 per night, €126 for 7 nights.

la fresneda

Partida Vall del Pi, 44596 La Fresneda, Teruel, Spain 0034 978 854 085 www.campinglafresneda.com

Picture this. The sky is a startling blue, save for a lonely cloud sweeping like a white paintbrush stroke across the distant horizon. A bird with a graceful wingspan weaves concentric circles above a small hill crowned in soft, matt-green foliage. The valley is a gently tiered landscape of olive and almond trees lined up like soldiers, flattening out into a yellow, parched terrain, before erupting into a distant wall of red rock. Sounds too good to be true? Wait, there's more.

In the foreground, the long afternoon shadows of a row of olive trees fall across the campsite, letting you know it's high time you drew up a pew on the little umbrella-studded patio. From the flat-roofed bar, fashioned from rustic timbers and rugged rock, a friendly face emerges with a glass of cold draught beer.

The Dutch couple who pulled this little piece of paradise together have figured out exactly what camping in Spain should be about. Jet Knijn and Joost Leeuwenberg purchased this 19-acre property in 2002. By recycling tiles and stonework from the original villa, the couple built a delightful family home in the style of the region. On the adjacent campsite, the washing area, bathroom and tiny bar were also specially constructed to help keep temperatures down and reduce environmental impact. The *finca* not only looks great, but its design got the thumbs-up from the locals, too.

During building, Jet and Joost lived in a caravan with just a solar shower and a composting toilet for company, an experience that turned them into camping converts. La Fresneda has only 25 pitches and, to keep the atmosphere relaxed, the couple discourage you from bringing your doggy companions, groups of friends or other appendages. They also don't have a swimming pool so instead built a shady garden atrium in which to cool down and relax.

There is plenty of exploring to be done. Ancient paths traverse local medieval villages, wild countryside, rugged canyons and mountainsides. Natural-rock swimming pools are 15-30 minutes away, and you can explore the scenic nature reserve of Los Puertos de Beceite; while the Via Verde, an abandoned railway track-turned-bike trail, gives you the choice of exploring by cycle or on horseback. Jet has catalogued these adventures in a handy campsite guide, so no excuses for not getting out and about.

Meanwhile, back at the campsite, Bar La Roca and the adjoining patio are well placed for early risers to get their espresso fix and pastries for breakfast and, in the evening, draught beer and wine from the local *bodegas* slips down a treat. Six nights a week, Joost gets busy in the kitchen making tapas, paella or a three-course menu, served up just as the sun goes down. In the off-season, when the campsite is closed, Jet and Joost harvest their own olives and save the big ones for scoffing, while the rest are bottled up to make edible souvenirs for the next camping season, along with local almonds: a perfect goodbye gift. A little piece of paradise. In a nutshell.

COOL FACTOR Perfectly and tastefully adapted site that gives a full-on Spanish experience.

WHO'S IN Tents, campervans, caravans, trailer tents – yes. Pets and groups – no.

ON SITE 25 spacious pitches with electrical hook-ups. Immaculate and tasteful bathrooms (including disabled facilities), a washing area with washing machine and basins. Bar "La Roca" with terrace – meals available every day (except Monday). Fresh bread available every day (except Sunday). Gas bottles on sale, telephone, postal service, safe, Wi-Fi available free of charge. Plus an amazing garden atrium in which to cool down and relax.

OFF SITE There's a ton of outdoor activities available in the local area – birdwatching, visiting a vulture observatory, hiking, mountain biking, rock climbing, horseback riding, 4 x 4 expeditions, canyoning and cycling on an abandoned and restored railway track. You can also visit monumental villages (like La Fresneda, with its medieval jail), the Picasso museum in Horta or admire the rice fields and birdlife in the Ebro Delta.

FOOD & DRINK Go no further than Bar La Roca, where the owners dish up tapas, paella and a 3-course menu 6 nights a week. Vegetarians are well catered for too. There's beer on tap, local organic wines and a handy espresso machine. Order fresh bread to be delivered to your tent each morning (except Sundays).

GETTING THERE Take the AP7 towards Tarragona/Valencia, and come off at exit 40 (N235/C42) to Tortosa/L'Aldea. Follow the C42 to Lleida, then C12 Amposta, and C12 Gandesa. Turn on to the N230B Vall-de-Robres (Valderrobres), then the T333 Vall-de-roures, then the T330 Vall-de-roures. From Valderrobres take the A231 towards Alcañiz. The campsite is signposted from here.

PUBLIC TRANSPORT Twice a day there is a bus from Alcañiz to La Fresneda, from where it's 3km to the campsite.

OPEN April–October.

THE DAMAGE €5.50 per adult/child, plus €14 per pitch. The price of the pitch includes vehicle, motorbike or bicycle and tent, caravan, campervan and electrical hook-up.

forest days

Navès, 25286, Solsonès – Lleida, Catalonia, Spain 0034 722 394 264 www.forestdaysglamping.com

When John and Montse left the corporate rush of central London a few years ago they had more than just a house in the suburbs in mind. Returning to Montse's roots in beautiful Catalonia, they ended up in the most contrasting landscape imaginable, with the skyscrapers of the city replaced by the crinkling peaks of the Pyrenees, stretching northward from their home, and the murky Thames now the Vall d'Ora, a wild swimmer's delight where river water cascades in sparkling waterfalls. Cars, tubes and double-decker buses are nothing more than a distant memory, supplanted by tractors and bicycles in their new rural paradise – a beautiful farmstead, poised on the divide between rolling, fertile farmland and steep, pine-clad mountains. Nestled among the trees, this brand new campsite captures much of what is great about a proper glamping holiday, with all the kit you need to simply kick back and relax. The shady canopy of pine needles and the views across the rolling hills beyond make it ideal for those who just want to hang out and not do much at all, while the easily walkable distance to the river, a nearby lake and a host of charming old towns mean explorers are just as well catered for.

The site itself comprises four fully furnished bell tents, raised on wooden platforms and well separated from each another so guests have a truly private camping experience. Inside, a super king-size bed is accompanied by bedside tables (made out of huge round logs) topped by charming old-style lanterns, a wood-burning stove in the colder months and a pair of indoor chairs. Outside, guests have their own dining space, and a hammock or two for reading and relaxing. On particularly hot days you can also roll up the lower section of the canvas bell tents, allowing the breeze to naturally cool the space.

While the bell tents have an adjacent private bathroom (with a composting loo and a solar shower upon request) there is another ablutions area down by the main house, equipped with flushing loos, showers and power sockets. By the house you will also pick up the Wi-Fi signal and can grab a little info on the local area while chatting to John and Montse. Their first port of call is normally to point you towards a pleasant walking route that descends to the river where an old lock has become a waterfall. The pools either side are perfect for swimming.

Those enticed into the countryside beyond the campsite by the wonderful views can hop on to the nearby C-26 road that wiggles down to the old town of Solsona. En route, take a detour for more swimming in Pantà de Sant Ponç or head straight into the town with its well-preserved old centre: the *Clos Antic*. Though boasting a towering Catalonian cathedral and a cluster of good eateries, the best thing about Solsona is that it's only the tip of the iceberg. A host of other small but historic towns pepper the surrounding area and many act as gateways into the mountains, the prime destination for lovers of the great outdoors.

COOL FACTOR A site that both soothes the spirit when you need to relax and has all you require when you want to explore the great outdoors.

WHO'S IN Couples, families and glampers – yes. Tents, campervans, caravans and dogs – no.

ON SITE 4 bell tents. Each sleep 2 in a super-king-size bed (bedding provided), 2 extra children's beds can be added if required. Each tent is furnished with hand-crafted wooden furniture and has its own private eco-bathroom with a composting toilet. There is another ablutions area by the main house with proper flushing loos, showers and electrical charging points. There's an honesty bar by the house and Wi-Fi. A central BBQ and cooking area is free for all to use and those looking to do more elaborate cooking can also ask for a cook-set to be provided.

OFF SITE Take a walk down the rough track to Vall d'Ora, a tiny river where an old lock now creates a cascading waterfall; an idyllic place to swim. Further afield, take the C-26 west towards Solsona and stop at Pantà de Sant Ponç, a beautiful lake that's perfect for wild swimming. The surrounding area has a network of excellent footpaths and the small roads around the lake are very quiet – ideal for cycling. You can kayak here too; just ask John and Montse for more information. In Solsona itself the Cathedral of Santa Maria de Solsona sits in the centre of the old town. Further south, Cardona is an equally beautiful place, overlooked by a castle.

FOOD & DRINK A continental breakfast is delivered to your tent each day and dinner can also be provided. There is a communal BBQ area or, if you don't want to cook, do the 15-minute drive into the town of Solsona.

GETTING THERE Ask when booking for specific directions. They'll also give you some recommended stops en route.

PUBLIC TRANSPORT There are around 4 buses a day from Barcelona to Solsona, from where pick-up can be arranged.

OPEN All year.

THE DAMAGE Prices start from €75 per night for 2 people including breakfast.

camping cala llevadó

Camping Cala Llevadó, Ctra. GI-682 Tossa-Lloret (pk.18,9), 17320 Tossa de Mar, Spain 0034 972 340 314
www.calallevado.com

Who says bigger isn't better? There's loads of space plus loads of campers at Cala Llevadó, but pitching your tent in the intimate cliff-hugging pine forest they have here makes you feel as though the view of the Mediterranean below is there for you, and you alone.

This sense of seclusion is all down to the setting: a glorious expanse of land on a sloping hillside draped in oaks and pines. On the seafront, giant walls of naked red rock alternate with not two, not three, but four beaches – all worthy of closer inspection. But far from being crowded, these sandy plots, or *calas*, are more like secret pirate coves, hidden between the rocks and almost undetectable until your toes are actually twiddling in their gorgeous sands, wondering if they'll come into contact with any buried pieces-of-eight.

Cala Llevadó itself is hidden away at the end of a tempting winding path, where kids with buckets and spades clamber amongst the rock pools looking for sea urchins. Further along, Cala d'en Carlos has a graveyard full of old boats that still feel the summer waves, and a little sheltered kiosk, an ideal spot for taking a refreshing beachside beverage. Cala Figuera is smaller, giving all you skinny-dippers a chance to have some privacy. At the other end, Platges de Llorell is a more active hub, which will certainly appeal if you're into scuba-diving, water-skiing, wind-surfing or kite-boarding.

A view on to one of these beaches should be a priority when you're wondering about the best place to pitch your tent. The idyllic beachfront plots are the ones that you'll find everyone else is heading for too, however, so it pays to arrive early. Plots A 67–87, above Cala Llevadó, are some of the best, beneath shady pine trees overlooking the cove. Similar pitches overlook the other beaches. If you happen to be lucky enough to score one of these, all you'll need next is a couple of deckchairs for a front-row seat, and perhaps a beer or two, as the setting sun bathes that distant blue horizon in dazzling reds, oranges and pinks.

Never fear if you miss out on the natural pleasures of the waterfront, because luxury of a different kind can be found by those who go for one of the glamping pitches – either eco-conscious bungalows or glamping pods or forest cabins, which are all built to the highest and greenest standards.

The campsite seems to go on forever, but Cala Llevadó strikes a nice balance between showing off its natural assets and providing you with everything you'll ever want or need (plus a few things you hadn't thought of). If you do grow weary of the beach, take your pick of the campsite's swimming pools, basketball court, children's playground, outdoor café or restaurant.

COOL FACTOR You can't get closer to a beach. In fact, you can't get closer to four beaches.

WHO'S IN Tents, campervans, caravans, dogs – yes. No pets in the bungalows.

ON SITE About 400 plots for tents and caravans, plus 30 ecological bungalows in a separate area of the site, 6 glamping pods (forest cabins) and 34 standard bungalows. Eco bungalows are made of wood and cork and built with low energy consumption in mind. Some have sea views and others have views to the forest of Cadiretes. There are 4 facilities buildings with toilets, baths and showers, laundry and ironing facilities. There is a swimming pool (and a children's pool), playground, games area, hairdresser, supermarket, basketball court, post office and internet café.

OFF SITE Llorell Beach has children's activities during peak season, or visit nearby Tossa de Mar (3km away) – a pleasant resort whose well-preserved old town is set within a walled enclosure dating back to the 12th century. If you're in need of exercise, take a 4-hour (9km) signposted walk between Tossa de Mar and Lloret de Mar. Sights include the Iberian settlement of Puig de Castellet and Santa Clotilde gardens.

FOOD & DRINK The campsite has a bar and café-cum-restaurant on an outdoor patio, which serves traditional meals and has particularly good paella. Work up an appetite by walking to Tossa de Mar, with its mix of local restaurants.

GETTING THERE You can spot the campsite easily on the roadside between Tossa de Mar and Lloret de Mar on Ctra. De Tossa a Lloret (around the 3km marker).

PUBLIC TRANSPORT Local buses shuttle between Tossa, Lloret, Barcelona and Girona.

OPEN April–end of September.

THE DAMAGE €5.75–€9.25 per adult and €0–€5.75 per child (4–12 years). Tent pitches €14.95–€31.50. Caravans €16.25–€33.50. Campervans €13.95–€27.25. Dogs €5. Forest cabins from €85 a night; standard bungalows €45–€75 a night; eco-bungalows from €115 a night.

can coromines

Ctra. de Figueres a Olot N-260 Km.60, 17851 Maià de Montcal, Girona, Spain 0034 972 591 108 www.cancoromines.com

Let's see – a beautiful setting at the base of the Pyrenees, the perfect location for exploring stunning Catalonia. A bucolic paradise brimming with wildlife and divine countryside views. Interested? We thought so.

Set around a 15th-century Catalan farmhouse, Can Coromines is a friendly, family-run site in the heart of rural Girona. It's a spacious place with many different areas to pitch your tent. Take your pick from a nice spot under the shade of a pine tree or a lush open space beneath the imposing panorama of Mont Mare de Deú. Wherever you choose, you're sure to enjoy this wonderful place. Your host Sara does an excellent job in creating a tranquil, relaxing environment.

Onsite activities are also plentiful, so whether you fancy a dip in the pool, a beer on the terrace or a game of table-tennis, Can Coromines should have something to offer. Off site, there's the nearby city of Figueres (an 18–km drive away), birthplace of surrealist art icon Salvador Dali and nowadays home to the fabulous Dali Theatre and Museum. Housing over 4,000 pieces of Dali's work including paintings, drawings and sculptures, it's pretty unmissable, whether you're a fan of the moustachioed maestro or not.

Many proud Catalans maintain that their corner of the country is a little bit closer to heaven than the rest of Spain. And with the soaring peaks, glorious countryside and sleepy small towns that surround this beautiful site, it's hard to disagree.

COOL FACTOR A family site in rural Girona, set around a 15th-century Catalan farmhouse.

WHO'S IN Tents, caravans, campervans, families, dogs (must be kept on a lead) – yes.

ON SITE 52 pitches, all with electrical hook-ups. Showers, sinks, toilets, washing machine and a sink for washing clothes. Restaurant (open end of June–August) and bar with terrace. Swimming pool, children's playground, zip-wire, badminton, table-tennis, table football and bikes for hire. Free Wi-Fi.

OFF SITE It's a 20-minute walk to the village of Maià de Montcal, where you can visit the church, the local shops or pick up a souvenir from the resident potter at his workshop. Catalonia's largest natural lake, Estany de Banyoles, is a brief drive away – it's a famous rowing location (used in the 1992 Barcelona Olympics) and popular with athletes and cyclists. If you visit Figueres, don't miss the Dali Theatre and Museum (972 677 500; salvador-dali.org) and the fun (if slightly creepy) Toy Museum (972 504 585; mjc.cat).

FOOD & DRINK Can Coromines' friendly welcome is matched by the tasty homemade food served in the café, whose menu features fresh local dishes using herbs and vegetables from the garden. Bread, croissants, milk and eggs are available to order every morning. There are dozens of restaurants in Figueres. Lizarran (972 506 667) offers a terrific range of tapas in a lively atmosphere.

GETTING THERE Girona airport is a 35-minute drive away. Maià de Montcal is 20km west of Figueres on the N260.

PUBLIC TRANSPORT Direct buses run from Barcelona to Besalú (3km from the site). The train station at Figueres is a major stop and you can take a bus from there to a bus stop just 1km from the site (Olot–Figueres route).

OPEN Easter bank holiday–November.

THE DAMAGE €7.50–€5.70 per adult and tent; €4.50–€3.20 for children; €4.60 per car. Special offers during low season.

la solane

Mas de la Solane, 66260 Saint Laurent de Cerdans, France 0033 4 89 81 64 14 www.solane.info

La Solane means 'on the sunny side' in Spanish, which says a lot about this marvellous site, hidden away in the French Pyrénées. Facing south towards the nearby Spanish border, it's perfectly placed to catch the sun as it rises behind the Spanish peaks. The simple pleasure of waking up to watch and feel the sun's golden rays as they filter through the site's chestnut, linden and fruit trees, and across the scenic mountain landscape, is reason enough to stay here. Plus the location is as remote as you could possibly wish for.

Dutch couple Eva and Jeroen converted the site from an overgrown tangle of mountain vegetation and a couple of abandoned farmhouses into the beautiful place it is today. They cleared the area and carved terraces into the hillside on which to pitch your tent. Being eco-minded, they collect water from a natural source and have constructed solar panels for electricity.

The eight generously sized atmospheric pitches are all well spaced out, and either well shaded by surrounding trees or nicely placed to catch the sun. Each pitch has its own wooden picnic table. Except for the large new swimming pool, there's just a reception area, a couple of hot showers, a washing-up area and a great campfire area, where guests can mingle at night. There's no playground as such, but the kids will lovebouncing on the trampoline or exploring the surrounding woods and splashing around in the nearby river.

At night, guests can enjoy a glass of wine on the terrace or join their hosts for home-cooked evening meals and pizza out of the traditional wood-fired oven. There's also a steady supply of fresh organic produce on site – although meat-eaters will have to suppress their carnivorous cravings as all meals are veggie/pescetarian.

The pièce de résistance, however, is without doubt La Solane's magnificent treehouse. Sitting seven metres above ground in the loving embrace of a 250-year-old chestnut tree, this feat of eco-engineering sleeps a family of up to six. It is fully equipped with kitchen bathroom (including shower and toilet), and even has a terrace for soaking up the breathtaking views. Elsewhere, there's a gorgeous, secluded wooden cottage (sleeping four) with its own kitchen, bathroom and conservatory. Finally, a caravan-under-canopy with outside kitchen is an ideal romantic retreat (or you could squeeze in a family of four). An indoor pool and sauna are also planned, but the owners promise that it won't impinge on the site's sun-kissed, natural vibe.

COOL FACTOR Remote camping right in the middle of the Pyrénées.

WHO'S IN Tents, campervans, tent-trailers, glampers – yes. Caravans, motorhomes – no.

ON SITE 8 pitches with wooden picnic tables but no electricity. Pitches are spacious and private, shady or with a view. Campfires allowed on the terrace and on site if the weather permits. There is a treehouse (sleeping 6), a wooden family cabin (sleeping 4) and caravan (ideal for 2 but can sleep 4) – all come fully equipped. 2 new showers and 2 toilets; washing up area with great views; a river with natural swimming pools and a waterfall. Indoor pool and sauna are planned. La Cantina stocks plenty of organic food (no meat) and serves evening supper on the terrace.

OFF SITE Hikers will enjoy the walks through the mountains, not least the GR10 – try the hike to the rocky peak of the Roc de San Salvador (1,234m). The lovely medieval Spanish town of Maçanet de Cabrenys is a 45-minute drive away.

FOOD & DRINK Basics are available on site alongside a well-stocked kitchen. Three-course evening meals available (€12.50; €7.50 for kids). The closest supermarket is in St-Laurent, a 25-minute drive. The best local market is in Céret (Saturdays). Can Mach (09 72 54 33 11; canmach.com) in Tapis serves hearty cuisine for good prices. Maçanet de Cabrenys also has several nice restaurants serving traditional Catalan/Spanish food.

GETTING THERE Take the last exit 'Le Boulou' off the A9, then the D115 into the Vallespir Valley; after Arles-sur-Tech take the road to St-Laurent-de-Cerdans. Follow the signs saying La Solane. GPS doesn't know the way!

PUBLIC TRANSPORT Train to Perpignan and bus (Courrier Catalan, Line 341, 6 times daily) to Amélie-les-Bains or (3 times daily) St-Laurent-de-Cerdans. Pick-ups can be arranged.

OPEN All year round, but depending on the weather in winter, so often from Easter to the beginning of December.

THE DAMAGE Family of 4 with own tent €35.

belrepayre airstream & retro trailer park

Nr Mirepoix, Ariége, Manses 09500, France 0033 5 61 68 11 99 www.airstreameurope.com

A couple of decades ago, Perry Balfour and his wife, Coline, set about transforming a beautiful part of the Ariege countryside into a themed trailer park. After locating an impressive collection of Airstreams, the pair painstakingly restored each one to its former glory, then decked them out in 1970s-era fabrics and flea-market paraphernalia. Most of these glistening beauties have come all the way from America, although one, transformed into a distinctive, colourful diner called Apollo Lounge, was discovered sitting under the Eiffel Tower.

Though the exteriors look majestic, the interiors look even better, with their cool bathrooms and showers, funky bedrooms and plethora of aptly psychedelic touches that includes floral curtains, retro crockery, black-and-white TVs and even an eight-track music system. Sliding in a scratchy Sly & the Family Stone cassette and putting your feet up on the sun lounger outside is a pretty cool experience, to say the least.

There's not much else on site save for an activities field, a nearby wood to explore and a small store at reception. In the evenings, all the action is centred around the Apollo Lounge, where Coline serves up tasty French food and wine, and Perry, cunningly disguised as DJ Bobby Lotion, spins everything from Motown to rock 'n' roll and disco on vinyl. If ever there was a campsite to help you trip back in time, this is it.

COOL FACTOR Europe's first retro Airstream trailer park, in the foothills of the Pyrénées.

WHO'S IN Tents, vintage caravans, camping cars, groups – yes. Pets – not in the Airstreams.

ON SITE 11 Airstreams for rent, each equipped with furniture and kitchen; a slightly old-fashioned but well-maintained block with 3 toilets and 3 showers; field next to reception caters for tenters and VWs. Retro Apollo Lounge with music, good food and drinks. Sauna, yoga room, table tennis, badminton, outdoor cinema screen, small shop. No campfires.

OFF SITE Hiking and mountain biking; bikes rented on site or delivered (06 31 94 24 91). There are medieval castles close by, the marvellous Château de Montségur (05 61 01 06 94; montsegur.fr) included. Discover Ariège by microlight with Partag'air (06 88 50 60 85; partagair.jimdo.com).

FOOD & DRINK Decent organic food on site in the evenings plus local produce. Apollo Lounge is well stocked with beer and wine. The Airstreams have cooking facilities. Mirepoix has a good farmers' market every Monday and great cafés.

GETTING THERE From Toulose follow the A66 south and exit at Pamiers on to the D119 to Mirepoix. From Montpelliers follow the A61 and exit at Bram in the direction of Mirepoix.

PUBLIC TRANSPORT Get to Pamiers or Toulouse by train, then hire a car or Perry may be able to pick you up.

OPEN May–End of September.

THE DAMAGE Pitch and 2 people €20–€30 per night. Airstream from €90 per night for 2 people, €160 for 4. Rates depend on how long you stay. 10% discount for visitors coming with a vintage car.

camping pré fixe

Route de Saint Gaudens, Cassagnabère-Tournas 31420, France 0033 5 61 98 71 00 www.camping-pre-fixe.com

Covering a region of over 45,000 square kilometres, the Mid-Pyrénées is the largest administrative region in France. In an area bigger than the Netherlands, visitors could be forgiven for feeling a little bit... well, overwhelmed in the shadow of such imposing mountains. But fear not Cool Campers, for this is also one of France's most sparsely populated regions. Daily life breezes along round these parts, with the Pyreneans renowned *gourmands* and unashamed exponents of that quintessential *joie de vivre*. We're happy to report that this laid-back atmosphere has extended to the local camping fraternity and, in particular, to the wonderfully easy-going Camping Pré Fixe.

Nestled next to the ancient foothill village of Comminges – the historical regional capital – the 3-star Camping Pré Fixe positively oozes peace

and tranquillity. Campers are spoilt for choice with a number of accommodation options on offer, including traditional tent pitches, luxury lodges and chalets as well as cute mini ridges tents on stilts – perfect for camping couples.

With an onsite swimming pool, tennis courts and more activities than you can shake a baguette at, there's plenty to keep you occupied (and that's not even mentioning the wealth of outdoor pursuits that await in the surrounding mountains). Our personal highlight is the camp's own *Le Bistro* bar: which is a labour of love for resident sommelier and owner Cyril, and stocks some of the finest local produce and wine.

So, with good wine, entertainment and even better views, Pré Fixe ticks all the most important Cool Camping boxes.

COOL FACTOR A perfect family site with a homely, welcoming vibe.

WHO'S IN Tents, campervans, caravans, glamping, camping, pets (only on camping pitches) – yes.

ON SITE This terraced site consists of 43 spacious (100m²) pitches separated by hedges and various trees for added shade. Electrical hook-ups are available on some plots. Fully furnished and equipped eco-tents and luxury wooden cabins are also available. Laundry facilities, onsite grocery shop, bar/bistro. Activities include a boules pitch, tennis court, badminton and volleyball, children's library, board games and ping-pong. No campfires.

OFF SITE With the Pyrénées just beyond your tent flaps, a wealth of outdoor pursuits awaits you: caving, rock climbing, paragliding, rafting, canyoning and kayaking, to name but a few. There are also plenty of walking/hiking/cycling routes and the beautiful ancient village of Comminges is just a short stroll from the site.

FOOD & DRINK Le Bistro offers quality wines and a fresh daily menu of homemade dishes. Cyril also organises BBQs, evening dinners and wine-tasting events.

GETTING THERE From Paris (by motorway), take the A10 (Paris-Bordeaux 582km) and then the A62 (Bordeaux–Toulouse 242km). Take the A64 in the Tarbes direction and leave at exit 21 (direction Aurignac). After 8km you will be in Cassagnabère.

PUBLIC TRANSPORT: Rail and bus transport is not particularly great for this campsite. By air, though, Toulouse-Blagnac Airport (located 1 hour from the campsite) is the nearest and serves many destinations in the UK and Ireland: London, Bristol, Birmingham, Manchester, Dublin and Shannon.

OPEN Start of April–mid October.

THE DAMAGE Pitch, 2 persons, 1 car: €13.50–€20.80; with electricity €17.50–€26.30. Extra adults €4.20–€6.20; extra child €3.20–€5.20; pets €2.10–€2.60.

camping la vie en rose

Escanecrabe 31350, France   0033 6 71 01 49 57   www.campinglavieenrose.com

Nestled on the undulating southern slopes of bucolic Gascony – a land famed for its *douceur de vivre* – Camping La Vie en Rose exhibits the fabled 'sweetness of life' and then some. Stretching over seven breathtaking acres of tranquil wildflower meadow fringed by enchanting oak woodlands, this beautiful Haute-Garrone glampsite hosts stunning views, with the peaks of the Pyrénées towering tantalisingly on the horizon.

After being met with the warmest of welcomes from hosts Emma and Jamie Fulton, the lucky glampers are leisurely delivered to one of the three spacious bell tents. Well, we call them tents... but that doesn't really do justice to the scale and style of these canvas palaces. Sat atop timber decking with rugs throughout, each tent boasts a staggering 45 metres of square footage. There's a lounge plus two separate bedroom tents including a deluxe 'superking' room that's ideal for parents. Outside, a fully equipped campsite kitchen has the answer to all your culinary needs, while the über-luxurious timber washing lodge is the very definition of high spec, with hot power showers, marble washbasins, organic soaps and fluffy towels. With an assortment of outdoor entertainment (pétanque, swingball, slides and swings), a well-stocked games room (books, pool table, ping-pong), and lots of other thoughtful touches (cots, high chairs and breakfast delivered fresh to the tent), it's clear that Camping La Vie en Rose is a site run by people who know the ingredients for a fuss-free family holiday. With all the comforts of a boutique hotel at a snippet of the cost, this is the ideal break for families looking to really get away from it all.

And when it's time to venture forth, this pocket of southwest France offers a wealth of things to do. Head to the beach at Lac de la Gimone for a refreshing summer swim, or take your little lords and ladies to the fortified city of Carcassonne – a UNESCO World Heritage Site that hosts jousting, troubadours and medieval fairs. And, of course, all you weekend Wigginses can test your cycling stamina on the Col du Tourmalet and Col d'Aspin.

The site is named after the signature tune of France's national songstress, Edith Piaf. Swinging lazily in the hammock in this Pyrenean paradise, we reckon France's iconic diva would approve.

COOL FACTOR It's a life through rose-coloured specs at this breathtaking slice of Pyrenean paradise.

WHO'S IN Groups, families – yes. Dogs, caravans, campervans – no.

ON SITE 3 bell tents (internal space of 45m²) with wooden flooring, separate lounge, decking and shaded canvas awnings. 2-bedroom tents (6m and 5m linked) one of which is 'superking' (luxury cotton sheets, netted inner tents and solar lighting as standard). Each tent has its own fully equipped outdoor kitchen with gas hob and fridge, plus private shower/ toilet room facilities with organic soaps and towels included.

OFF SITE Head up the mountains for a spot of wild swimming. Les Laquettes, Lac de Mondeley and Lacs de Bastan are all less than a couple of hours drive away. There is parking and the latter boasts a café and beach. France's fourth largest city, Toulouse, is an hour away and has plenty of museums and sights, including the fine art collection at the Musée des Augustins (05 61 22 21 82; augustins.org), while a visit to the Cité de l'Espace (05 67 22 23 24; cite-espace.com) national space centre is out of this world. A gentle river cruise along the city's Canal du Midi is a fantastically peaceful way to round off your day-trip. Finally, why not treat yourself to a day of restorative pampering at the Balnéa spa at Loudenvielle (08 91 70 19 19)?

FOOD & DRINK A continental breakfast of fresh fruit, breads, pain au chocolat and croissants is delivered to your tent each morning, as well as complimentary welcome gifts on arrival. The surrounding farms and markets boast a wealth of fantastic local produce and Emma will happily point you towards the finest regional charcuterie, meats and cheeses. Restaurant-wise, the village of Saint Andre boasts 2 real gems in the Chez Fourcade Bistrot (05 61 98 92 20; chez-maryse-fourcade.fr) and Auberge Champêtre (05 61 88 22 71; auberge-champetre. com). 10 minutes away in Aurignac, Hôtel St. Laurans (05 61 90 49 55; hotelstlaurans.fr) brasserie and garden restaurant serves refined dishes in sophisticated surroundings. Their wine list is also pretty extensive.

GETTING THERE Driving directions will be provided by the site when a booking is made.

OPEN June–September.

THE DAMAGE High season: €170 per night (minimum of 1 week's stay starting on Friday or Saturday). Low season: €132 per night (minimum 4 night's stay starting on Friday or Saturday). Tents can accommodate 4–6 people.

glisten camping – col d'ibardin

220 Route d'Olhette, 64122 Urrugne, France 0844 344 0196 www.glistencamping.com

Some otherwordly structures have landed in the Labourd countryside with their geodesic shape and striking white outer shell. In fact, visitors to these parts could be forgiven for thinking they've stumbled upon southwest France's very own Roswell. Well, the little green men could do a lot worse than the dome village at Glisten Camping...

An innovative new holiday experience, Glisten Camping brings some truly unique glamping accommodation to sunny southwest France. Like the domes themselves, the concept is simple. The brainchild of Cornwall-based camping nut Simon Thomason, Glisten selects the best locations in southwest France and then sets up these distinctively stylish geodesic domes, which can sleep a family of up to six. As Simon succinctly puts it, 'the great outdoors deserves a beautiful indoors'. Inside, the domes are a triumph of ergonomic design that would have even Kevin McCloud struggling for superlatives. These stylish pods come complete with partitioned bedrooms, king-size beds and proper mattresses, hanging beds for the kids and ultra-comfy Fatboy bean-bags. There's also a cool yet functional 'plancha' gas cooker and a spacious covered al fresco dining area for those long, lazy, holiday meals. So chic are these dextrous dome-iciles, it wouldn't surprise us if the St Tropez set soon migrated westward along the coast for a spot of glamping.

As all cool campers know, location is everything and Glisten certainly scores top marks

for that. Col d'Ibardin, the first campsite on which the Glisten domes have been located, is a relaxed, family-friendly retreat that boasts all the bells and whistles we've come to expect of campsites in this part of the world (clean, modern facilities; swimming pools; decent bar-restaurant). This bucolic Basque bolthole lies at the foothills of La Rhune and is ideally located to explore the other natural delights the region has to offer. With the sweeping golden sands, enchanting pine forests and traditional mountain villages of Le Pays Basques, it isn't hard to see what makes this such a magnet for camping fans. And while it also boasts some of Europe's warmest temperatures, the cooling sea breeze of this breathtaking Atlantic coastline means the only thing you need sweat over is which corner of this region to explore next.

COOL FACTOR Space-age domes that offer serious comfort.

WHO'S IN Glampers, familes, couples, kids – yes. Caravans, dogs – no.

ON SITE 6 geodesic domes sleeping up to 6. Swimming pools (2 for kids and 1 for adults), children's play area, onsite bar/restaurant, kids' club, small farm, plus plenty of games including pétanque, table tennis and basketball.

OFF SITE Explore the surrounding hills and forests or take to 2 wheels – Glisten can organise bike hire for the whole family, as well as surf hire and lessons. For something less labour intensive, take the vintage Train de la Rhune (05 59 54 20 26; rhune.com) to the first summit of the Pyrénées – the views from over 900m high are spectacular. There are plenty of beaches to choose from too, with St Jean de Luz, Socoa and Hendaye among the nicest and nearest. The Basque region straddles some of the most spectacular sites in southwest France and northern Spain. Take in the glamour of Biarritz or chic San Sebastián across the border.

FOOD & DRINK With a wealth of delicious local produce to be sampled (including Bayonne ham and Gâteau Basque), most dome-dwellers opt to cook their own on the *plancha*

grill provided. La Kantina – the onsite bar-restaurant – serves up decent, good-value meals and regional specialities such as *axoa*. Eat al fresco on the terrace or enjoy some private fuss-free dining with the takeaway service. Basic provisions can also be purchased from the onsite shop, open 7 days a week. For something extra special, make the short pilgrimage to gastronomic San Sebastián. If your budget won't stretch to the haute cuisine heights of Arzak (09 43 27 84 65; arzak.info), saddle up at a harbourside tavern for some traditional *pintxos* and some good Rioja.

GETTING THERE From the north, take the RN10 and the A63. Take exit 2 – 'St Jean de Luz south-Urrugne-Col Ibardin'. At the roundabout, leave by the exit for Urrugne. Turn left and continue along the D4 to Ibardin D4 for 4km. At the intersection, continue straight towards Ascain. The site is located 200m down the road on the right.

OPEN April–September.

THE DAMAGE Minimum stay 2 nights and prices per night start from £75 in low and mid season. Weekly rentals are run from £399 in low season to £856 during peak months.

quirky camping

Chez Devalon, 24320 Nanteuil Auriac de Bourzac, Dordogne, France 0033 5 53 91 82 42 www.quirkycamping.com

Hard as it may be to believe, just over 10 years ago this charming Dordogne farmstead was little more than a dilapidated smallholding, complete with a rustic farmhouse. The romantic idea of transforming the space into a rural idyll, including scratching chickens and a flourishing garden, enticed Matt and Wendy Meers to move here in 2002 to begin a new life in the French countryside. Matt's successful willow-weaving business had previously seen him working at some of the most prestigious garden shows in the UK. Little did he know, however, that the 25,000 willow cuttings they had just planted in France would be the origin of what is now Quirky Camping. Showing their business at a local eco-festival, the couple was struck by a new use for their willow plantation and Matt returned to the farm to try his hand at yurt building.

Matt and Wendy's stylish, eco-friendly creations are furnished for those who like camping in comfort. The natural canvas makes it light and airy, while the lovingly-restored furnishings allow plenty of storage space. There are sofas, a coffee table and a bookshelf that is well stocked with interesting reads and information on the local area. Each yurt has its own kitchen, private eco bathroom with basin and solar-powered shower, as well as a separate compost toilet.

When dinnertime beckons, glampers need look no further than the BBQ provided. Wendy has plenty of recommendations for local food producers, from ice cream and duck to foie gras

and trout. She can also offer fruit and veg from the kitchen garden and farm-reared lamb and pork on most days. And with your very own fragrant herb garden to pick from, you'll be able to rustle up a delicious, mouth-watering, regional feast to enjoy on the terrace – with the stunning views as the perfect accompaniment.

When you've finished the cake and wine that awaits you on arrival and have put down the guide that's tempting you to explore the area, why not borrow a bike from Wendy and Matt? The busy village of Verteillac lies a couple of clicks away and has all the amenities you'll need, along with a couple of decent bars and restaurants. And there's a handful of idyllic little towns just waiting to be discovered a short bike ride away. Brantôme is a particular highlight, sitting on the verdant banks of the River Dronne, its peaceful charm epitomised by the Benedictine Abbey founded there in 769. You can rent a canoe and paddle downstream in the afternoon sun, or venture into prehistoric caves and underground grottos.

Ultimately, though, you may well find the allure of the campsite too much. Once you are tucked away in your own private clearing, Quirky Camping will capture you in the same way it did Wendy and Matt all those years ago. If the willow-work of your yurt leaves you inspired, then you can also join Matt for a lesson in pole lathe wood turning. He's a patient teacher, which is handy if you're not blessed with beginner's luck!

COOL FACTOR Chilled-out yurt glamping in idyllic, blissfully rural isolation.

WHO'S IN Glampers, couples, friends, families with young children, well-behaved dogs (by prior arrangement). Exclusive site hire and wedding hosting available. No tent camping.

ON SITE 3 yurt hideaways (plus a smaller yurt for an additional cost). All sleep 2 in a double bed with the possibility to add an extra bed on request. There is additional accommodation for larger groups (a two-bedroomed gîte, tipis and also bell tents) but only by pre-arrangement. Each yurt has a fully equipped kitchen including cool boxes (freezer in garden shed), dining terrace and BBQ, solar bathroom with shower and basin and a separate compost toilet. Brand-new solar bathroom in the vegetable garden. Mobile phone charging available. Garden with plunge pool and campfire.

OFF SITE The lively local markets of Riberac (Friday) and Villebois Lavalette (Saturday) offer an authentic slice of Dordogne culture. Breathtaking Brantôme – 'the little Venice of the Dordogne' – is a leisurely cycle away. Take a paddle down the River Dronne to the Château de Bourdeilles, stopping off at Le Moulin de L'Abbaye (05 53 05 80 22; moulinabbaye. com) for a chilled glass of wine.

FOOD & DRINK Most guests opt for self-catering, but those looking for a totally hassle-free holiday can order a breakfast hamper or 3-course evening meals, served on your private deck. The Périgord is renowned for its cuisine and nearby Verteillac (6km away) boasts some fabulous restaurants.

GETTING THERE Take the D708 to Gouts Rossignol and then follow the D100 for 6.7km and turn left at the Moulin Poirier. Chez Devalon is situated 1.4km up the hill on the right.

PUBLIC TRANSPORT The nearest train station is Montmoreau; the nearest TGV train stations are Angouleme and Périgueux. Pick-ups are possible by prior arrangement.

OPEN Mid April–mid October.

THE DAMAGE Yurts £455–£555 per week depending on season; 3-night stays £250–£300 for 2. The extra yurt is an additional £50–£60 per night. Minimum stay 2 nights.

manzac ferme

Manzac, 24300 Augignac, France 0033 5 53 56 31 34   www.manzac-ferme.com

Listen... can you hear it? No? That, camping compadres, is the sound of complete silence. Unadulterated peace and quiet in the heart of the tranquil French Dordogne. That, people, is the sound of Manzac Ferme.

Nestled smack-bang in the middle of the sprawling Perigord Limousin National Park (eight scenic hours' drive from Calais), Manzac Ferme is the very epitome of rural seclusion. Fringed by thick woodland, this is a true oasis of tranquillity, accessible via near-deserted roads which snake their way to this herbaceous hideaway.

This adults-only, dog-friendly site caters to the canvas contingent as well as the caravan and motorhome mob. The conscientious owners have limited their field to just 10 pitches, so there's ample room for everyone to relax. What's more, the immaculately clean facilities (proper loos, laundry and hot showers) are more than able to cope.

The surrounding Perigord Vert is abuzz with all manner of wildlife. From vibrant butterflies and patrolling eagles via the abundant trout and grayling in the nearby River Bandiat, to the graceful deer emerging at dawn from the thick forest pines, a stay here offers a real back-to-nature experience.

Despite the calming sense of remoteness, Manzac Ferme lies just seven kilometres from one of the Perigord Vert's loveliest towns, Nontron – home of the famous folding knife and a number of other great attractions and culinary gems (the region is renowned for crêpes and *confiture*). The farm is also around an hour away from the legendary Cognac. And without any kids to worry about back at camp, it would be rude not to indulge in a tipple or two...

COOL FACTOR A tranquil, adults-only woodland hideaway in the beautiful Dordogne region.

WHO'S IN Tents, trailer tents, motorhomes (up to 9m), caravans (both single and twin axle), well-behaved pets – yes. Sorry, no kids. Maximum 4 to a pitch so group bookings are subject to availability.

ON SITE 6 hard-standings with electric hook-ups for caravans and motorhomes. A separate woodland camping area by the River Bandiat offers 4 secluded and large tent areas, all with hook-ups. This area has a separate car-parking area, around 30–50m from the tents. Free Wi-Fi across the site. Free hot showers, UK-style toilets, washing-up, a book swap, information area, plus a dumping-point for septic tank friendly loos/grey water. Laundry available for a small fee. Campfires and charcoal BBQs not permitted but gas BBQs are allowed.

OFF SITE The Périgord Limousin National Park is brimming with excellent walking and cycle trails – your hosts can provide maps. Just 25 minutes' drive away lies the stunning town of Brantôme from where you can take a boat trip or hire a canoe to cruise down the River Dronne. Nearby, the ancient network of caves at Villars is home to some remarkable prehistoric paintings. You can also visit the battlefield where Richard the Lionheart was killed, in nearby Châlus. The village of Nontron is well worth a visit too, particularly if you happen to be camping in April when the annual Masquerade Soufflaculs takes place. If visiting in July, be sure to find out where in Périgord the annual Félibrée will be taking place. This celebration of Occitan language and culture is a huge occasion for the region, with the chosen town decorated with vibrant flowers, as revellers enjoy traditional music, dancing and singing along with Occitan dishes and drink.

FOOD & DRINK There are plenty of excellent eateries just a short drive from the site. Your hosts are full of decent recommendations and will call ahead for reservations. Nontron, 10 minutes' drive away, is home to 3 large supermarkets that are open all day, while you can stock up on some of the region's celebrated produce at the Piégut market, which runs every Wednesday morning. There are also 2 excellent bakeries within a 5 minute drive for fresh croissants in the morning.

GETTING THERE In the village of Augignac there is a crossroads with an iron gated house. Here a white Manzac camping sign points you in the right direction. Turn here (also signposted for Abjat s/Bandiat and Savignac de N). Soon after turning on to this road (around 100m), turn right, following various signs including 'Manzac'. At one point the road appears to go straight on, but the main road is sharp right (again there is a Manzac sign here). Keep following the road from Augignac for approximately 4km, through a small village and over another crossroads until you arrive at an avenue of conifers and, straight in front of you, there is a property (Manzac Château) with a pointed roof. The campsite is on the right, just before it.

PUBLIC TRANSPORT The site is a bit tricky to reach by public transport. The nearest train station is Angoulême, a 45-km drive away. Folks on a cycling holiday would be able to manage this, but there are no viable bus routes nearby.

OPEN Mid may–mid September. If you would like to visit outside of these times, please contact for availability.

THE DAMAGE 2 people sharing one pitch €22–€24 (low/high season). Price includes showers, water, electricity, Wi-Fi, pets, awnings. Extra people are €5–€6, up to a maximum of 4 people per pitch.

la ribière sud

87230 Pageas, Limousin, France 0033 5 55 78 58 62 www.la-ribiere-sud.com

Known as France's Lake District, the Limousin is celebrated for its wonderful rolling hills, fox-red cattle and hordes of Brits trying to escape their compatriots from the Dordogne. It's also an area integrally tied to the history of the Crusades and Richard the Lionheart, who met his end in the village of Châlus.

Camping de la Ribière Sud is just a few minutes away from there, set in nine hectares of sleepy woodland and meadow on the former site of a tree nursery. It's run by two northerners (from the north of England, that is): Ann and Harry. Harry is an electrician by trade, so everything works like clockwork. Ann is gaining a reputation as a painter, and her work appears in the local gallery as well as back home. The site's centrepiece is a wonderfully painted, genuine Mongolian yurt; inside this is a hobbit-hole of gypsy chic with wooden struts delicately illustrated by the hands of nomadic craftsmen; outside is a wonderful canvas dome bound in camel hair. But you don't have to stay in here if you've brought your own canvas – there are plenty of pitches in the shade of the towering poplars, all with electrical hook-ups. Wild boars sometimes pop in for a sniff and snort around, as do the local deer, beneath the ever-present shadows of buzzards circling majestically above. By night you'll be sung to sleep by the soporific hoots of owls and coos of wood pigeons. The nice thing about La Ribière is the scale of the grounds – you can wander in wild glades and prairie grass without meeting a soul.

COOL FACTOR Mongolian splendour meets woodland serenity in this simple, immaculate campsite.

WHO'S IN Tents, campervans, dogs (on leads) – yes. Caravans, motorhomes – no.

ON SITE There are 6 generously sized pitches with separate power points. The wash-block is brand new and has piping-hot, eco-friendly power showers. There are disabled facilities. They plan to add some kids' amusements, such as swings and climbing frames, but for the moment the wild grounds are rich pickings for their imaginations. Campfires are allowed.

OFF SITE The capital of Limousin is Limoges, famed for its pottery and gastronomy (Limousin beef is delicious, as is its indigenous cream and cherry tart), and is a short drive away. The ruinous Château de Châlus-Chabrol (open to the public) is where Richard the Lionheart met his maker when he was struck in the eye by a crossbow bolt. Northeast of Limoges (between Guéret and Bourganeuf) the Forêt de Chabrières is not only a wonderful place to go walking and picnicking, but home to the Les Loups de Chabrières animal park (05 55 81 23 23; loups-chabrieres.com), where you can see wolves close up. The area is dotted with lakes, some of which have beaches with swimming and picnic areas. There you can go kayaking in Aixe-sur-Vienne and Brântome, while other activities in the area include fishing, cycling, walking, horseriding and go-karting.

FOOD & DRINK Hôtel du Centre in Châlus (05 55 78 58 62) does great daily specials such as escargots, quiche Lorraine and salads and steaks – as well as regular plats du jour for €11. There's also an Intermarché supermarket, butcher and bakery in town for all your self-catering needs.

GETTING THERE From Limoges head south towards Périgueux on N21, through Séreilhac. Camping de la Ribière Sud is 8km south on the left, just past Domaine de la Ribière (fishing lake) and just before a right-hand bend.

OPEN All year.

THE DAMAGE Tents and campervans from €15–€20 per night, including 2 people and electricity. Extra person (older than 5 yrs) €3. See their website for more details and yurt prices.

camp laurent

Le Fournet, St-Laurent-de-Ceris, Charente 16450, France 0033 6 02 22 37 15 www.camp-laurent.com

The River Charente may not be the longest or most famous of French rivers; it doesn't have the same iconic status as mighty Rhône or Loire, with their vineyard-filled valleys. However, this languidly meandering waterway has its own unique charms. Once decreed by no higher authority than French monarch François I as 'the most beautiful stream in the kingdom', La Charente snakes its way through some of southwest France's most ancient counties. It is also where visitors to this enchanting corner of the country can find the region's newest and (dare we say) loveliest new campsite, Camp Laurent.

When ex-pat Tracey first laid eyes on the Poitou-Charentes, it was love at first sight. Setting up camp (quite literally) in the summer of 2013, Tracey's vision was of a tranquil retreat – easily achievable due to the adults-only admittance policy. Nestled in eight unspoilt acres just outside the sleepy village of St-Laurent-de-Ceris, Camp Laurent has ample room for just ten emplacements with six hook-ups. The pitches overlook the river and valley below, while butterflies, rabbits and the odd roe deer dominate the scene. Facilities are more than adequate, with wet-room style bathrooms featuring hot showers, modern toilets, laundry and a washing-up adjacent to the 200-year old stone barn. With the river on your doorstep, you could be forgiven for neglecting the new, open-air pool which is just the ticket for cooling off in France's second sunniest region.

With 400 metres of river frontage, the site makes an ideal base from which to fish for trout, carp, pike, perch and eels. A lazy paddle in a canoe or a cruise in one of the numerous pleasure boats makes for a great way to explore the idyllic nearby towns and villages. You'll take in such famous names as Angoulême and Cognac – yes, the very same. Just be sure to appoint a designated skipper for the journey home.

COOL FACTOR Idyllic riverside camping in a relatively little-known part of France – for adults only.

WHO'S IN Tents, caravans/motorhomes, dogs – yes. Kids – no (sorry nippers, it's adults only).

ON SITE Ten grass pitches. Swimming pool with seating area. Electric hook-ups available. Modern bathrooms with hot showers, washing-up, laundry. Disabled facilities.

OFF SITE There are plenty of cycling and walking routes in the surrounding area, including route 48, which is on Camp Laurent's doorstep. The River Charente offers a wealth of great activities including canoeing, fishing or simply taking a leisurely barge cruise. The Lacs de Haute Charente and River Vienne promise similar waterside fun – including a beach. If you're visiting in August, the historic nearby town of Confolens hosts its annual world music festival, a 5-day summer event that attracts around 30,000 visitors. Confolens itself is beautiful, intersected by the idyllic River Vienne and 2 historic bridges. The Château de Rochechouart (05 55 03 77 77; musee-rochechouart.com) is also well worth a visit, as is the interactive science theme park, Futuroscope (05 49 49 59 06; futuroscope.com).

FOOD & DRINK The nearest bar/restaurant is Le Marronnier (05 45 30 68 53), in St-Laurent-de-Ceris, about 4km away. There are also lots of surrounding villages that offer an authentic French culinary experience. Several large supermarkets can be found in Roumazières-Loubert and in Confolens. About 40 minutes' drive away, in the regional capital Angoulême, you'll find an eclectic, trendy mix of places to eat and drink. La Ruelle (05 45 95 15 19; laruelle-angouleme.fr) is an eccentrically decorated restaurant in a converted transport depot that serves refined French cuisine with a contemporary twist. No visit to the region could be complete without sampling Cognac's famous brandy and the town's lesser-known aperitif, *pineau*. Try some Limousin *boeuf* too if you get a chance.

GETTING THERE From Angoulême take the N2141 north, and then left on to the D951 tp to St Claud. Beyond St Claud, take the D15 left and then the D345 north to the site.

OPEN Mid May–late September.

THE DAMAGE €25 per pitch per night based on 2 persons sharing (€20 without hook-up). Additional people pay a supplement of €5 up to 4 per pitch.

les quatre saisons

Chignat, nr Bourganeuf, 23250 Soubrebost, France 0033 5 55 64 23 35 www.les-4-saisons.com

Ah yes, the Four Seasons. Great pop band. No? The hotel chain? No. The Vivaldi concertos then? No. The pizza? No, no, no... Les Quatre Saisons campsite, of course. There's been a campsite on this classic *aire naturelle* site for ages, but it's only in the last few years, since it was taken over by Andrew and Bernie Carnegie, that it has really taken off. The new owners dug flat pitches into the sloping field and turned one of the barns into a games room and campers' shelter for the occasional spells of inclement weather (ah, so that's why it's called the Four Seasons!).

And what they've produced is a great little getaway in the heart of the Creuse region of Limousin. It sits among rolling hills just 4 kilometres east of the little town of Bourganeuf, which was supposedly founded by the Knights Templar and was one of their favourite French hangouts – though you probably wouldn't guess this because it didn't feature in *The Da Vinci Code*.

The main camping area is fairly open and fringed with trees but with a few hidey-holes if you want to keep out of site of the neighbours. Off to the side are a couple of smaller, more discreet areas behind farm buildings for the Howard Hughes and Greta Garbos among you. But if you are happy to show your face, you could do worse than sign up for one of Bernie's evening meals. She's a qualified chef and, when the weather's nice, will serve up a fabulous four-course feast on the lawn. Just don't ask for a *quattro stagioni* whatever you do!

COOL FACTOR A discreet, serene hideaway in the heart of the Creuse region of Limousin.

WHO'S IN Tents, campervans, caravans, dogs (for a fee and if the owners are notified in advance) – yes. Large motorhomes – no (they get stuck on the steep drive).

ON SITE 25 level pitches on 5 acres of meadow, with special areas in July and August for quiet camping. There's one central facilities block with 3 showers/WCs, and 1 disabled toilet and shower. There's also a washing machine (€4) and electricity can be made available at every pitch. Elsewhere there's a barn for shelter, table-tennis, fridges and free Wi-Fi.

OFF SITE The site is on the GR4 walking trail and there are over 150km of trails around the region. There's also horseriding, biking and fishing and, slightly further afield, is the huge Lac de Vassivière (lelacdevassiviere.com) – one of France's top water sports venues.

FOOD & DRINK Evening meals available on site at €25 per person for 3 courses. Wine €6 a bottle. Homemade bread and croissants in the morning (order the night before). There are 2 small brasseries in the square by the church in Bourganeuf – Le Central (05 55 64 05 67) and La Mezzanine (05 55 64 31 17), which both serve standard French fare.

GETTING THERE From the N145 between Guéret and La Souterraine, take the D912 for Bourganeuf. At the roundabout in Bourganeuf follow the D8 towards Lac de Vassivière. After 3.5km turn left on to the D37 (there's a blue site sign) and follow the road down the hill and turn right (there's another site sign). Carry on up the hill and the site is dead ahead.

OPEN Officially April–September, but by arrangement you can probably stay any time.

THE DAMAGE Pitch price per night is €8 + adults €4, children up to 6 years €2, electricity €4, dog €2. Fixed tents cost €245 per week.

tipis at folbeix

Folbeix, 23270 Ladapeyre, France 0033 5 55 80 90 26 www.vacanesdetipienfrance.com

Not far to the east of this site, the little town of Treignat claims to be the geographical centre of France. It's not the only place to make the claim, and there are dozens of villages, fields, and hilltops bearing plaques and flags making the same claim. Quite how you calculate the centre point is complicated and all to do with how you define the borders of France, whether you include Corsica, and so on. Anyway, staying at Nigel and Sheila Harding's tipis in the hamlet of Folbeix is as close as makes any difference to staying right in the heart of France.

For centuries this region was so dark and dense that it was virtually bypassed by roads, commerce, modernity – you name it. No one since the Romans had really ventured in. During the Second World War even the occupying Germans knew better than to try to police such an impenetrable area. They simply threw a cordon around it and tried to stop people from getting in and out, although this didn't prevent a couple of plucky British agents parachuting into a nearby field to make contact with the *La Résistance*. What they got up to after that has never really been clear, but Nigel found an old service revolver in the attic of the farmhouse, so they must have come here for more than a walk in the woods and to check out the local cheese.

When the first edition of *Cool Camping France* was published, the site was ending its first season and Nigel was busy up ladders with a hammer in his hand, still building the facilities. Now that it's all complete it's even more impressive than it was first time around.

Adjacent to the picture-book, ivy-clad farmhouse, a piece of ancient natural woodland houses the six tipis, each one situated in a different part of the wood. They sleep up to five people (two adults and three pre-teen kids), though there's one tipi, the one furthest from the others, which is reserved for couples (where two's company and three's a crowd). Such is the charm of the place that it's become a huge hit with families. The natural boundaries of the site make it an ideal spot for the kids to roam around and get mucky. Nigel can provide bows and arrows if you want to play cowboys and Indians, and he organises midnight walks, where he leads a gaggle of petrified children through the dark woods.

Despite the greater emphasis on family fun, the site remains a haven of environmental consciousness. Solar power and candles provide the lighting, waste is composted and recycled, and biodegradable products are used wherever possible. Meanwhile, Sheila's a dab hand at *table d'hôte* and serves a mean dinner in the restored barn. And, just so that you're ready for it, in addition to the three courses and wine, plus a fantastic cheese board, you'll be offered one of Sheila's homemade liqueurs. So make sure you've left room for one because they're delicious. Particular favourites are the strawberry and walnut, described by Sheila as 'tasting like Christmas in a glass'. If you could distil the essence of a great campsite into a single dinky liqueur, you can bet the result would taste something like this.

COOL FACTOR Peaceful and natural woodland site with an environmental conscience.

WHO'S IN People under 7 feet tall – yes. Campervans, caravans, dogs – no.

ON SITE Bedding is provided but you need to bring your own towels. Outside the sanctuary of your tipi there are separate male and female washing facilities. There's also a handy kitchen (with a fridge and cool-box with ice packs, plus everything else you'll need) and a day room in the restored barn, which doubles as the breakfast and dining room. There is also a relaxation room with comfy chairs and cushions. There are herbs for picking in the garden and various jams, chutneys, and home brews available from the house. There are two communal firepits and tipis are allowed off the ground or in the specially constructed stone BBQ pits. Mountain bike and canoe hire, plus other equipment is possible and games can be used for free.

OFF SITE This area is pretty remote, which makes for some great walks and cycle trails. You can hire bikes from the campsite or Nigel and Sheila can point you in the right direction if you fancy a walk. Nearby is an area known as Pays de Trois Lacs, a collection of three lakes, and further afield is Lac de Vassivière, a huge man-made lake that's celebrated as one of France's top water-sports centres.

FOOD & DRINK In this distant spot it's best to come prepared to cook for yourselves or to partake of Sheila's *table d'hôte* (€15 for adults and €10 for kids; under-3s eat for free). Meals are usually on Fridays and Sundays, though you can make a special request. There are plenty of herbal pickings at the site and drinks are available from the house and a local market every Friday in Châtelus-Malvaleix, along with a *boulangerie* and *pâtisserie*. Further afield there are plenty of restaurants in the medieval part of Montluçon, particularly on rue Grande, which goes up to the castle. Try L'Eau de la Bouche (04 70 03 82 92), whose owner also runs a saucy cabaret revue bar called Le Royal Avenue if you fancy it. It's cheaper than the Moulin Rouge.

GETTING THERE Heading east from Guéret on N145, turn onto the D11 at the sign for Ajain, and follow it to Ladapeyre. If you're coming west from Montluçon via Gouzon then turn on to D990 to Ladapeyre. From Ladapeyre take the D990 towards Châtelus-Malvaleix through Folbeix, which is little more than a few houses on either side of the road. One of the first is an ivy-covered house on the right. Pull in there and shout 'Bonjour'. If you're coming from the north on the D940, take the D990 just past Genouillac, through Châtelus-Malvaleix and the ivy house is on your left in Folbeix. You should still shout 'Bonjour', though.

PUBLIC TRANSPORT The nearest train station is at Guéret (with services from Paris).

OPEN May–September.

THE DAMAGE 3-night breaks are around €135/€170/€225 in low/mid/high season; full weeks are €270/€350/€435. Prices are based on 2 adults; the supplement for kids is €5 per night or €30 for a full week. Breakfast is included.

camping les ormes

Lieu Dit Fauquié, 47210 St. Étienne-de-Villeréal, France 0033 5 53 36 60 26 www.campinglesormes.fr

Out of Africa meets Ibiza chic in this leviathan of taste and scale. It's hard to imagine a more stylish campsite, but don't be fooled by the über-cool bar complete with shiny chrome taps, de rigueur grey tables, Ben and Jerry's fridge and leafy piazza – Les Ormes is as rough-and-ready as you want it to be. Apart from the high-luxe tents, there are 100 great tent pitches for traditional camping in shady meadow areas. Of course, you could indulge in a bit of fantasy glamping if you fancy it, and we wouldn't blame you, with the choice of 25 safari tents, each individually finished, hidden in mature groves, and perfectly set apart so as to nurture your Robert Redford/Meryl Streep delusions.

Each 'Gibson' tent has its very own verandah, twinkling candelabra, and lavish interior that seems to jump right out of the pages of *Tatler*; chaise longue, scatter cushions, fresh flowers, retro furnishings, and cool self-catering facilities, all finished off with a dash of élan. There's even a raised outdoor platform with a tent atop, should your kids want to escape you, but it's close enough should the bogeyman come a-calling. For the best valley views be sure to ask for the Mojave tents. By the restaurant, on a gentle elevation, there are hammocks strung between the trees so that you can make the most of the splendid sunsets. The crowd is mid-thirties to forties, the atmosphere decidedly laid-back; perhaps something to do with the chillsome tunes wafting by, along with the smell of deliciously grilled food from the bar. As for facilities, there's a great deal to keep

you busy and ensure you never need to leave the site. After a faux African sunrise and delicious breakfast in the whiter-than-heaven café, head off to the tennis court, or to the pond for a spell of fishing, or maybe it's volleyball, or a wander over to the petting zoo… oh now they're just showing off! And I didn't even get to the black granite swimming pool with the hip silver bus that doubles as a snack bar.

Kids are in their element here, perhaps because the site is huge but secure, so their parents are able to really relax, safe in the knowledge that if one of the children tries to escape, the chances are they'll be spotted by one of the many staff who drive around in ancient Renaults. Apart from the kids' pool there are swings and climbing frames and, if they really want to go feral, there's a mature elm woods – from which the place takes its name – to run wild in. There's even a kids' restaurant, where they can eat with their new buddies, undisturbed by annoying crinklies. As to the final hundreds and thousands on this magnificent gâteau, there's a very tasteful boutique where you can buy jewellery and pashminas in the event you get a little romantic or have forgotten your other half's birthday.

Yes, if Carlsberg did campsites it would probably look something like this. For a bunch of Dutch travellers who came together through their wanderings in Indonesia and the Far East, Camping les Ormes is quite a production – a beautiful place that sets high standards of service and creative imagination.

COOL FACTOR Les Ormes redefines camping, with its laid-back ambience, efficient facilities and general panache.

WHO'S IN Tents, campervans, dogs (on leads), glampers – yes.

ON SITE 100 pitches on a large, beautifully landscaped site; choose between forest and field. 2 large toilet and shower blocks, laundry, a tennis court, granite swimming pool, and stylish pool bar as well as a kiddies' pool. There's a sandy beach by a lake rippling with fish, a petting zoo, a Mediterranean-style restaurant with the best steaks this side of Argentina, a well-stocked bar and a boutique selling jewellery. Yoga classes, kids' art courses, and onsite massage are all also available.

OFF SITE The nearest town of interest is beautiful Bergerac, which shares its name with the celebrated gentleman with an oversized proboscis. You can see a statue of him in the old town – that is if you're not too busy stocking up on wine in one of a clutch of excellent wine shops. The region is famous for its red wines and there are great deals to be had. The old town makes for a lovely morning visit, wandering through the narrow alleys and getting lost. Closer to home there are a number of fortified medieval villages (*bastides*) including Villeréal, Monflanquin and Monpazier, all vibrantly French with arcaded squares and weekend markets selling everything from foie gras to local produce. Come August, the towns recall their medieval past with the costumed festivals of the Vallée du Dropt (medieval.dropt.org). If you fancy a wine dégustation in a beautiful historic setting, head to the Château de Monbazillac (05 53 63 65 00; chateau-monbazillac.com) to try their sweet white wine. There's also an 18-hole golf course right next to the campsite.

FOOD & DRINK Étincelles (05 53 74 08 79; gentilhommiere-etincelles.com) in nearby Ste-Sabine-Born village has a Michelin star and is celebrated for its authentic French fare. To be honest, though, the campsite restaurant has a terrific menu, with staple dishes such as steak and couscous, and you may not need to go anywhere else.

GETTING THERE Take the A10 towards Bordeaux; just before Orléans take the A71 direction Paris/Blois. After around 80km– just before Vierzon – turn on to the A20 to Toulouse/Limoges. Near Brive-la-Gaillarde, pick up the A89 to Bordeaux and exit at J15, direction Bergerac, then follow N21 and D121 through Bordas and Castillonnès to Villeréal, from where the site is clearly signposted.

OPEN Early May–mid September.

THE DAMAGE Pitch + car €12; adults €8; children (up to 7 yrs) €4.50; electricity €5; no pets in high season but €5 in low season. Safari tent rates vary depending on the tent and the season but you can reckon on paying €300–€475 a week in May and June, and €660–€1000 in July and August.

le capeyrou

24220 Beynac, Dorgogne, France 0033 5 53 29 54 95 www.campinglecapeyrou.com

In the heart of the Périgord Noir region, along one of the most jaw-droppingly perfect stretches of the Dordogne Valley, is the village of Beynac-et-Cazenac. Nestled under the vigilant gaze of the Château de Beynac, this magical little village clings to the hillside as if it's been flung there by a giant. With its turreted witch's hat buildings and storybook red-tiled roofs, it's clearly medieval, though people have lived here since the Bronze Age. Pull up a chair at a riverside café, order a cool beer, and ponder Viking longships prowling up-river as they penetrated the valley in the 9th century. Head upstream to La Roque-Gageac to hire a kayak, then paddle downstream past cliffs and castles peeking through the vernal river bank.

Situated in this 'five castles valley' in the heart of the Périgord Noir, Camping Le Capeyrou sits beneath the fortress of the Château de Beynac. Waking to the sound of the nearby Dordogne River, it's hard to imagine a more enchanting view. The site itself is well catered for, with a generously sized swimming pool, volleyball court and homely bar, and 120 pitches enjoying plenty of mature shade. Pitch up by the river or in the meadow, away from civilisation. Come evening, the bar, with its exposed stone walls and outside patio, is a pleasant spot for sundowners. Inside the recreation room, its walls festooned with old bicycles, there's a huge hearth and grill, where people bring their own meat to BBQ (there's a butcher a few minutes from the site). And if you're feeling decidedly British there's even a darts board.

COOL FACTOR Huge lush grounds beside a gently flowing river and one of the best castle views in the south of France.

WHO'S IN Tents, campervans, glampers – yes.

ON SITE 2 shower blocks, disabled facilities, baby-changing rooms. No food on site but an inviting swimming pool, toddler pool and kids' climbing area. The best pitches are by the river. Volleyball court plus table-tennis tables and laundry facilities. 3 safari tents recently added. Campfires allowed.

OFF SITE The surrounding area is famed for the presence of Cro-Magnon Man some 20,000 years ago. Within a 30-km radius there are plenty of troglodyte caves to explore, including world-renowned Lascaux. There are also more than 100 castles to visit. Fishing is a must, with local rivers choking on trout, salmon and pike. If horseriding (€16 per hour) and canoeing from Canoe Dordogne (05 53 29 58 50) don't grab you, why not take a gentle river ride in a traditional *gabarre* from neighbouring La Roque-Gageac (€8.50 adult/€6 child)? Hot-air ballooning can also be arranged.

FOOD & DRINK There's a little supermarket by Le Capeyrou's entrance, beside which is a pâtisserie; it might not look like much, but their walnut cake is exported all over the world. In Beynac, head for the impossibly romantic restaurant, La Petite Tournelle (05 53 29 95 18; restaurant-petite-tonnelle.fr) up a higgledy-piggledy street. Try the grilled duck. The chocolate cake is pretty sumptuous, too. Prices from €16.

GETTING THERE Head towards Sarlat-la-Canéda. Beynac-et-Cazenac is 8km southwest of the town, off D57. Coming from Bergerac, just follow the River Dordogne.

OPEN April–September.

THE DAMAGE Pitch €5.80–€11.10; Adult €4.40–€6.90; children (up to 7 yrs) €2.40–€3.95; pets €1–€2.50. Electricity €3.50–€4.55. Tourist tax (for those over 13 yrs) €0.55.

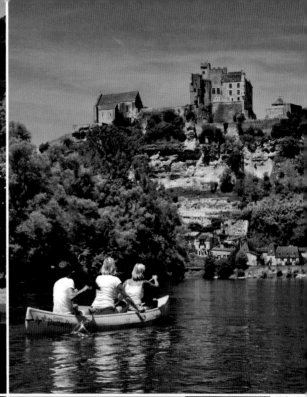

camping domaine des mathevies

24200 Ste-Nathalène, nr. Sarlat-la-Canéda, France 0033 5 53 59 20 86 www.mathevies.com

The medieval town of Sarlat-la-Canéda is a maze of cobbled squares and imposing turreted buildings – in no time you'll be lost like Theseus in a benign labyrinth. Follow the nostalgic music of the accordion... didn't you pass that chap in the beret just a moment ago?

Losing your bearings is half the fun. The alleyways bulge at the seams with foie gras shops, for this is the home of the hallowed pâté, and renditions of geese abound at every turn. Take in the 12th-century cathedral over a cool *pression* at one of many al fresco bars before weaving your way through rolling countryside to Camping Domaine des Mathevies.

Natalie and Patrick McAlpine, the campsite's owners, first met in India. Their subsequent travels brought them to this neglected campsite and they set about tastefully transforming it into the eco-minded sanctuary it is today. A labour of love, it's a place where adults are as well catered for and contented as their kids and where you can sit back with a frothy latté or play pétanque over a leisurely glass of St-Émilion as a paraglider is swallowed up by the salmon-pink sunset below.

Set on a gentle incline with masterful views over the wooded valley, there are 40 pitches, many of which enjoy shade from walnut, cherry, fig, apple and plum trees, and all of which have electricity hook-ups. If you're arriving late and don't fancy pitching up for the night there are four brand-spanking new cabins, pitched to savour the best view over the hills, plus seven more well-furnished cabins dotted around the edge of the site that can sleep up to six. There are also two self-contained gîtes with all mod cons, which still retain exposed stone walls and beamed ceilings and are perfectly sized for families, with two double bedrooms. The real ace, though, is the spectacular sunset view.

The site itself is a real playground for kids, with a toddlers' play area near the Cosy Nook Café (so you get to relax with them in plain view). Natalie and Patrick have two kids and it's this empathy for the little ones that seems to have led to so many thoughtful details to keep them happy. There's a tree house for older kids and a terrific climbing area, a children's pool, as well as a larger swimming pool for adults beside the tennis courts and table-tennis table. The Cosy Nook Café lives up to its name, with swallow-you-up couches and delicious bar snacks. Fresh bread and croissants are delivered every morning; the best spot to take breakfast is under the shade of the linden trees. And, just in case you sneaked your computer in with you, the Nook has Wi-Fi as well as satellite TV for movies or sport in the evening.

With all this, and with the gastronomic mecca of Sarlat so close, you may well find yourself staying much longer than planned – at what is by any standards the most charming, friendly campsite in the Dordogne.

Aujourd'hui 34°

Demain 33°

Lendemain 29°

COOL FACTOR One of the friendliest sites in the south. The hosts are delightful, the views stunning and there's bags of stuff for you and the kids to do.

WHO'S IN Tents, campervans, glampers, caravans, dogs on leads – yes.

ON SITE 40 pitches, 7 wooden cabins and 4 mobile homes, plus 2 gîtes. This is a friendly, but restful place, so be prepared to while away a few hours with a glass of red wine. The café-bar houses a good selection of holiday reads, has Wi-Fi, and sells a selection of basic supplies such as milk. There's a brand-new shower/wash-block with baby-changing facilities and toilets for disabled campers. Apart from the playground and swimming pools there's also a tennis court. If the unthinkable happens and it rains, the yoga barn morphs into a kids' area with board games, drawing materials, and plenty more things to keep everyone busy.

OFF SITE There are stacks of things to do locally if the mood takes you – from lunching in Sarlat-la-Canéda or popping into a roadside wine-seller's for a quick dégustation. Wine here is great value and Patrick can advise you on where to stock up. The owners can also organise pony rides at a local farm or you can take Maisy, the campsite dog, for a walk. Canoeing is a must; the Dordogne River is lazily paced and a wonderful adventure for your kids (lifejackets provided) as you pass wildlife and fairy-tale châteaux.

FOOD & DRINK The Cosy Nook Café turns out tasty snacks as well as a bevy of barista-style coffees, organic teas and alcoholic drinks. Breakfast is perfect here, but for lunch you'll want to head off for an adventure. Sarlat-la-Canéda takes its cuisine very seriously and its winding streets are full of restaurants and bistros. For something different tucked away in the centre of the old town, Chez le Gaulois (05 53 59 50 64) serves rustic platters of sliced cheeses and charcuterie, boiled potatoes, salads and melted raclette. Service is great and the atmosphere superb. It's small and

popular so booking is advisable. Out of town, try the Pech de Malet, Vitrac – a family owned restaurant with a fab terrace and views across the valley. Open-air tables make it ideal for kids. The Hotel Delpeyrat, in Carsac is a traditional French dining room, with Madame in the kitchen producing homemade delights. It's a great favourite with the locals who know good food when they taste it. Finally, the closest option to the site, a 2-minute drive down the hill, is L'Escale, Sainte Nathalène (05 53 59 22 18), with a nice terrace and a family-friendly menu including, pizzas, steak frîtes and ice creams.

GETTING THERE Follow the A20, take exit 55 and follow signs for the D703 in the direction of Sarlat, St Julien de Lampon. Turn right on to the D61 in the direction of Carlux. In Carlux take the D47B to Sainte Nathalène. At the end of the D47B you will come to the D47 – turn left and go through the village of Sainte Nathalène until you reach the only bar in the village (with a large terrace and awning). With the bar on your right, take the first road on the right (you will see an old petrol station/garage and agricultural materials) and follow it up the hill, where you will pick up signs to the diminutive hamlet of Les Mathevies.

PUBLIC TRANSPORT By train, Sarlat-la-Canéda (7km) is at the end of a branch line. Souillac (20km) has direct trains from Paris-Austerlitz. From other parts of France, it is best to head for Bordeaux (from where most of the trains to Sarlat start their journeys) or Libourne.

OPEN April–September.

THE DAMAGE Tents (pitch + 2 persons) per night low/high season: €16.50/€45 (high season tariff includes 2 adults, 2 children under 5 yrs and electricity). Children (under 5 yrs) €3.50–€6.50. Electricity €4.50. Gite Les Mathevies (sleeps 5) €360–€1080 per week. Gîte le Point de Vue (sleeps 8) €390–€1180 per week. Chalet Cabins (sleep up to 6) €260–€880 per week. Mobile homes (sleep 4–5) €210–€780.

camping fans

Lieudit Fans, 12390 Rignac, France 0033 5 65 64 49 56 www.camping-fans.com

In the words of Björk, 'It's, oh, so quiet'. Yes, we're in the heart of the Aveyron, one of France's largest, least-populated, départements – and, we might venture, one of its most beautiful. Yet there's hardly a soul to be seen. It's high season, after all. A time when, at most tourist hotspots, the roads are choked with traffic and café tables are permanently occupied by the hungry hordes.

At Belcastel, though, you can enjoy a slice of France unspoilt by mass tourism. This fabled medieval settlement, home to just 200 residents, sits on the tranquil banks of the River Aveyron. Its 11th-century château and spread of ancient houses, set on cobbled streets, nestles on the wooded slopes along the river bank. The town's humpbacked Gothic bridge positively demands an impromptu game of Poohsticks. It's easy to see why this has been officially voted one of the most beautiful villages in France.

Just down the road from Belcastel, in the idyllic hamlet of the same name, Camping Fans is set within 55 acres of tranquil riverside valley meadows. This picturesque family-friendly site is the pride and joy of wonderful campsite chiefs Pieter and Marcelline Quartero. Essentially, it's a tale of two campsites: the *aire naturelle* caters to the bulk of campers, while The Secret Valley is secluded between the wooded slopes of the valley, with space for just eight pitches, including a couple of lucky groups in the fully furnished Canadian Wilderness Resort Tents. To call the pitches spacious would be an understatement – they range from 200m² to 350m². So even in the height of the summer season, this place never feels crowded.

The main draw here, though, is undeniably the river. The gently flowing waters are safe for all children of swimming/paddling ability, and there's a small sandy beach to help you navigate your way in. With the summer sun in full beam, there's a steady stream of parched campers lining up to jump off the jetty into the cooling waters of the tranquil Aveyron; and the river is teeming with wildlife, from herons and coypus to trout and the sweet-tasting *écrevisse* (crayfish, to you and me) – the perfect addition to a summer salad.

There's a pleasingly lazy pace to life round here. There are no *animations* for children ('we think children are much more capable of amusing themselves than we adults are'), and Pieter and Marcelline pride themselves in their daily break between 12.30pm and 3pm. Fresh bread and croissants are delivered from the village *boulangerie* every morning in high season – the perfect accompaniment to the excellent morning coffee to be had in the communal barn.

Camping Fans by name; camping fans by nature – Pieter and Marcelline know exactly what campers want out of an Aveyron holiday under canvas. And no doubt this gorgeous, unspoilt riverside site will be winning a few more fans, season after season.

COOL FACTOR Unspoilt riverside camping in the heart of the Aveyron countryside.

WHO'S IN Tents, trailer tents, well-behaved groups, dogs (outside of high season) – yes. Caravans/motorhomes, campervans, dogs (in high season) – no.

ON SITE 33 pitches spread over 2 adjoining sites (*The secret valley* and the *aire naturelle*). The Secret Valley has an ablutions block with 1 shower, 1 sink and 2 toilets for up to 8 tents; the *aire naturelle* has 2 showers, 4 toilets and 6 sinks for up to 25 tents. No electricity in the Secret Valley; Aire Naturelle has 17 hook-ups (2 amp). Fridge and a washing machine available. Free Wi-Fi available at the café in the Small Barn. The Secret Valley also boasts 2 fully furnished Canadian Wilderness Resort Tents (sleeping 6 and 4).

OFF SITE Aveyron is a dream for the outdoor enthusiast. There's canoeing just an hour from Camping Fans and plenty of great hiking routes, with the Grande Randonnée 62B directly accessible from the site. The gorgeous village of Belcastel is just a short drive away; its quaint cobbled streets, distinctive 15th-century stone houses and medieval castle sit on the tranquil banks of the Aveyron River. Every Friday night its *marché nocturne* brims with plenty of stalls for eating, drinking and good company. Villefranche de Rouergue boasts many historic buildings and a famous Thursday morning market. Enchanting old Rodez also boasts a market on Saturday morning. The atmospheric medieval village and ruined twin towers of the château inférieur at Peyruss-le-Roc are also an essential visit. A good hour's drive away, the Tarn city of Albi hosts a UNESCO World Heritage Site in its cathedral and the renowned Musée Toulouse Lautrec (05 63 49 48 70; museetoulouselautrec.net) in honour of its most famous son. Toulouse is also a couple of hours' drive away.

FOOD & DRINK Fresh bread and croissants are delivered from the village *boulangerie* every morning in high season.

Home-cooked hot meals are offered twice a week. There's a great little market in Rignac every Tuesday morning – perfect for basic and artisan produce. You can also order takeaway pizzas from the village. The hotel restaurant Du Vieux Pont in Belcastel (05 65 64 52 29; hotelbelcastel.com) offers stunning views and impressively refined French cuisine. For something a little less grand, Chez Anna (05 65 63 95 61) serves easy but good food from its delightful terrace. The famous wine region of Marcillac is just 20km to the northwest of Rignac. Be sure to visit for the Sunday morning market and pick up a nice bottle of red to accompany the local specialty, *tripoux* (stuffed sheep's tripe).

GETTING THERE Coming from Paris on the A75, follow the signs for Clermont-Ferrand. Continue in the direction of Montpellier and leave the motorway at Sévérac le Château. Then follow the signs to Rodez on the N88, and then Montauban at all roundabouts. After almost half an hour you will arrive at a roundabout named Giratoire de Rignac-Centre. Turn left on the D997 in the direction of Colombiès and Belcastel (do not go into Rignac). After about 5km you will arrive at Le Pont Neuf; just before the bridge you will see a narrow road turning sharply to the right, with signposts indicating Fans and Camping de Fans. Follow this, keeping the river on your left-hand side for about a kilometre to the first buildings. You have arrived at the farmhouse. If you find that you have crossed the river you've gone too far!

PUBLIC TRANSPORT The nearest train station is in Rodez or Villefranche de Rouergue. However, there is virtually no public transport in this region and taxis are consequently quite costly, so this is definitely a place to arrive with a car.

OPEN Start of May–end of September.

THE DAMAGE €5.50 per tent pitch; small supplementary tent €2.75. Adults €6; children under 9 years €3. Hook-ups €2.50. Tourist tax (for those over 13 yrs) €0.33.

étang du camp

12320 Sénergues, France 0033 5 65 46 01 95 www.etangducamp.fr

Situated on a mountain plateau beside a lake ornamented by a Monet-style bridge, Étang du Camp was a once-neglected municipal site that was rescued in 2006. The views are serene, but consider this: you'll be camping by a reed-fringed lakeside, with honeyed African light dappling the canvas of your safari tent, and, through the elephant grass, spying the hulking form of water buffaloes. Check your GPS and you're actually in Aveyron, home to ten of France's most beautiful villages; and the buffaloes, well, they belong to a neighbour. But the lake and the safari tents are all real and very alluring, plus they come fully-equipped with a real bed and cooking facilities. There's a fleet of mountain bikes you can freewheel to the valley floor on and be picked up if needed. There are evenings dedicated to story-telling around the fire, enjoyed with a glass of vino and *aligot-saucisse* (local-style sausage and mash).

Stuart and Christine are great hosts and, conveniently, exceptional cooks when breakfast time rolls around. Together they are the go-to source of knowledge on how to make the best of the area. Medieval Conques looks as if it's stepped straight from In the Name of the Rose; the cliff-huddling town is unforgettable. Sit in the peaceful Abbaye de Ste-Foy (best visited in early evening as the light is fading) and listen to choral music before walking the labyrinthine streets. You'll be following in the footsteps of thousands of Santiago de Compostela pilgrims, who have been coming through here since the 11th century.

COOL FACTOR An exotic-tinged mountain-top retreat with views, walks and medieval towns to die for.

WHO'S IN Tents, caravans, campervans, dogs – yes.

ON SITE The site has mature shaded areas and a maximum of 60 pitches. A clean wash-block also caters for babies and disabled campers, and has a washing machine (€4). Café, table tennis. Lake is home to pike, carp, and perch. Fishing free. Weekly campfire nights. All safari tents have real beds, cooking facilities, a BBQ and picnic table.

OFF SITE Aveyron's wooded valleys, poppy-flecked mountain meadows, honey vendors and pottery workshops are all nearby. One of the loveliest walks is the 7-km ramble in La Vinzelle (ask Christine for details and a map). Views of the valley and glittering River Lot are life-affirming. Pick up a kayak and paddle down the river from Entraygues-sur-Truyère.

FOOD & DRINK Christine serves up continental/full English breakfasts (€6.50–€7.50) with fresh bread. On certain evenings the campsite also holds evening meals on a long table with local food and wine. In July and August there are several evening markets in the area. The nearest town is St-Cyprien-sur-Dourdou, which has plenty of cafés and grocery shops. In Conques, Hervé Busset (05 65 72 84 77; moulindecambelong.com) is a 1-star Michelin restaurant in a magnificent historic setting.

GETTING THERE By car from Brive-la-Gaillarde, head to Figeac on the D840, then to Decazeville. From here it's easy to reach St-Cyprien-sur-Dourdou, then follow signs to Sénergues (D502 then D46) and L'Étang du Camp is signposted.

OPEN April–September.

THE DAMAGE Safari tent (2–4 people) low/high season 2 people €227/€255 per week or low/high season 4 people €249/€305 per week. Tent (2 people, electricity) €18.50 per night.

domaine de pradines

Route de Millau, 30750 Lanuéjols, France 0033 4 67 82 73 85 www.domaine-de-pradines.com

If you like your campsites to come with a healthy dose of history, check out Domaine de Pradines. According to official documents, the site was once owned by a certain M. Cambacères, a key official in Napoléon's government. Indeed, Napoléon is said to have stayed here, for which Cambacères planted some trees following the outline of the imperial eagle as a welcoming gesture. Not impressed? Well, architectural evidence shows that the site harks back at least to the Knights Templar. Still not enough? Okay – how about the discovery of a 4th-century Roman coin on the grounds?

Today's incarnation of the campsite is in the capable hands of Virginie (from France) and George (from Scotland), who have been in charge of the place, along with their respective families, since 2006. Situated slap-bang in the middle of the Parc National des Cévennes and Parc Régional des Grands Causses, Pradines is as idiosyncratic as they come. It boasts Turkmen yurts, a series of vaulted buildings that date back to the 13th century, wooden chalets and an almost unbelievably large tract of land (150 hectares) that's mostly left wild. Mostly. Thirty hectares have been reserved for the main camping site a vast and fairly unruly space that has a touch of the savannah about it, helped by the African-style BBQ area and tall, blonde grass.

Campers can choose to take one of the huge spaces around the periphery of the field, or lose themselves completely in the woods. Either way, it's unlikely you'll be disturbed by your neighbours unless they're shouting through a megaphone; and

unless you have powerful binoculars, you won't be seeing many of them either.

While the owners admit that the rugged feel of the site isn't for everyone, it'll certainly suit anyone with a sense of adventure or with a liking for nature. Besides, it's not so rough really – the amenities include a shower block ensconced in a charming old vaulted stone barn, a kids' playground, a pool, a restaurant, a reception with a well-stocked shop... and you can even get Wi-Fi if you need to.

The real idea, though, is to take a memorable hike or adrenalin-pumping raft trip through one of the nearby gorges – the Tarn, Jonte and Dourbie are all within easy reach – and other outdoor playgrounds that offer a multitude of activities, from climbing and hiking to kayaking, rafting, and canyoning. You can even paraglide if you want to see the area from a bird's-eye perspective. Or explore the forests, granite hills and magnificent caves of the Cévennes – a decidedly different landscape, but also in close proximity. There are places like the charming holiday town of Meyrueis to visit. Or try Millau, home to the marvellous Millau Viaduct, the highest bridge in the world.

Guided walks and maps are available from reception. Plus there's the campsite's expansive terrain, where you can spot wildflowers (including several species of rare orchid), birds and butterflies. Maybe you'll find something older than a coin from the 4th century BC. A dinosaur footprint maybe?

COOL FACTOR Wild-style camping in the middle of two great national parks.

WHO'S IN Tents, caravans, campervans, cars – yes. Groups by arrangement.

ON SITE 3 communal BBQ areas, 50 huge pitches, 48 of which have hook-ups, some close to the sanitary block, others further away, while finally there's semi-wild camping for the more adventurous or complete tranquillity seekers. Facilities include 9 hot and 2 cold showers (including a hot shower with disabled access), washbasins in cubicles, washing-up sinks, washing machine and dryer. Swimming and paddling pool, 2 tennis courts, boules court, children's playground. Restaurant with a beautiful vaulted ceiling, takeaway food options, shop, Wi-Fi, volleyball and badminton courts. No campfires.

OFF SITE There's the Grotte de Dargilan caves (46 6 45 60 20; grotte-dargilan.com) as well as the caves where they make Roquefort cheese (05 65 58 56 00; visite-roquefort-societe.com), while the Micropolis Insectarium will appeal to creepy-crawly lovers (05 65 58 50 50; micropolis-aveyron.com). Fremyc (06 58 13 48 48) in Meyrueis, organise rafting, canoeing, walks, bike-rides and potholing. Airzone Parapente (06 60 84 76 23; parapentemillau.com) can sort out tandem rides over Millau and the Grands Causses. Randals Bison (04 67 82 73 74; randals-bison.com) offer cowboy-style riding on their bison farm. Great walks and wild river swimming are easy to find and there is a variety of activities such as canoeing down the Tarn river, hiking, horseriding and visiting Templar strongholds.

FOOD & DRINK Pradines' own auberge serves food in July and August in an ancient building with an impressive stone vault (formerly a Templar chapel). It has a pleasant grassed terrace and there's also a small shop on site which serves fresh bread daily. The village of Lanuéjols has a hotel-restaurant and bar – Hôtel Bel Air (04 67 82 72 78) – which is informal and family-run. Meyrueis is a bustling village in the summer with a weekly market, shops and wide range of cafés, restaurants and bars such as Hôtel Family (46 6 45 60 02; hotel-restaurant-family-48-12.com) and the Hôtel du Mont Aigoual (04 66 45 65 61; hotel-mont-aigoual.com), both of which have good food and atmosphere. Among other local restaurants, try the Ferme Auberge de la Tindelle (05 65 59 18 39) or the wonderful Lou Puech in St André de Vézines, which serve excellent hearty meals.

GETTING THERE Pradines is 35km east of Millau. From Millau follow the D991 towards La Roque St Marguerite and then take the D41 towards Lanuéjols. Pradines is 4km outside the village.

OPEN Camping officially from start of June–mid September; May too depending on the weather. Yurts can be rented mid April–mid October. Gîtes and chalets are open all year.

THE DAMAGE Tents: 2 adults €12–€16 (electricity €3); large yurts (sleep 4) €350–€550 per week; small yurt (sleeps 2) €170–€280 per week; bell-tent (sleeps 4) €55 per night, minimum 3 nights high season. Gîtes and chalets (sleep up to 6) also available.

camping chantemerle

Lieu dit La Pontèze, Bédouès 48400, Florac, France 0033 4 66 45 19 66 www.camping-chantemerle.com

When author Robert Louis Stevenson penned *Treasure Island*, his colourful plot drew on a life peppered with interesting travels. Decades earlier, his adventures in the south of France inspired *Travels with a Donkey in the Cévennes*, a classic of outdoor literature. Meandering through the tree-clad mountains, Stevenson's idea of cool camping was a little different from ours today, not least because his shabby homemade sleeping bag was so heavy a donkey was required to carry it. But, all the same, he knew a stunning location when he saw one – 'a smooth sandy ledge... the Tarn below... a thin fringe of ash trees... a faint sweet perfume which pervaded the afternoon air'. We couldn't have put it better ourselves. Stevenson captures the timeless beauty of this exact spot more than a century ago. Things have changed a little since then and the idyllic setting Stevenson found is now a resting point for fellow travellers known as Camping Chantemerle. However, the Tarn still frolics through its sandy channel, and the ash and Spanish chestnut trees remain, although they now provide a shady canopy for tents. Echoing the traits of the languid young wanderer, this riverside spot is unpretentious and relaxed a campsite where time passes you by as gently as the water's flow.

Beneath ancient trees, camping pitches are spread around, indiscernibly divided from one another, all with electrical hook-ups, if required. Around 25 of the 69 pitches are along the riverfront, although the rest still have easy access to the water, where a private beach reaches down to the Tarn, good for paddling and bathing, though not quite deep enough for a proper swim. There's a great swim hole at the far end of camp that's perfect for proper wild swimming. Choose between sunning on the beach beside an old bridge or hopping along the rocks that cluster on the river banks as you head upstream towards a deeper gorge. Head this way in the evenings to perch quietly on the bank and catch a glimpse of the resident beaver family, bobbing along in the water, pushing branches on their noses.

Back at the campsite, there is plenty to entertain you, with an outdoor play area, table tennis and a pétanque court, along with an established bar/restaurant serving good, local food in a simple café setting that reflects the friendly personalities of Claudio and Nicole, the inimitable campsite owners, who make Camping Chantemerle the place that it is. The former is French/Italian and the latter German/American so there's no need to worry about any language barriers. Warm, welcoming and full of local knowledge, they are the go-to couple when you finally drag yourself away from the river and decide to explore the surroundings. Deep in the Parc National des Cévennes, with picturesque rural settlements dotted among the hills, it is difficult to go wrong here. Like our wayward traveller Stevenson, tie your laces, point your finger and explore. A wondrous landscape awaits.

COOL FACTOR Relaxed riverside camping and wild swimming in the beautiful Cévennes mountains.

WHO'S IN Everyone: caravans, campervans, tents, families, couples, dogs.

ON SITE 69 pitches, 8 mobile homes, 1 tipi and 1 caravan. Riverside pitches are just a few metres from the water, with rocks to the edge and a sandy beach. The River Tarn is ideal for paddling and bathing, though not deep enough for a proper swim (making it particularly safe for children). The RL Stevenson long-distance footpath goes right through the campsite into Florac. There is a free Wi-Fi hotspot at reception, tourist info, basic grocieries and ice creams for sale. Showers and toilets are relatively old and simple but immaculately well kept. There is also a laundry room, games room, playground, swimming pool, table tennis, table football, pétanque, book exchange and bikes for hire. Campers can even hire a donkey for a spot of Stevenson-style trekking.

OFF SITE The Gorges du Tarn, 5km away, is a far more tumultuous section of the same river that slides lazily past the campsite – perfect for wild swimming. Cévennes Évasion Voyages Nature (04 66 45 18 31; cevennes-evasion.com), based in Florac, arrange walking, climbing and potholing trips, while Canoe 2000 (04 66 48 57 71; canoe2000.net) organise canoeing trips. Both operators have excellent English and campsite guests get a 10% discount.

FOOD & DRINK Fresh bread and croissants are available at reception. There is an excellent bar/restaurant overlooking the river serving regional specialities as well as pasta dishes and pizza. In Florac, 4km away, they serve probably the best crêpes in the region at Au Pecher Mignon (04 66 45 14 28). La Lozerette (04 66 45 06 04) in Cocures (800m from the site) serves refined French cuisine in a gorgeous setting.

GETTING THERE The site is 4km outside Florac on the D998.

PUBLIC TRANSPORT Take a train to Ales station and then a bus to Florac.

OPEN April–November.

THE DAMAGE 2-person pitch with vehicle €12.50–€18. Children: €2.50–€3.50. Electrical hook-up (10 amp) €4.

cosycamp

Les Ribes, 43800 Chamalières-sur-Loire, France 0033 4 71 03 91 12 www.cosycamp.com

Picture the scene: a French summer's evening at dusk, the heady scent of wild herbs and flowers lingering in the soothing air, a glass of chilled Chenin Blanc in hand and the gentle lapping of the nearby Loire soundtracking this idyllic scene. Throw into this picture an array of quirky accommodation options alongside traditional tent camping and you have one seriously super-luxury campsite.

Opened in May 2013, Le Cosy Camp is shaping up to be one of the Loire Valley's best new eco-sites. Occupying an enviable riverside location in the picturesque village of Chamalières-sur-Loire, this is a place positively charged with history – the most evident example being the 12th-century Romanesque church. Surrounding the peaceful villages which adorn the lush valley floor

are highland plateaus and rocky gorges, which attract no end of walkers and enthusiasts of all things outdoorsy. You can hike, bike, trek or climb your way around this unspoilt, under-explored region of Central France. They have routes and prices on site. With safari and Canadian tents, gypsy caravans and treehouses to choose from, it really doesn't matter where you decide to lay your head. The main draw here is the wonderful riverside surroundings. Your considerate hosts have designed the site with relaxation in mind. From the various gardens (flower, vegetable, orchard, botanical labyrinth, even a 'garden of fragrances'), to the onsite bird sanctuaries and 'wellness centre', a stay at Le Cosy Camp will definitely recharge the batteries.

COOL FACTOR Real riverside camping on the banks of the historic Loire.

WHO'S IN Tents, caravans, vaccinated pets, large groups – yes.

ON SITE 63 camping pitches, 1 gypsy caravan, 2 treehouses, 10 safari lodges, 10 Canadian tents and 5 cottages. 2 shower/toilet blocks (one is heated during cooler months). Laundry, baby-changing facilities, electric hook-ups. Heated outdoor swimming pool and paddling pool. Fishing equipment can be rented on site. Campfires in designated area in the evening.

OFF SITE The picturesque village of Chamalières-sur-Loire and its 12th-century church are well worth a visit. Besides the countless river-based activities, the region is brimming with lots of other outdoor pursuits. There's rock climbing in the village while, for the more intrepid, high altitude walking on the Via-ferrata des Juscles in Pertuis is 19km from the site. Les Ravins de Corboeuf, known as 'Le Petit Colorado de l'Auvergne', is a geological curiosity of coloured clays. There's also a leisure park, Le Neyrial, Yssingeaux, 17km away (04 71 59 04 62; leneyrial.com), with quad bikes, trampolines, mini-golf and archery, among other activities.

FOOD & DRINK An onsite snack bar serves up simple local dishes, using organic and fairtrade products whenever possible. There's also a daily specials dinner menu and the likes of 'pancake family party', plus burgers from the grill. Special breakfasts and picnics can be arranged by request. There are many local markets during the day and in the evening in the summer, making it easy to stock up on produce. Chamalières-sur-Loire boasts 3 bars and restaurants, including the excellent Le Cham's (04 71 03 71 44; le-chams.fr), which has a choice of good-value menus.

GETTING THERE Follow the N88 north towards Saint Etienne from Le Puy en Velay: take the D103 left from Yssingeaux – the 'road of the river Loire' – up to Retournac. Then cross the bridge and turn right to Chamalières-sur-Loire.

PUBLIC TRANSPORT Chamalières-sur-Loire train station is just 300m from the campsite.

OPEN Start of March–early October.

THE DAMAGE Basic tent pitch + 2 people €15.50–€27; extra adults €3–€4; extra children (3–6 yrs) €2–€3; pets €3. Safari tents from around €245 a week, gypsy caravans from €335 a week, cabins and cottages from €450 a week, lodges from around €400 a week.

camping le clapas

280 Chemin de la Vernède, 07150 Salavas, Vallon Pont d'Arc, France 0033 4 75 37 14 76 www.camping-le-clapas.com

Le Clapas might sound like the kind of thing you'd do to a Ricky Martin track – but 'clapas' is actually an old Occitan name for a pile of stones, or a building made from a pile of stones. In the case of Camping le Clapas, the stones come from a beach on the Ardèche River – the robust river that forged the beautiful gorges in this area and which gave the département its name.

A former municipal site, Le Clapas was taken over in 2005 and transformed into something a little more special. Trees were planted, small walls were built using the eponymous stones, which still line the river bank and the site's private beach, and the facilities were expanded to make the site more comfortable. You'll find the 75 decent-sized pitches beneath a swaying miscellany of acacias and pines, and many offer views of the Ardèche. It's a family-friendly place with boules, table-tennis and volleyball on offer, and regular group entertainments, such as BBQs, themed evenings and karaoke. The adults are catered for, too, with a small onsite bar.

Canoeing and kayaking are big draws here. And, there is something for everyone – gentle stretches of river for beginners and feisty rapids for adrenaline fiends. Le Clapas works in partnership with a local tour operator to arrange canoe and kayak tours, for individuals, groups and families, that leave directly from the site; these range from a leisurely 8-km paddle to a more strenuous 32-km trip. If river-related shenanigans don't grab you, there are plenty of other diversions. The most obvious – the Gorges de l'Ardèche – feature limestone cliffs that reach up to 300m high; one of the most popular sights along the way is the natural 60m stone arch known as the Pont d'Arc, which appears on much of the local publicity material. It happens to be a particularly pleasant hour's stroll from the site and it also has a beach.

Amateur geologists and other interested parties will no doubt be aware of nearby Chauvet – a Paleolithic network of caves containing paintings and engravings that are thought to be over 36,000 years old. Easily rivalling the more famous sites of Lascaux and Cosquer, the cave's priceless geological value means that visitors cannot currently visit, but the excellent Grotte Chauvet-Pont-d'Arc Cave Exhibition is the next best thing. The local region is also studded with timeless villages. Balazuc and Vogüé, in particular, are worth heading to. The former hangs off a steep hill and clifftop and is surrounded by trees; the latter is a similarly stunning collection of stone houses huddled together beneath an imposing 17th-century château.

The site really comes into its own as a chilled retreat from the summer-time masses. With over 100,000 tourists descending on the area throughout July and August, it can be difficult not to feel a bit smug as you chill on a hammock or paddle in peace, while the 250 plus pitch resorts across the river milk the masses with over-priced activities and tacky discothèques.

We have to say, it's much better to be doing Le Clapas; let the others do Ricky Martin.

COOL FACTOR Killer site right on the Ardèche River with its own private beach.

WHO'S IN Tents, caravans, campervans, glampers, dogs – yes.

ON SITE 67 camping pitches, most with electricity, 2 pre-erected tents and 16 mobile homes for rent. All the amenities you'll need are here, except a restaurant. There are 2 modern sanitary blocks with hot water plus washing machines, grocery store and snack bar – and everything is clean and functions well.

OFF SITE For via ferrata climbing, try Vert Tige (04 75 88 02 61; vert-tige-ardeche.com) in Vallon Pont d'Arc. And kids will love exploring the caves at Aven d'Orgnac (04 75 38 65 10; orgnac.com).

FOOD & DRINK Pizza and frîtes are served up on site throughout the summer, but for pukka Provençal food check out Les Tilleuls (04 75 37 72 12) in Lagorce. Consider also the *table d'hôte* menus served at the striking Château de Balazuc (04 75 88 52 67; chateaudebalazuc.com). For self-catering supplies, Vallon Pont d'Arc has a regular market every Thursday and a food market every Sunday in high season.

GETTING THERE From Aix-en-Provence, take the A8 to Salon-de-Provence, then the A7 towards Orange. Continue through Orange on the E15 and turn off towards Vallon Pont D'Arc. Follow the signs to Salavas and then keep a look out for signs to Le Clapas.

PUBLIC TRANSPORT The closest you can get on public transport is Vallon Pont d'Arc, which is accessible by train or bus. From there, the site is a 25-minute walk or a taxi ride (about €13).

OPEN Mid-April–September.

THE DAMAGE Pitch for 2 people is €15–€27.50, depending on season. An extra adult costs €4.70–€7.50 and a child (2–10 yrs) €3.20–€5.80. Equipped tent €245–€539 depending on season. Mobile home €245–€775 depending on season.

le grand bois

Col de Boutière, D233, 26460 Le Poët Célard, France 0033 4 75 53 33 72 www.legrandbois.nl

Peek through the trees of this nature reserve woodland and, behold, a cluster of humungous safari-lodge tents looms into view. Situated among limestone scenery of the Parc Régional du Vercors, this settlement pioneers next-level glamping, with sturdy canvas homes perched on wooden decks hidden in woodland behind an 18th-century inn. These constructions are simply huge; you'll stretch your legs just fetching a glass of water and families can hang out here all day without feeling claustrophobic. Choose between a covered or uncovered terrace porch, then tie back the front flaps to create an open-plan abode filled with double and bunk beds and full-sized wardrobes. Look outwards towards a view of arboreal wilderness. A cheaper camping option is to book a tunnel tent sleeping five, with awning, bedding, towels, and gas stove, or just to pitch a tent in the camping meadow near the pool, snack bar, dining patio, and wash-block. Once acclimatised, you can explore the park by way of a hiking, cycling or motorcycling package. Otherwise just enjoy your house in the woods; it's too special to leave for too long.

COOL FACTOR Taking camping in the woods to a whole new level, this campsite is too special to leave.

WHO'S IN Campervans, caravans, dogs, large groups, young groups (all low season only) – yes.

ON SITE 40 sheltered pitches all with electric hook-ups for tents, caravans and campervans. A few pitches are available in the sunny meadow. Most pitches located in the woods offer plenty of shade and privacy. Amid the pitches, Le Grand Bois offers 10 fully-equipped luxury safari-lodge tents. *Table d'hôte* dinners, pizzas and breakfasts are available. Swimming pool, playground, volleyball, Wi-Fi and bread service. Bar 4pm–10pm. No BBQs or campfires.

OFF SITE Mountain bikers can take on the challenge of Mont Ventoux and the Vercors, infamous climbs from the Tour de France. Bike storage on site.

FOOD & DRINK Stuffed ravioli is a local speciality, and the Auberge de l'Éstang (04 75 76 05 70; laubergedelestang.fr) in the village of Saoû is a good place to sample it.

GETTING THERE From the A7, take exit 18 to Montélimar Sud and follow the D540 to Dieulefit, then Bourdeaux. Follow the signs to Vers Pascalin and Le Grand Bois on the D233. The campsite is after 250m on the D233.

PUBLIC TRANSPORT TGV to Valence or Montélimar, then the train to Montélimar or Crest, and the bus to Dieulefit.

OPEN Start of May–mid September.

THE DAMAGE 2 adults with tent €19; children (2–7 yrs) €6.00; extra adults €8. Safari lodges €350–€770 per week, €50–€75 per night (not July/August). Dogs €3.50. Hook-ups €3.50. B&B €55–€85. Gîte €560–€725 per week, €85 per day. *Table d'hôte* dinner €25.

camping la source

05140 Saint Pierre D'Argençon, Hautes-Alpes, France 0033 4 92 58 67 81 www.lasource-hautesalpes.com

There's something very wholesome about Camping La Source. Firstly, there's the air. Clean, pure breezes roll off the mountains and filter through the trees to fill every inch of the expansive sky that dominates this charming campsite. Secondly, with a manageable 25 plots, it's never crowded, which explains the tranquillity. Birdsong and crickets provide a steady background chatter, adding to the natural ambience. A walk through the campsite's woods reveals a surprising variety of trees, including pine, cherry, lime and walnut, but the stars of this woodland show are the giant sequoias. These towering trees are genuinely impressive; their thick trunks rising so high from the pine-needle-strewn ground that you have to crane your neck to follow them.

Whether you're just relaxing or using La Source as a base for hiking, fishing or swimming in the lakes, you never tire of the view that greets you every morning. And whichever plot you pick, you'll be overlooked by mountains close enough to glide from – a fact that some hang-gliding regulars take advantage of by flying from the peak and landing right back at their tents. As for nightlife, well, it's as quiet at La Source as you might expect, and they ask you to pipe down after 11.30pm in any case. But who needs carousing when you can simply get a bottle of wine, lie down on your back and gaze at the fantastic light show that greets you here every night? Star-gazing really doesn't get better than this.

COOL FACTOR Peaceful, spacious tranquillity with a spectacular backdrop. You half expect Julie Andrews to come running out of the woods.

WHO'S IN Tents, caravans, campervans, dogs (under control), groups (booked in advance) – yes. Noisy folk between 11.30pm and 7.30am – no.

ON SITE 22 pitches with a further 3 woodland pitches allocated to luxury Tipis. A cute wash-block has 2 hot showers with sinks, 3 bathroom sinks and 3 washing-up sinks. A separate toilet block has 4 WCs. Washing machine €5. Badminton court, boules pitches, table tennis and communal BBQ. No campfires or charcoal BBQs are allowed on pitches, but electric or gas BBQs are permitted.

OFF SITE It's all about the Great Outdoors. Nearly 7,000km of walking trails cover the Hautes-Alpes region, so pack your hiking boots.

FOOD & DRINK La Source has its own restaurant, offering breakfast, afternoon tea with homemade cakes and evening meals. At Aspres-sur-Buëch (7km) there is a small supermarket, *boulangerie*, café/bar and butcher. For eating out, try the Auberge de la Tour (04 92 58 71 08) or Pont La Barque (04 92 53 80 10), both within 10 minutes' drive.

GETTING THERE Follow the N75 to Aspres-sur-Buéch and then the D993 to Valence. Continue past the turning for St-Pierre-d'Argençonand and soon you'll see signs to La Source.

PUBLIC TRANSPORT From Grenoble you can get a local train to Gap, Aspres-sur-Buëch or Veynes.

OPEN Mid April–mid October. But the Chambre d'Hotes (B&B) is open all year, so get in contact for winter ski holidays!

THE DAMAGE Tent/caravan/campervan €4.50 per night; adults €4.50 per night; children (under 10 yrs) €2.50 per night; dogs €1.50. Electricity €4 per night. Car and Tent supplements €1 per night.

CAMPING

GÎTES DE FRANCE

les olivettes

Hameau les Pourcelles, 04190 Les Mées, France 0033 4 92 34 18 97 www.campinglesolivettes.com

Nora and Michel met and fell in love while working in Paris; she was a web designer, he a documentary cameraman. They both wanted to escape the bustle of inner-city life and so began their three-year search for the perfect campsite. Les Olivettes was a winner for such a visually acute couple; this staggering mountainside vista, in the heart of Provence, bursts with colour all year.

The site is over 50 years old but Nora and Michel only took up the reins in 2009, bringing a touch of Parisian chic to its rural setting and giving it a boutique, bohemian vibe. The most recent additions are a solar-powered pool with a meditation area, a stylish BBQ spot with tables and chairs and tastefully painted cornflower-blue modern amenities. Michel, whose other love affair is with wood, has further plans for bespoke fixed tents and cabins. Yet there will always be a place in this olive grove for campers; as Michel admits they like their 'temperament'. Each camping and caravan pitch has been carefully considered and levelled, offering a variety of east- and west-facing options, with some olive trees shading you from the Provenal sun.

Ecology is important to Nora and Michel; both the showers and pool are solar powered and all rubbish can be recycled. The only additional lighting comes in the shape of small solar lights, which are just about light enough to guide you through the site at night. They certainly don't pollute the view of the staggering star-flecked sky, which is said to be the clearest in Europe. If you need more proof then, from July to mid-September scrutinise the night sky further at the astronomical observatory in nearby Puimichel.

This star-crossed couple left life in the fast lane – and they believe that you should change down a gear, too. Nora and Michel want you to empty your mind and breathe in the natural surroundings. Inevitably teenagers may find this dull, but Les Olivettes is perfect for young families. The site is dotted with wooden toys, including a mini kitchen, perhaps to prepare little ones for future Provençal cooking. Although there is a supermarket in nearby Les Mées, in summer fresh bread and croissants are delivered and potatoes can be collected directly from the farmer. Twice a week delights such as quiche Lorraine and homemade *confiture* are brought back from the bountiful local markets; at some point you'll want to experience these treats firsthand.

Nora's little office at the entrance is stocked full of suggestions of what to do further afield, and Les Olivettes is a perfectly placed jumping off point. Just a 20-minute drive to the A51 means it's a good base for a wide range of activities – from gliding and hot-air ballooning in the east to swimming and water sports in the west.

Just down the road from Les Olivettes is the mill where Michel and Nora press their olives into oil in March. There's also a small museum that celebrates this special 'elixir of Provence', which, of course, is locally sourced and lovingly made.

COOL FACTOR Superb views with boutique chic and a personal, loving touch.

WHO'S IN Tents, campervans, caravans, mobile homes, young families, couples, dogs (upon presentation of a rabies license) – yes.

ON SITE 31 pitches, all with hook-ups, and 4 mobile homes. 2 excellent amenities blocks with washrooms, a coin-operated washing machine, 4 solar-powered showers (free), baby-changing, disabled toilet/shower, playground and swimming pool. Baguettes and croissants must be pre-ordered (available July–August). Information point. Great BBQ area with tables, chairs and sculptures. No campfires. Provençal bistro open in July and August from 17.00–19.30.

OFF SITE From 1 July to 15 September you can visit the Observatoire de l'Alifant in Puimichel (puimichel.obs.free. fr). The Ecomusée l'Oliver is the place to go to find out about the history of the precious olive (04 92 72 66 91). The Paragliding school Haut les Mains often does flights around Oraison (04 92 34 34 00; haut-les-mains.fr), and there's also Hot Air Balloons Provence (04 90 05 76 77), 55km away as the balloon flies, who charge €245 for a long flight and €175 for a short trip. For kids there's Jungle Parc in St Pons (06 86 73 37 57; jungle-parc.fr), though parents will have to venture further to Maillemoisson's Forêt Domaniale (04 92 35 29 79) for adult-orientated versions. For those who like to climb a mountain and jump off it, there's Fusion Paragliding near Gap (6 80 02 54 39; fusion-parapente com).

FOOD & DRINK There are plenty of restaurants in Les Mées. The best is La Marmite du Pecheur (04 92 34 35 56; lamarmitedupecheur.com), specialising in seafood. The local baker delivers in July/August but La Boulangerie de Lurs (04 92 79 17 68) is worth visiting for the wide variety of specialist regional breads. Chez Jules in Puimichel (04 92 74 98 10) offers a changing menu based on seasonal availability. Further into the mountains, 13km from the site, in Entrevennes, is Le Paradiso (04 92 77 25 92) a very reasonable bistro with an extensive vegetarian menu. Find regional specialities at the markets in Oraison (Tuesday morning) and Gréoux-les-Bains (every Thursday).

GETTING THERE From Grenoble follow the A51 and take exit 20; at the first roundabout head in the direction of Les Mées on the D4a and, at the second roundabout, turn right in the direction of Oraison on the D4. After 11km turn left and go throught the hamlet of Les Pourcelles. From Aix-en-Provence take exit 19 off the A51; turn right in the direction of Oraison on the D4b. At the next crossing, turn left in the direction of Les Mées on the D4; after 4km turn right and head through the hamlet of Les Pourcelles.

OPEN Mid April–late September.

THE DAMAGE Espace pitches €15–€28; electricity €4.90; large pitch with bathroom €21–€45; large pitch with kitchen €21–€41; adults €3–€6.50; children under 7 yrs €3–€5; children under 2yrs free; pets €3.50.

camping du brec

Le Brec, 04320 Entrevaux, France 0033 4 93 05 42 45 www.camping-dubrec.com

If the French Alps boast some of Europe's most awe-inspiring scenery, then the Maritime Alps in the country's remote southeastern corner are truly a sight to behold. The southernmost tip of this mighty mountain range, the Maritime Alps straddle the border between *l'hexagone* and the Italian regions of Piedmont and Liguria – an epic landscape of lush, craggy mountains and vast gorges bejewelled with sparkling lakes. And surveying this breathtaking vista, beside one such lovely waterside scene, you will first lay eyes upon one of the region's most enviably located campsites: Camping du Brec.

Managed by wonderful English-speaking hosts Clare and Eric Rondeau, Camping du Brec is 7.5 acres of idyllic family camping. With a mixture of shady pitches catering to tents, campervans and caravans (as well as the obligatory French camping bungalows), it's big on facilities, though with a refreshingly uncommercial slant. After navigating the serpentine roads that snake their way around the meandering River Var, arrival at Camping du Brec is akin to finding an oasis – water, sands, the lot. For the jewel in du Brec's already resplendent crown is a gorgeous lake and beach. A hive of swimming, fishing, canoeing and general aquatic escapades, the private lake is the focal point for campsite life – helped in no small measure by the lakeside bar.

As if the lakeside locale wasn't enough, Camping du Brec is also mere minutes from some of the best attractions that southeastern France has to offer. There's the sprawling Mercantour National Park (home to wild boar, golden eagles and wolves); the heady vineyards and perfumed lavender fields of Provence; and the picture-postcard town of Entrevaux, its citadel a marvel of medieval construction. The site is also not too far away from the glamorous Côte d'Azur (although it's a million miles away in terms of pretentiousness).

Natural wonders are really the thing here though: Les Gorges de Daluis and le Lac d'Allos – there's an epic scale to everything. And for those brave (or foolhardy) enough, there's always cycling the Col de la Bonette, Europe's highest road and the bane of the world's greatest cyclists during the Tour de France.

However you choose to spend your break, just let the invigorating mountain air, a panacea for all the ills of modern living, do its thing. And as the sun descends over the surrounding mountains and you kick back with a beer on the lakeside terrace as the glinting rays dance on the gently lapping waves, you'll be glad you navigated those winding Alpine roads.

COOL FACTOR A family-camping paradise in the Maritime Alps... with its own private lakeside beach.

WHO'S IN Tents, campervans, caravans (not double axle), well-behaved dogs – yes. Groups are welcome during the low season but must make prior contact for group rates and availability (no stag or hen weekends).

ON SITE 88 pitches (all with electric hook-ups) including 76 pitches for short-stay campers (of which 3 are tent-only pitches); 6 self-contained bungalows and 6 pitches for year-round campers. 2 shower blocks with ample toilets, showers, washing-up sinks and separate clothes washing sinks. A baby room has a bath and shower, while the newer of the 2 blocks has disabled facilities. Washing machine and dryer (€3 each). Ironing board and iron available at reception. Caravan/camper service area. Freezers for ice packs; Wi-Fi connection on 80% of the site (€1 for 24h); computer with free internet connection; European electrical adaptors can be borrowed from reception, as can hiking maps and guides, table-tennis bats, boules and badminton raquets. Fresh bread service running from Easter to the end of September and 2 communal BBQs available for use.

OFF SITE The site is an ideal base for all kinds of outdoor pursuits, and Base Sport Nature (04 93 05 41 18; basesportnature.com) can organise rafting, tubing, canyoning, via ferrata and climbing trips – campers get a 10% discount on all activities. Nearby Entrevaux is a charming medieval town with historic ramparts; and an hour's drive away lies the Mercantour National Park (04 92 81 21 31; mercantour.eu), with peaks reaching 3,000m and the Lac d'Allos, the largest natural high-altitude lake in Europe. The famous Gorges du Verdon is also only about an hour away. The 14km-long Martel Trail follows the course of the River Verdon, taking in some of the country's most stunning scenery.

FOOD & DRINK There's a well-stocked supermarket less than 2km away for any provisions, and an onsite snack bar overlooking the lake, which serves draught beer, hot and cold drinks, ice creams and light snacks. Every Monday evening in July and August the site is visited by a pizza van. There's a choice of restaurants in Entrevaux (1.5km away), among which the Auberge du Planet (04 93 05 49 60; restaurant-leplanet-entrevaux.fr) serves traditional French cuisine and pizzas. In Annot (8km), the ever-popular La Table d'Angele (04 92 83 88 50) is worth a try. For local delicacies, be sure to sample some *secca de boeuf* – a dried slated-beef speciality particular to in Entrevaux. The region is also famous for its apple juice – a great accompaniment to the area's famous sweet *pain d'épice* (ginger bread).

GETTING THERE From Nice, follow the N202 in the direction of DIgne-les-Bains for about 75km until you reach Entrevaux. Drive through Entrevaux and stay on the same road for approximately 4km until you cross the River Var. Immediately after crossing the river turn right down a side road (signposted Camping du Brec, Intermarché, Base Sport et Nature). Drive to the end of this road (approximately 2km) and Camping du Brec is at the end. From Digne, take the N85 in the direction of Nice for approx 17km until you reach Barrème. At Barrème take the N202 towards Nice. Approximately 4km before Entrevaux – and before crossing the Var River – turn left down a side road (signposted Camping du Brec, Intermarché, Base Sport et Nature). Drive to the end of this road (approximately 2km) and Camping du Brec is at the end.

OPEN Mid March–mid October.

THE DAMAGE €8.10 per pitch per night. Adults €5.10, children (2–13 yrs) €3.45, electricity €1.60–€3.25, pets €1, tourist tax €0.35 per person.

ferme noemie

Chemin Pierre Polycarpe, Les Sables, Bourg d'Oisans 38520, France 0033 4 76 11 06 14 www.fermenoemie.com

Mention Bourg d'Oisans and many travellers will think of Alpe d'Huez, the world-famous ski resort that sits 21 hairpins above the bustling town. Advanced cyclists are likely to froth with excitement; they view these mountain bends in the same way that Catholics view Lourdes, making it their lifelong ambition to visit. Not for the actively challenged, the climb is steep: it can take three hours to pedal to the top (under an hour for the pros), but once there you can buy a certificate testifying that you've conquered what was the first alpine climb introduced to the Tour de France, in 1911.

Alpe d'Huez also boasts the longest black ski run in the world, the 16-km 'La Sarenne' but, as thrilling as the snow-covered mountain range is, it's summers here that are truly special. Regardless of whether cycling is your bag or not, time spent sprawled out on the lawns of Bourg d'Oisans' outdoor swimming pool, surrounded by the scenery of the magnificent Alpes, will do wonders for your limbs. It will bronze them at the very least, and the toddlers' pool and fun slide will entertain the tiny tots for hours. After a *tartiflette* lunch in town, march off the frighteningly calorific potato, cream and cheese dish along the 680km of walking trails of the Ecrins National Park – the largest of France's six national parks. Mountains loom from all angles, cutting into the landscape like a helter-skelter of peaks and valleys, visible, in all their glory, from the campsite at Les Sables, just up the road from Le Bourg d'Oisans.

Ferme Noemie has around 21 numbered pitches, in homage to the Alpe d'Huez hairpins.

The owners Melanie and Jeremy are great skiers. They met working for a UK ski-holiday company in the late 1980s and basically never returned home. He's good with his hands; the chalet shower block and loft apartments are all his own work. And Melanie is a consummate hostess. Should the nights turn chilly at this high altitude, warm blankets are handed out. The reception is crammed with information leaflets, a coffee-making machine, microwave and fridge. If you've run out of beer, the couple will give you theirs; they won't want anyone to go without. In fact, they'll give away cider made from their own apples, gratis. Plastic tables and chairs are allocated to most pitches, so you can picnic under the gaze of the national park. The adjacent cliff face is striking and majestic. Caravans have to park on the right of the driveway so that they don't spoil the alpine serenity. 'Camping for softies' is the couple's latest project: bell tents with beds, duvets, wine glasses and a sheltered cooking stove. So successful are these tents that there are now four on site, cosy and contemporary-cool in green and cream.

It's not hard to find things to do here. As well as walking, cycling and swimming, how about trying rock climbing, rafting, canoeing, horseriding or even parapenting? The latter involves running off the side of a nearby mountain with a large gliding canopy attached to you. Whether you're brave enough to try this or not, this certainly isn't a campsite for the bone idle; you'll be fighting fit and ready to tackle those hairpins yourself by the end of your stay.

COOL FACTOR Everything about the site is cool: the location, the view, the British owners, the fresh air.

WHO'S IN Tents, campervans, caravans, dogs, large groups, young groups – yes.

ON SITE 16 pitches, plus 4 for caravans/mobile homes. Park next to a field of grazing horses, who are living out their twilight years in the most beautiful spot imaginable. The owners' wooden chalet house blends in with the various apartments for hire that the couple have built. The camping field is triangular in shape, with lush green grass, a few dainty blossoms and the mountains towering sky high in the background. 4 bell tents can each fit up to 4 beds (all singles), with solar lamp, kettle, wine glasses and portable stoves kept in an outside dining shelter; 2 mobile homes (April–October) sleep 6; 4 chalet apartments, including 1 loft conversion, sleep 6, with cot and baby bath. One wash-block, gorgeous inside and out, with hot showers and disabled WC. In the reception there's a coffee machine, fridge, freezer, microwave and PC. Breakfast bread and croissants can be delivered to your pitch in high season. Washing machine and drier €4. Play area. Badminton net. Free Wi-Fi. Communal BBQ next to the kids' play area. No campfires.

OFF SITE Aside form all the obvious outdoor activities, you can cycle the Alpe d'Huez which is a 13-km climb from Bourg d'Oisans, renting a bike from any of the town's cycle-hire shops from €25 for 1 day, €125 for 6 days. There's also the Domaine de Vizille which is an 18-km drive (04 76 68 07 35; www.domaine-vizille.fr) and also has exhibitions dedicated to the French Revolution, set in a stunning deer park.

FOOD & DRINK Make a detour to the right to stop off at the kind of bonkers art-deco restaurant that you'd expect to see on a film set – Hôtel de La Poste in Corps-la-Salette (04 76 30 00 03; hotel-restaurant-delas.com) serves a 5-course set lunch that you'll not forget in a hurry. Chintzy decorations fill every inch of space inside and huge serving plates of oysters, pastry canapés, sweet roulades, and shellfish are presented on the balcony terrace or indoors.

GETTING THERE The 'Romans' route is very easy; most of it is a long, straight, fast road that leads you on to the Grenoble bypass, the Rocade Sud and up to the Oisans Valley. Follow A48, A41, or A51 into the region and you will find the town on the D91/D1091. More windy, but with spectacular scenery, is the route de Napoléon that runs via Corps-la-Salette.

PUBLIC TRANSPORT From Grenoble and Lyon, buses run to Bourg d'Oisans (€15). Pick-ups can be arranged if the owners are available, otherwise take a taxi for the 4km to Les Sables.

OPEN April–October.

THE DAMAGE 2 adults and tent (or caravan or mobile home) €22–€44. Bell tents from €400–€450 per week; dogs free. Hook-ups €3.50. Mobile home weekend/week €90–€400. Children €2.50. Prices may vary during the Tour De France.

camping les dômes de miage

197 Route des Contamines, Saint-Gervais-les-Bains 74170, France 0033 4 50 93 45 96 www.camping-mont-blanc.com

There are not many campsites out there that can rival this one for views. Situated 900m high, in the Haute-Savoie region of the French southeast, Camping Les Dômes de Miage boasts unparalleled, breathtaking vistas of the mighty Mont Blanc and surrounding Rhône-Alpes.

Managed and maintained by the charming multi-lingual hosts Stéphane and Sophie, this Alpine Eden is a veritable institution. Welcoming campers for more than 50 years (that's three generations), Camping Les Dômes de Miage doesn't go in for the bells and whistles ('no noisy swimming pools, no static-caravans... no *animation* programs'); and why would it need to with a setting like this?

It's a site of happy contrasts – sprawling yet remote; wild yet well managed. Kids can ride their bikes with abandon, unencumbered by the tents and caravans occupying the spacious, shady (if you prefer) pitches that align the site's wooded fringes. Facilities are first-rate, free and open long hours, with the shop and reception available until 8.30pm. For those wishing to really indulge, Les Dômes de Miage also boasts a lovingly-restored *mazot* (that's a Savoyard chalet to you and me). With Italian marble floors and hand-crafted wooden furniture, a stay in this timber-clad former granary is the height of luxury.

Unlike many purpose-built ski resorts round these parts, Saint-Gervais-les-Bains has a uniquely authentic Savoyard heritage and charm. And then there's the view – the sublime mountainscape that launched a thousand brush strokes and stanzas of Romantic verse. A campsite on the roof of Europe? We think that's a height worth scaling...

COOL FACTOR Site boasting breathtaking views of Europe's highest mountain.

WHO'S IN Tents, motorhomes, dogs (if vaccinated and kept on a lead) – yes.

ON SITE 150 pitches (3 high altitude): all are a minimum of 100m²; 100 with electric hook-ups. 2 facilities blocks; free unlimited hot water showers open 24 hours a day; baby-changing/family facilities; disabled facilities. Motorhome and camper van chemical waste disposal point. Laundrette with washing machines and dryers; 2 play areas; basketball area, volleyball area, table tennis. TV room, library. Free internet access point and free Wi-Fi. Shop selling essentials. Free ice for cool-boxes.

OFF SITE It's all about the mountains. Mont Blanc (literally) looms over everything. While a climbing expedition will be beyond most campers' means, you can hop on the Mont Blanc Tramway (04 50 53 22 75; compagniedumontblanc.co.uk) from Saint-Gervais-les-Bains-Le Fayet station, to savour the views from Nid d'Aigle (2,380m), in front of the Bionnassay glacier. Saint-Gervais-les-Bains also boasts an ice rink (04 50 93 50 02) and leisure centre with heated pools, tennis courts, crazy golf and beach volleyball. You can also hire mountain bikes from here. The market in Saint-Gervais-les-Bains takes place every Thursday. Bask in the healing mountain waters at Les Thermes de Saint-Gervais Mont Blanc (04 50 47 54 54; thermes-saint-gervais.com), a thermal spa that's just the ticket for recharging those batteries. Some of the French Alps' most famous ski resorts are all within easy reach of Saint-Gervais, including Megève and Chamonix. Further afield, Lake Annecy (France's third largest) makes for a wonderful day trip and is a popular spot for swimming and water sports. Why not extend your trip to Switzerland? Geneva is only 80km away.

FOOD & DRINK The onsite shop sells bread, wine, snacks and other basics, plus there's a supermarket 7km away for all other needs. There's also the Hotel Restaurant les Dômes de Miage (04 50 93 55 62), a stone's throw from the site entrance a cosy timber-beamed bar/restaurant. The costly Le Galeta restaurant (04 50 93 16 11) has a proper spit BBQ and a lovely terrace for al fresco libations; Lou Grangni (04 50 47 76 39) boasts mountain views and traditional Savoyard specialities, such as *reblochonnade tartiflette*, grilled meats and, of course, cheese fondue.

GETTING THERE Travelling on the A40 motorway, take exit 21, in the direction of Le Fayet, and then towards Saint Gervais. At Saint Gervais village take the D902 to Les Contamines. The campsite is located 2km down here on the left.

PUBLIC TRANSPORT There's a bus stop at the campsite entrance (regular service) and a free St Gervais shuttle during the high season. Tramway du Mont Blanc station is 2.5km away; while the TGV railway station 5.5km away.

OPEN May–mid September.

THE DAMAGE 2 people, plus tent (without electrical hook-up) and vehicle from €21.20-€26.60 (depending on season). Caravans with hook-ups from €25.80–€31.20. Extra person €4–€6.20; children (under 10 years) €2.90–€4.80; Dogs €2. Credit cards are accepted. Booking is advisable, particularly during July and August.

camping terre ferme

386 Chemin des Baisses, Le Petit Condal, 71480 Condal, France 0033 3 85 76 62 57 www.terreferme.eu

The owners of Terre Ferme, Matthijs and Renske Witmans (yep, they're Dutch), bought this place years ago while they were still living in the Netherlands and, over years of long-distance commuting, have slowly and painstakingly turned what was an old maize farm into a new and stunning campsite. They restored the magnificent long farmhouse and designed and built a facilities block in the local rustic style. Eventually, a few years back, the couple were finally ready to make the big move south and it was 'so-long Holland' and '*bonjour La France*'. Now that all the works are complete, Matthijs and Renske can sit back and admire what they've achieved, which is a really charming little *aire naturelle* campsite.

Terre Ferme is situated in Le Petit Condal, a tiny *hameau* in rural Burgundy that is as small as the name implies. Condal is pretty small, but this place is so tiny that it hardly features on the map at all. Mind you, the property here covers seven hectares, of which some have been cleared to make the camping field; the rest has been penned off to keep donkeys, sheep and chickens, or has been left as natural woodland and a spring-fed pond. The camping field has only 20 pitches, and cars are kept off the grass, so there is plenty of space to stretch out. The one slight downside of the site, a consequence of its recent conversion from a field growing maize, is that there's little or no shade to be found. Some trees have been planted, but it's going to take a few years for them to offer any relief from the summer sun. So, in the meantime, if you ask nicely, you can get a tarp set up to offer you some temporary cover if the sun (or the rain) is particularly fierce.

And, if you don't fancy sticking up canvas yourself, you can always hire a pre-erected safari-style tent in the field. This sleeps four and has its own cooking facilities and fridge. Or there's a compact wooden chalet, which sleeps four in a double with two bunks set off to the side, behind the facilities block.

Most of this area is still given over to maize farming and its quiet back roads are a maze too, perfect for idling around on bikes, which are available to hire from the farmhouse – including a tandem, if you're that way inclined. But this is also the *terroir* that breeds the renowned *poulet de Bresse*, the most famous chicken in the world. These beauties are reared outdoors on small, dedicated farms and are protected by the same kind of *Appelation d'Origine Controllée* that governs the production of wines. They don't come cheap but, let's face it, half the reason you come to France is for the food and drink (the other half's probably a combination of the weather and the scenery), so it's worth giving one of these especially edible chooks a spin around the rotisserie. They are to your standard cellophane-wrapped supermarket chicken what a *filet mignon* is to a takeaway burger. And much the same can be said for the delicious little site at Terre Ferme. This place is to your standard French campsite what a boutique hotel is to a Blackpool B&B. It's a class apart and you can't go far wrong with that.

COOL FACTOR A blissfully quiet hideaway – all just a convenient couple of miles from the autoroute.

WHO'S IN Tents, campervans, caravans, dogs (for a fee) – yes.

ON SITE 20 pitches, all with electricity available. 1 central facilities block, built in rustic style, with free hot showers and WCs (both unisex). Outdoor, but covered, washing-up sinks and a washing machine (€4.50). Round the front is a covered terrace with tables and chairs. A minute's stroll down the hill is a quiet pond fed by a spring, and there are various domesticated animals.

OFF SITE This is a fairly remote farming area and there isn't a decent-sized town for miles around. Neither is there a huge number of activities available. You can hire bicycles from the site at €9 per day. If you can make it that far (it's about 10km away) it's worth visiting St-Amour, a little town of narrow, colourful streets, ivy-clad houses and an impressive old church.

FOOD & DRINK There are various facilities (fridge, coffee-maker) on the terrace, and all kinds of goodies on sale from the farmhouse – eggs, cheese, wine, beer. You can order fresh bread and croissants for the morning or arrange a continental breakfast. The owners cook up a communal BBQ on Saturdays and Wednesdays are pizza night during the peak season. In Varennes there's a *boulangerie* and butcher and a small Proxi supermarket, plus a decent little restaurant.

GETTING THERE Between Lons-le-Saunier and Bourg-en-Bresse, leave the A49 at exit 10 and, just after the péage booths, take the first right at the roundabout. Follow the road towards Petit Condal. Just before the village, turn left and the campsite entrance is on your left.

PUBLIC TRANSPORT There's a railway station at St-Amour. You can arrange for the campsite owners, Matthijs and Renske, to pick you up from here.

OPEN May–October.

THE DAMAGE A pitch is €4–€6 (depending on season), plus €4.70 per person; dogs €1. The safari tent is €260–€295 per week and the wooden chalet €100 for 2 nights or €325–€395 per week. Minimum 3 night stay.

domaine du bourg

Chemin des Terriens, 03230 Gannay sur Loire, France 0033 4 70 43 49 01 www.domainedubourg.com

Domaine names are a tricky business. Not those double-yew double-yew double-yew dot internet domain names, but the names of little French estates. Call them something fancy like Domaine de Beauregard and the neighbours think you're pretentious. So this place keeps it pretty simple. Domaine du Bourg, it says on the gate: 'Small Market Town Estate'. And what's inside's fairly straightforward, too. Dutch owners, Peter and Trudi de Lange, have converted some old farming buildings into a cracking, pretty sizeable home, along with four gîtes, three chambres d'hôtes and some gîte d'étape dorm rooms. Beyond the huddle of buildings are 2½ hectares of camping ground with only 25 pitches (so you can do the maths to work out how much room there is).

The small market town in question is Gannay-sur-Loire, a pretty sleepy little place, if the truth be told, but the quiet roads and gentle countryside are ideal for exploration by bike. These are available for hire from the site and come equipped with maps. There are plenty of gentle water sports to do and kayaks are available for hire from the site. The site's also on the new EuroVelo 6 cycle route, stretching across six countries from the Atlantic coast to the Black Sea. The French section starts at St Nazaire and follows the Loire through Orléans and Nevers, before swinging north through Switzerland, Germany, Austria, and Slovakia and south through Hungary and Serbia, finishing in Romania. So there's no real excuse for coming here and just lounging around.

COOL FACTOR Smallsville camping with plenty of room in which to stretch out.

WHO'S IN Tents, campervans, caravans, dogs (as long as you scoop any poop) – yes.

ON SITE 25 car-free pitches (electricity available). There is also a 3-person gypsy wagon to rent, plus 3 safari tents (sleeping 4–6), and a gîte d'étape or 'hiker's cabin' (sleeping up to 8). A brand-new half-timbered building houses free warm showers toilets, washbasins and dish-washing facilities. Toilet paper is supplied so you can leave your rolls at home. There is also a disabled room and baby-changing facilities. Elsewhere there's a small pool and a covered seating area (where meals are served), which is handy as a day area.

OFF SITE This is a fairly quiet site, so the best thing to do is capitalise on that quietness and hire a bike or kayak. Bikes can be rented from the site at €10 per day and kayaks are available at €14 per half-day and €23 per full day, including transport to and from the river.

FOOD & DRINK There's a small Proxi convenience store, a *pâtisserie*, a butcher and a 'very local' cafe-bar in the village.

GETTING THERE From Nevers take the D13 and D116 to Decize. Head out of town on the D978a and turn left on to the D116 for Gannay-sur-Loire. Once in the village cross the river and you'll see a triangular green with a road veering off to the left. Follow that road for 100m and the site is on the right.

PUBLIC TRANSPORT The closest you can get to the site is 12–16km away, at one of several nearby railway stations at Fours, Cercy-la-Tour or Decize.

OPEN April–November.

THE DAMAGE Pitches €6–€10. Adults €2.50–€3.50, children (up to 12 yrs) €1.50–€2.50. No charge for dogs. Hiker's cabin €10 per person per night; gîtes €345–€625 per week in high season, €150–€190 in low season.

domaine les gandins

1 allée des Gandins, 03140 St-Germain-de-Salles, France 0033 4 70 56 80 75 www.domainelesgandins.com

Un gandin, you may or may not have known, is a dandy, an aristo, the kind of guy who lost his head to the guillotine when the French Revolution rolled into town. There were loads of them who lived lives of quiet luxury on little estates, just like this one, until the Revolution came along and recommended that that kind of thing ought to come to a stop.

The estates, of course, remained, even though their owners went the way of Louis XVI and Marie Antoinette. Of course, once the dust had settled and the cobbles were hosed down, most of them eventually found their way back into the hands of a new aristocracy, as is the way with so many revolutions, but thankfully many of them are now little hotels, B&Bs, gîtes and campsites, open to the *sans coulottes* – like us lot. And of all the similar domaine-style campsites in France, this one, at Domaine les Gandins, is surely the dandiest of the lot. A magnificent house, dating back to long before the Revolution, sits at the centre of a glorious little estate comprising various gîtes (including one in a converted pigeon loft), a stretch of sleepy river, a raised wooden swimming pool, a fantastic tree house and – this is where you come in – a spacious and leafy camping field.

The main house, with its red-tiled roof and deep-green shutters, is postcard perfect, and the grounds are all immaculately kept by the friendly French family who own and run the campsite. With all its attendant facilities, Domaine les Gandins is really something of a one-stop shop of a campsite, so much so that you might be forgiven for pitching your tent on the day you arrive and

staying for a whole week without ever venturing beyond the confines of the site.

For a start, the river of La Sioule is a minute's stroll through the meadow behind the complex of buildings and past the tree house. It's not the raciest of rivers, so it's perfect for a paddle or for just for cooling off on a hot summer's day, and there are plenty of shady places in which to lounge around and listen to the birds or the gentle sound of the water. That's assuming you can block out the sound of the kids. Then there's the busy kitchen, which is at the heart of the site and always seems to have steam and smells emanating from inside. Whether you just want a morning cuppa to go with your croissant or fancy taking part in the communal *table d'hôtes* meal in the evening, you'll find that the kitchen is the social hub around which everything else revolves.

If you do venture off the site while you're here you could do worse than head down to Vichy. This old sulphur spa town gained notoriety during the Second World War, when it became the seat of Marshal Pétain's government. Thankfully, now it's reverted to being a thermal spa town next to the wide Allier River, where folk come to take the waters in search of a cure for rheumatism or gout, or just for a stroll through the leafy riverside parks.

However, there's no reason why you can't do much the same thing by the quiet waters of La Sioule at the campsite. It might not have the same kind of sulphurous healing powers, but the peace and tranquillity will surely have much the same restorative effect on the mind.

COOL FACTOR Dandy camping in upper-class surroundings by a sleepy river.

WHO'S IN Tents, campervans, caravans, groups, dogs (on leads) – yes.

ON SITE 25 grassy camping pitches. There's 1 large chalet-style block tucked off to the side of the site with a row of WCs and hot showers, which is perfectly serviceable. There are also laundry facilities. There's a great tree house between the estate and the river and, down at the bank, there's a communal firepit and some wooden furniture for lazing about by the water. There is a raised, wooden, heated swimming pool. BBQs off the ground are permitted on the camping field.

OFF SITE The site is rather out in the boonies, and the nearest town of any note is Vichy, which is worth a visit if you're a fan of thermal waters. Unsurprisingly, perhaps, there are few reminders of the town's collaborationist past under Marshal Pétain. Otherwise, if you're looking for inspiration, you could do worse than check out Les Gandins' website, where you'll find suggestions of things to do in the local area listed under 24, yep 24, separate headings, ranging from parachuting and where to browse the best bric-a-brac shop, to thermal bathing in Vichy and bike hire. It's an impressive list – it even has a volcano in there – so if you can't find something useful to do with yourself after browsing that, then take a walk along the river and give yourself a stern talking to.

FOOD & DRINK You can pick up bread from the van that visits the site and there are coffees and ice creams available from the kitchen during the day. Or why not treat yourself to a 4-course *table d'hôte* meal in the evenings, which is €26 for adults, including wine and coffee. Guests can even get a takeaway to eat back at camp for just €15. There's also a 2-course kids' dinner at €9, including lemonade. These meals are available every night during high season (July and August), but not on Mondays and Thursdays outside those months. If you want to self-cater, there's a small Proxi convenience store a couple of miles away in Étroussat, but it's only good for the basics. The town of Gannat has a better range of shops. For a real treat, though, head into Vichy to Maison Decoret (04 70 97 65 06; maisondecoret.com), a kind of French-fusion restaurant with set menus from €40, made up of whatever the chef chooses to give you, to €165 for a multi-course meal with selected wines for each course.

GETTING THERE Midway between Gannat and St-Pourçain-sur-Sioule on the N7/D2009, turn left on to the D36 to Étroussat. Just over the bridge and before a large metal agricultural building, turn left at the red and white houses. There's a signpost saying Les Perrets. Follow the road over the old railway track and the site entrance is on your left.

OPEN Late April–early October.

THE DAMAGE Low season (per day): pitch €6, adults €5, children (up to 9 years) €4, pets €5, electricity €4.50. High season (per day): pitch €10, adults €8, children (up to 9 years) €5, pets €5, electricity €4.50.

mathonière

03350 Louroux-Bourbonnais Frankrijk, France 0033 470 072 306 www.mathoniere.nl

Don't you just hate it when you turn up at a campsite and the owner whips out a red marker pen and a site map of numbered pitches and plonks a big fat cross on No.127? It's usually way down the far end, between the fence and the bins, and with a long, desperate walk if nature calls. It's really not what you want.

How much nicer, then, when instead of that kind of welcome, a campsite owner stands in front of a green field, opens his arms out wide and says 'Anywhere you like. Just don't scare the donkeys.'

Thankfully that's more the kind of welcome you'll find at Mathonière, a complex of buildings and a campsite set amid the forests and lakes in the heartland of the old Dukes of Bourbon. Behind the fine old rustic farmhouse there's an expanse of green field, broken up here and there with the odd hedge and tree, but essentially an open area, where you can pick a pitch to suit your mood. There's a large tree in the middle, which usually shelters some kind of makeshift wooden fort the kids have cobbled together, and there's a pool, too – one of those freestanding things that looks like the kind of giant cooking pot cannibals use. Elsewhere, closer to the farmhouse, there's a great little café-cum-bar with a sheltered seating area. Here you can enjoy a café au lait or something stronger, and there's a menu with a range of meals. The best bit, though, is a covered cooking area, with a huge paella pan, where the owners throw together communal meals for everyone to enjoy.

It's a tried-and-trusted French formula, this. A few old farm buildings converted into a lovely owners' home, some gîte accommodation and an open field for the camping and the cooking of communal meals. There's also another common feature of these kinds of places: a large pre-erected tent that sleeps six and comes complete with gas and electricity.

This makes Mathonière sound a little formulaic, but honestly, it's not. It's a simple, wholesome, unpretentious site that's a great place to bring the kids to, but with enough space to stretch out if you don't want to be pestered. The surrounding region is dotted with forests and copses and has loads of interesting old towns and villages to explore. While it is possible to get to places on foot, by bike or by donkey, the farther-flung destinations are really only accessible by car. If the cooking-pot pool doesn't tickle your fancy, there's a sandy beach in the vicinity and loads of forest trails that are great to explore either on foot or by bike.

Just don't get lost. Because you will want to find your way back to Mathonière, and probably more than once. The site may be based on a simple formula, but then all the best formulae are simple. Like $E=mc^2$; and it doesn't come much simpler than that. At least in theory it doesn't. Making things look as effortless and simple as this is often the hardest trick in the book. And you really don't need to be Einstein to figure that out.

COOL FACTOR Middle-of-nowhere peace and quiet and a great safe haven for the kids.

WHO'S IN Tents, campervans, caravans, dogs – yes.

ON SITE There are all sorts of goodies. In addition to the usual facilities of hot showers, WCs, and washing facilities, there's a great little café-cum-bar with a sheltered outdoor seating area, where communal meals are served and where you can sit and play some of the games available, from chess to board games. Next to it is an area with a huge paella cooking pan. Then there are the animals, the pool, and the homemade fort to keep the kids happy.

OFF SITE Where to start? There are some great little towns and villages in the vicinity, such as Hérisson and La Salle. In the former there's a wonderful ruined 14th-century castle with a crumbling keep. For something a little more adventurous, head to the Plan d'Eau de Vieure (04 70 02 04 46), a T-shaped lake just off D11, north of Les Magnoux, that boasts a small section of sandy beach, but also offers kayaks, canoes, and pedalos for hire. In the opposite direction is the 11,000-hectare Forêt de Tronçais which is so ancient that Julius Caesar is said to have passed through.

FOOD & DRINK If you don't fancy the café on site, head into Cosne-d'Allier, where you'll find a large Carrefour supermarket with everything you need to cater for yourselves. Unfortunately, the town's not that hot on restaurants or bars. For these, you're better off going to Montluçon, where there's a much better choice on rue Grande in the medieval part of the town.

GETTING THERE The site is off the D16 north of Cosne-d'Allier. Come off the D16 on to the eastbound D251 and go through Louroux-Bourbonnais, keeping left and heading along D57 to Theneuille. About 2km beyond the village, turn left at the crossroads. There's a small sign for the site. Follow the road up the hill and the site is on your right.

OPEN May–October.

THE DAMAGE Low/high season per night: Adults €7/€8, children (up to 13 years) €4.50/€5.50, dogs €0/€2, hook-ups €3.50. Gîtes €345–€515 a week; mobile homes €285–€385, pre-erected tents €265–€300.

au bois joli

2 Route de Villeprenoy, 89480 Andryes, Burgundy, France 0033 3 86 81 70 48 www.campingauboisjoli.com

Au Bois Joli means 'in the pretty wood' and is a fine indication of where you're heading with this site. Perhaps all woodland areas have their charm, yet there is a little extra magic about this site and the trees that arch over it. Approaching Andryes on meandering roads, dissecting vast farmscapes that blend at the horizon with rich blue skies for much of the summer, it is impossible to resist a smile. Perhaps it's the wealth of Burgundy sunflowers arching aloft before the summer harvest that makes even the most inanimate entity appear jolly. Or it could be the inspiring, vast skies. Whatever the explanation, it's blindingly obvious why Robert and Henriëtte de Vries elected to settle here, amid the cheerfully swaying branches.

Au Bois Joli was created with a sharply observed philosophy in mind: respect for nature, for peace of mind, and for a carefully nurtured atmosphere of goodwill. The site layout, its location and ambience merge effortlessly towards this end, yet only a daily investment of hard work and passion maintains the balance. The camp is quietly adjusted around the campers all day, with the owner's high expectations catapulting the site way ahead of 'average'. It has been awarded a prestigious 'Clef Verte' for its ecologically sound methods and reverence for nature. In turn, nature seems to be thanking Au Bois Joli, with Robert and Henriëtte proud to record each new winged visitor or blooming flower. If you're lucky and catch either host during a quiet moment, it's nice to learn about the site's unique micro-environment and how they tend it. For example, more than a dozen varieties of orchid have blossomed under their watch, a total of 110 wild plants have been noted and 61 different types of bird have paid a visit thus far.

Consideration for the environment is also extended to Robert and Henriette's human guests. Parents on holiday with young children can often endure more work than relaxation, but Camping Au Bois Joli tries to address this with a site built for safety. A tree that lends itself to climbing has a stone-edged entrance guiding children towards the lower branches and soft wood chippings below. The ample play areas have the same soft precautions, with enough corners, obstacles, and hideaways to feed fertile minds. Children even have a wash-block of their own. Adults can luxuriate in the shade of mature trees or blister in the sun beside the pool, all the while soaking up epic views. For a small deposit, books can be borrowed from the library or a magazine borrowed from the racks outside reception. At the highest point of the site a gate leads to a wild wood and, within moments it's possible to be quite alone. Alternatively the prepared welcome pack, tailored to the length of your stay, has suggestions for offsite activities.

It is difficult to be critical of a campsite like this, especially when plans are afoot to make it even better by improving safety on the site road. But we're not ones to gush, so we'll end on a critical note. The site isn't open all year. That's it. Otherwise it's perfect.

COOL FACTOR Relaxation and tranquillity, in contact with abundant nature. Exceptional views and open pitches.

WHO'S IN Tents, campervans, caravans, nature-lovers, families – yes. Loud, busy people, night owls – no.

ON SITE 95 pitches, with a wide, open area among trees for pitching tents. There are also 3 large nature fields for 'free camping' (unmarked pitches without electricity), plus a fully equipped Cotton Lodge Nature Tent that sleeps a family of 4. Weekly campfires are lit by the owners. 15 superb shower booths, ample toilet blocks, disabled access for toilets, showers and washing-up, dedicated wash-block for children/seniors with low access facilities. 3 washing machines (€4.50 including powder), tumble drier, free spinner. Excellent climbing frame, children's playground, slides, sand pit, table tennis, volleyball, skittles and giant outdoor chess. Swimming and paddling pool. Café, shop selling organic produce, daily bakery delivery, library, local information. Free Wi-Fi in an all-weather marquee, with independent power sockets.

OFF SITE One must-see is the astonishing contemporary construction of a medieval fort at Guédelon (03 86 45 66 66; guedelon.fr), using only 13th-century tools and materials. Work began in 1997 and completion will happen around 2035. Auxerre, Avallon, and Clamecy all have farmers' markets once a week. The campsite is also an official start-point on the newly renovated cycle paths beside the Canal du Nivernais, running from Auxerre to Decize.

FOOD & DRINK Auberge des Sources (03 86 41 55 14; auberge-des-sources.com), beyond Clamecy, has a good reputation, as does the warm and inviting 2 Pieces Cuisine (03 86 27 25 07; 2pieces-cuisine.fr) in Clamecy itself. The latter has a great candle-lit terrace and a wonderful family feel.

GETTING THERE From Auxerre, take the N151 to Bourges. In Coulanges-sur-Yonne, take the D39 to Andryes, 3km away, and in the centre of the village you will see the Camping signs.

OPEN April–November.

THE DAMAGE Car, caravan, pitch: 2 people €16–€29, children (up to 11 yrs) €3.50–€5. Cotton Lodge Nature Tent from €150 for 2 nights.

les grèbes du lac de marcenay

Rue du Pont Neuf 5, 21330 Marcenay, Burgandy, France 0033 3 80 81 61 72 www.campingmarcenaylac.com

Marcenay, in the Châtillonnais area of Burgundy, is one of 23 villages famed for its Chardonnay and Pinot Noir wines. At one time the lake here was used by local monks as a source of piscatorial sustenance. Today, however, it attracts a more diverse collection of people, who come to sunbathe on its sandy banks, row, paddle across the large expanse of water, or watch the wildlife. And, fortunately, there's also a lovely campsite nestled right next to it.

Les Grèbes du Lac de Marcenay is everything that a campsite should be. It's got all the ingredients for an old-school camping experience: a remote location, far away from any road noise, a substantial lake, an incredibly friendly and helpful welcome in the guise of Dirk Jansen, the owner, and a laissez-faire attitude to where you pitch your home for the duration of your stay. That it's off the beaten track won't appeal to people who like to be within walking distance of a choice of bars and restaurants, but this isolation is all part of its appeal.

When Dirk took on the site it was a tired municipal affair in desperate need of renovation. One of the first things he did was remove the barrier at the entrance and throw away the rules and regulations telling campers what they could and couldn't do. 'People don't want to see that when they are on holiday', he explains in his dulcet Dutch tones. Since then, he's been quietly turning it

into a relaxed lakeside idyll, attracting a mixture of people: young couples touring around France who just want to stay for a few days, and older folk who come back year after year and stay for weeks at a time. It also seems to attract cyclists, who use it as a base to explore the area. Also, being away from any traffic, the site feels like a safe place for kids to run around without causing undue parental anxiety.

It's a lush, green, wooded plot with reasonably spacious pitches. Each one is set in a clearing that is partially surrounded by shrubs or trees, so there is a real sense of privacy. On one side are open fields and vineyards and on the other is the lake, which is about 5km all the way round and the site's greatest asset. There is something very special about living near the water and the tall trees that line its banks. Unfortunately you can't actually camp on the lakeside itself, but you are literally a hop, skip and a jump away, so you can very easily take a bottle of wine and a blanket and sit on the sand, watching the sun set. Campfires aren't usually allowed next to the pitches, but there is a communal area just outside the main site overlooking the lake, where Dirk regularly sets up a fire and BBQ for everyone to enjoy.

All in all, Les Grèbes du Lac de Marcenay is a very special campsite. Its relaxed, welcoming atmosphere and beautiful setting somehow capture the true spirit of camping in France and make the experience of staying here a real joy.

COOL FACTOR Relaxed, remote, lakeside chilling. Les Grèbes du Lac de Marcenay is everything that a campsite should and could be.

WHO'S IN Tents, campervans, caravans, dogs, large groups (owner checks details before confirming) – yes.

ON SITE 90 pitches, all with electric hook-ups, if needed. There are 13 clean toilets and 17 good showers, free for residents, 2 disabled toilets and showers and a baby-changing room. A small play area is provided for children, with kids' bikes and a free-standing outdoor pool. In the main reception there is a games area with a pool table and free Wi-Fi. The laundry area is also in the main reception building and there is a backpacker-style kitchen along with a wood-fired stove. There is a facility for freezing ice packs. There is a communal fire just to the side of the main site. Outside the reception there is a windsurf you can take up to the lake and some oars and paddles. Ask for a key and you can also unlock one of the 2 rowboats, a canoe or even a sailing dinghy moored at the waterside, free for all campers to use.

OFF SITE There are 3 different walks you can do around the lake, ranging from 5km to 10km in length. You can also borrow the Canadian canoe for free if you want to get out on the water. Dirk will rent bikes to you at a reasonable €3.50 for 2 hours and lend you some local maps, and the quiet roads are ideal for cycling and not too hilly. Or you can try pony-trekking next door for €18 an hour (ask at the reception). There's also a hidden bird-watching tower for the more ornithologically inclined. And if the attractions of the lake aren't enough, there's a recently opened assault course in the trees at Forêt de l'Aventure d'Auxerre-Laborde (06 69 06 34 17; foret-aventure-auxerre.com), which is a 45-minute drive and costs €14 for kids and €22 for adults.

FOOD & DRINK You can pre-order fresh bread and pastries at reception every day and the site carries a very small selection of food and drink, including the local tipple – Crémant de Bourgogne. Dirk is also a fan of hosting traditional crêpe evenings every now and then, whipping the pancakes up outside reception. For those interested in fully immersing themselves in local culture, there is free wine-tasting in Marcenay courtesy of Monsieur Guilleman (03 80 81 40 03). Just around the corner, in Balot, there is a snail farm, which you can visit and even taste the produce for €7 per person. For traditional French food served in what feels like someone's front room, complete with dressers and a mounted boar's head, Auberge de la Baume, also in nearby Balot (03 80 81 40 15; aubergedelabaume.com), is well worth a visit for its friendly welcome and reasonably priced fare. For a special treat, why not try the Michelin-starred, 12th-century château-hotel, Abbaye de la Bussière in Bussière-sur-Ouche (03 80 49 02 29; abbayedelabussiere.fr)?

GETTING THERE The site is on the D965 between Laignes and Châtillon-sur-Seine. Follow the signposts to Lac de Marcenay and 'Camping'.

OPEN May–September.

THE DAMAGE 2 adults and a tent €15.50; extra adults €5; children (2–11 years) €4.

camping de troyes

7 Rue Roger Salengro, 10150 Pont-Ste-Marie, France 0033 3 25 81 02 64 www.troyescamping.net

There's something extremely appropriate about the medieval town of Troyes – the capital of the Champagne region – having a town centre that's shaped like a champagne cork. It's a lovely centre, too: a huddle of medieval buildings that stand out proudly against the town's workaday charm. Though the town was formed in the Roman era, most of Troyes' architecture dates from the Middle Ages when it was an important trading post.

Just along the road, in Pont-Sainte-Marie, is Camping de Troyes, the town's official campsite. Though it's former municipal spot, the owners here have done everything in their power to transform it into something much more alluring than the word 'municipal' suggests and today it is a surprisingly green site that's just a 20-minute walk away from Troyes' centre.

When you first arrive at the campsite you could be forgiven for thinking that you were walking into a motorhome nightmare. But keep the faith and head to the back of the site, where you'll find a tent haven surrounded by shrubs and trees. Suddenly you'll realise why it's worth a few nights' breather. Although you can easily feel you have your own private space, the plot itself isn't exactly sprawling, so being at the end of the site doesn't mean a long walk if you get caught short in the middle of the night.

The site is modern, but not overly manicured, and the pitches aren't regimented. Squirrels rustle among the old trees, flowers splash colour around the perimeter and a swimming pool injects some playful fun into it all, accompanied by evening campfires arranged when the weather permits.

The overall feel is 'organised' and those using it as a handy stop off point on the way to Southern France will leave thoroughly refreshed and ready to get on their way.

Campers hanging around for longer can busy themselves in the centre of Troyes and, when they feel they've exhausted the local charms, they can try the more natural attractions of the nearby Parc Naturel Régional de la Forêt d'Orient, just 20 minutes away by car. The forest's natural lakes proffer plenty of outdoor activities and can be accessed by *la vélo voie* verte ('Green Bicycle Path') – detailed maps of which are available at reception.

COOL FACTOR A handy stop-off point when journeying across France but a bit of a gem in its own right.

WHO'S IN Tents, campervans, caravans, dogs — yes. Large groups allowed, but owner checks details before confirming.

ON SITE 104 pitches (all with electricity), 26 for tents. Heated outdoor swimming pool, inflatable giant-cushion-style trampoline, games room, restaurant. 12 free showers, 11 toilets and a wash-block. Disabled facilities and baby-changing room. Bike hire, small shop and daily bread-delivery service. Small play area, kids' bikes for hire. Ice-pack freezing. No campfires.

OFF SITE Troyes is one of Champagne's historic capitals and has a lovely medieval centre. Visit the Cathédrale St-Pierre-et-St-Paul, hard to miss in the centre of the town, which frequently houses small exhibitions that often provide a little insight into the spectacular series of 180 stained-glass windows that glisten along its walls. Elsewhere, Troyes has a number of decent museums, including a particularly good modern art collection at the Museé d'Art Moderne, based on the collection of the Lacoste clothing dynasty (03 25 76 26 80; musees-troyes.com). The town even has its own beach at Lac de la Forêt d'Orient.

FOOD & DRINK The onsite restaurant is fairly basic but Bistro du Pont (03 25 80 90 99; bistrodupont.com) is 300m away and serves decent local dishes. For something a little different, Libanais (03 25 70 60 68) serves homemade Lebanese food.

GETTING THERE From central Troyes, head 4km north to Pont-Ste-Marie (signposted), along Avenue Robert Schuman, then follow signs for Municipal Camping. Just after a set of traffic lights you cross a river and there is a big blue camping sign directing you to your right.

PUBLIC TRANSPORT Troyes is easily reached by train or bus from most major French towns. A bus service runs from the centre to within 50m of the site.

OPEN April–mid October.

THE DAMAGE 2 people, vehicle, tent €18.30–€22.70; extra adults (13 yrs plus) €5.50–€6.50; children (2–12 years) €3.60–€4.70; dogs €1.50; electricity €3.50.

ferme de prunay

41150 Seillac, France 0033 2 54 70 02 01 www.prunay.com

Gazing at the turrets and gleaming towers of Azay-le-Rideau, Villandry or Valençay, which are so picture-book pretty that they look more like Disneyland Paris than anything real, it's easy to forget that not all of the châteaux decorating the Loire Valley exemplify state-of-the-art Renaissance luxury. Chinon, by contrast, is a fortress, all practical purpose and no frippery, while Amboise was heavily defended long before François I made it a centre of culture and learning. The château at Blois (like Amboise, it's no more than 20 minutes' drive from Ferme de Prunay), was also built with defence in mind, a reminder that this region was fought over for many centuries, not least by the English.

Ferme de Prunay looks perfectly peaceful now, but the farm originally formed the core of a Gallo-Roman fortified village. The ancient moat that curls around two sides was built to keep marauders out, but now it provides a gentle afternoon's fishing practice. Similarly, when the owner, Michel Fouchault, dug out the swimming pool, he unearthed many graves and bones, but hopefully that won't bother campers as they dive into the heated piscine.

The farm has been in the Fouchault family for six generations and is a large undertaking, and its feeling of spaciousness extends to the enormous pitches, some of which are big enough to accommodate a car, a caravan and a few badminton courts as well. There's never any danger of feeling hemmed in between caravans and motorhomes here, and there's a real variety to the pitches, too. The French tend to prefer privacy, with hedges and trees around them. The Dutch, who live in a relatively small, crowded country, like open space and expansive views, so they usually opt to be next to the fields. As for the British, well, they may go for one or the other.

Many of the pitches have their own plum or apple trees, which campers are welcome to plunder, or you can join the Dutch overlooking a huge bank of wildflowers (planted to attract butterflies and bees) and the open fields. Those who choose the views should know that their freedom comes with a price tag, as those pitches are further away from the wash-block. But it's worth it.

The Ferme de Prunay also operates as a *ferme pédagogique*, or teaching farm, with school visits off season. Those opportunities continue throughout the summer, so children and their parents may learn how corn is ground and how to bake bread, for instance, or go on guided walks to a local goat farm or vineyard. The bikes around the site are all free to use, as are the volleyball and basketball areas.

It's an easy-going place, especially for families. Kids will really love the tractor-train rides and walking up the forest path to see the animals – take your pick from pigs, rabbits, chickens, donkeys, goats, turkeys and a horse. The site is extremely well located too. Just 10km away is the turreted wonder of Château de Chaumont and you are but a short drive away from some of the finest grand Loire châteaux and gardens.

COOL FACTOR Camping on the farm just a short ride away from the grand castles of the Loire Valley.

WHO'S IN Tents, campervans, caravans, motorhomes, families, dogs (on leads) – yes.

ON SITE Pitches varying in size with cabins and gypsy caravans also available. The brand new wash-block has the option of family and disabled shower rooms, and fits the superbly organised feel of the site, which has welcome letters and information in English, French, Dutch and German. The bar is open from 8am (for bread and croissant deliveries) until 9pm and also sells ice creams, basic bar food and pizzas. There are tractor-train rides around the site (high season), animal petting and a kids' play area, table tennis, volleyball court and basketball areas at the front of the site, which is where (supervised) campfires take place. No unsupervised campfires, but BBQs are okay.

OFF SITE There are discount vouchers available on site to get you into many tourist locations in the Loire-et-Cher département for a reduced price, including the wonderful château at Blois (02 54 90 33 32; chateaudeblois.fr), 16km away, where Joan of Arc was blessed in 1429 before she left with her army to drive the English from Orléans. There's also the Maison de la Magie (02 54 90 33 33; maisondelamagie.fr), a spectacular magic museum, opposite the chateau, and the beautiful town of Amboise is also well worth the 20-minute drive along the river, both for its chateau (02 47 57 00 98; chateau-amboise.com) and Le Clos Lucé (02 47 57 00 73; vinci-closluce.com), the house where Leonardo da Vinci lived his final 3 years.

FOOD & DRINK The farm is a member of the regional tourist organisation 'Bienvenue à la ferme' and can recommend many local suppliers, including La Cabinette for goats' cheese in Onzain, 8km away (which also has the best range of shops locally), or their favourite organic Touraine wine produced at Domaine Château-Gaillard in Mesland, 3km from the site. Among the many local markets the farm recommends are those in Amboise on Friday and Sunday mornings. There are many restaurants to choose from in Blois, and just about anywhere near the castle is good, but L'Orangerie du Château de Blois (02 54 78 05 36; orangerie-du-chateau. fr) stands out as a special gastronomic treat, housed in a beautiful building with stunning interiors and a lovely terrace; its menus start at €34.

GETTING THERE From the A10 take the Blois exit, then follow directions for Angers and Château-Renault until you reach Molineuf, then follow the signs for Chambon-sur-Cisse and then Seillac on the D131, where you'll pick up the roadside signs to Ferme de Prunay.

OPEN Late March–early November.

THE DAMAGE 2 adults plus pitch plus electricity €20 (€33 in high season). Extra adults €8 (€10.80), under-5s €4 (€4.80).

le chant d'oiseau

49390 Mouliherne, France 0033 2 41 67 09 78 www.loire-gites.com

The open grassland and forests surrounding Le Chant d'Oiseau make an ideal habitat for the barn owls and tawny owls that live in the loft above one of the three gîtes. All sorts of other birds, from herons to buzzards and goldfinches, also love it around here, which is surely how the house got its moniker. The name appears on a map from 1750 but the house could be centuries older – the date 1626 was incised into the stone walls of the hayloft by workers tallying up bales. Stu and Syb Bradley are passionate about the house and the region, learning its history and photographing its finer features – and they are, of course, a knowledgeable source of recommendations of places to visit.

The Bradleys moved their family here from Doncaster in 2005 and brought an easy-going Yorkshire conviviality that blends in perfectly with the Loire region's reputation for good living (Flaubert called it 'the most sensual river in France'). They're relaxed about campers arriving late and offer to come find those searching for the site after dark, even making them a nice cup of tea on arrival – just the ticket after a long drive from a channel port. An earlier arrival means you can join your hosts for a glass of wine in the beautifully rebuilt open barn, which serves as an al fresco Wi-Fi area, communal eating space, shady retreat and home to two barbecues and a bread oven that Stu has installed.

It was worth the effort: the wood-fired oven makes a superb pizza oven once a week, when campers can meet each other, under the vast roof of wooden beams. On Mondays and Fridays during the summer the owners serve a four-course French meal here, too, and they heat up the oven on Sundays to bake the troglodyte (and Angevin) favourite, *fouée*: small parcels of bread dough with savoury or sweet fillings such as goats' cheese, pork pâté, *rillettes*, *confiture*.... These events are all optional, but it's an option that can make camping so much more appealing. The Bradleys had decades of experience of camping and caravanning before coming here, and have tried to incorporate all the best features of sites they've experienced, as well as just giving the chance for campers to get together to socialise. Animals are very much part of the Bradley ménage, meaning that guests' pets are no longer accepted on site. But the family do have their own that you can adopt for your stay. Bracken the dog, ably assisted by the cats Splodge and Wisp (not to mention the hens) will always give you a friendly welcome. Deer are a common sight and wild boar live in the woods, so it's not surprising that the sport of kings, which originally attracted French royals to the Loire, now draws *chasseurs*. Fortunately shooting doesn't begin until September, so the forests are perfectly safe throughout the summer. Cycling is a prominent feature of the area, with safe country roads and lanes to explore. Stu is happy to lead keen two-wheeled fans out on local excursions when time permits. Otherwise he has plenty of maps and advice on the best places to go. A sociable campsite in a beautiful location, with loads to do? What's not to like?

COOL FACTOR Birdsong and conviviality in the heart of the Loire Valley.

WHO'S IN Tents, campervans, caravans, large groups (by arrangement) – yes. Pets – no.

ON SITE 10 pitches, all with 6-amp hook-ups. The 2 showers and 2 toilets (plus 3 basins) are freshly tiled, clean and homely, with wheelchair access. There may be a wait in high season. There are 2 stone BBQs available, which campers are welcome to use, plus a gas cooker, fridges, kettle, microwave and food-preparation area in the Kampers' Kitchen. Stone-cooked pizzas are cooked once a week and 4-course meals, prepared by Syb and Stu, are available 2 nights a week during the season, so cooking need not be an everyday chore. Wi-Fi, table tennis, a pool table, a small swimming pool, bikes and book exchange are all available, and there's a kids' play area. 3 gîtes on site means multi-generation family/friends holidays are easy.

OFF SITE Medieval Mouliherne and its twisted-spired church is 5km away and there are peaceful walks and bike rides through the woods and fields. The elegant city of Saumur, with its fortress-château, multi-arched bridges and houses built in local tufa limestone, is a 25-minute drive. Stu (and the Michelin Guide) rate the Musée des Blindes tank museum (02 41 53 06 99). The town also has a great market on Saturdays on Place St. Pierre and is renowned for its sparkling white wines. There are lovely châteaux at Gizeaux, Montgeoffroy and Montsoreau (all around 30 minutes away) and the abbey at Fontevraud (02 41 51 73 52; fontevraud.fr) is impressive – Richard the Lionheart, Henry II and Eleanor of Aquitaine are all buried there.

FOOD & DRINK Cooked food is available twice-weekly on Mondays and Fridays, as well as pizzas (Wednesday) and fouée (Sunday). Milk, fresh eggs, ice creams and wine are also for sale, as are daily bread and croissants (when booked the night before). Le Grand Bleu (02 41 67 41 83; legrandbleu-saumur.fr) is a lovely family-friendly seafood restaurant on rue du Marché in old Saumur. Alternatively (and closer), there's La Chaumière in La Pellerine (02 41 82 38 19), where Stu and Syb's daughter is co-owner, along with her French partner, the chef!

GETTING THERE It's easiest to get to the nearby village of Mouliherne and follow the signs to Le Chant d'Oiseau, 5km from there. Otherwise, the site is off the D58 between Vernantes and Mouliherne, but it's very easy to miss. Count 5km from Vernantes or Mouliherne and then look for a crossroads. If it says Plaisance on one side and you can see an advertisement board for Le Chant d'Oiseau on the other, follow the direction of the sign for about 1km.

OPEN March–November.

THE DAMAGE Pitch free plus 2 adults €10–€20. Extra people over 5 years old €5 in high season. Electricity €5 (available in high season only).

bot-conan lodge

29170 Beg-Meil, France 0033 6 11 05 19 43 www.botconan.com

While there are many reasons that campers consistently return to Brittany, one is undeniably the glorious beaches. From the stunning clifftops at Perros-Guirec, to the opulent north coast of Dinard, Brittany has a seemingly endless stretch of majestic, unpredictable coastline.

While there's no doubting the region's epic quality, we know of a tranquil, secluded cove where soft, white sands meet the azure waters of the sea. A place that's the very essence of rest and relaxation. Welcome to Bot-Conan Lodge.

Just a flip-flop away from the bay, this über-luxurious new glampsite boasts some of the region's most enviable ocean vistas. But these are not the crashing Atlantic swells of maritime lore. At Bot-Conan's secret beach, a meditative calm pervades – kids are safe to paddle and lovers free to contemplate the endless seascape before them. Pure bliss. After a day's frolicking in the temperate waves, cataloguing the local wildlife, or simply lazing on the beach with a good book, retiring to your safari-lodge dwelling is simply wonderful. As well as safari lodges, four 'atoll' tents are available, combining the pleasure of camping with the luxury of your very own sun deck and outdoor kitchen. Whatever accommodation you choose, you're sure to enjoy this beautiful, Breton bolthole.

Welcoming host Arnaud has ensured the site blends perfectly into the local landscape – even the two bathhouses integrate seamlessly, with their green roofs and wooden facades. Although it's tough, do try to drag yourself away; the local area is spectacular. Brittany's deep, mysterious interior is there to be explored – from Arthurian woodland (the fabled Brocéliande) to canals and rivers that are ideal for hiking, cycling or cruising lazily. For something more adrenaline fuelled, surf junkies can get their fix at La Torche, some 30 minutes away.

As well as a shared Celtic heritage (not to mention landscape) with their Cornish cousins across the water, the Breton's share a love for cider, and Fouesnant is the spiritual home of Breton *cidre*. It's generously endowed with fertile orchards which produce the very best brews. If you're staying in July, the annual 'Fête des Pommiers' (Festival of the Apple Trees) is a must-visit for all cider connoisseurs.

COOL FACTOR Luxurious comfort a pebble's throw from a secluded Atlantic cove.

WHO'S IN Glampers, campers, groups, and dogs – yes. Campervans, caravans, tent campers – no.

ON SITE 12 'Archipel' safari tents, and 4 'Atoll' bell tents. 2 bathhouses with hot showers, toilets, washbasin and sinks. 2 safari tents have private showers and toilets. Each tent has its own private deck, outdoor kitchen with 2 gas stoves, wood stoves, utensils, cooler box and dining area. Bed linen and towels are provided. High-chair and baby cots available. Electricity and Wi-Fi available. Bicycles to borrow.

OFF SITE Overlooking La Forêt-Fouesnant bay, the Cornouaille Golf Club (2 98 56 97 09; golfdecornouaille. com) is the oldest course in southern Brittany and remains a challenging place to play. Concarneais only a short drive away; it's a charming walled town that still makes its living from the fishing industry, catching more than 100,000 tonnes of tuna every year. The Musée de la Pêche (298 971020; musee-peche.fr) is an interesting spot to find out more about this.

FOOD & DRINK There are no onsite catering options, but local produce can be sourced if requested and a pub is soon to open on the farm directly next door. For cider lovers, the annual 'Fete des Pommiers' ('Festival of the Apple Trees') takes place in July and features music, dancing and plentiful amounts of the celebrated brew. The nearby village of Beg Meil has a lovely local market, crêperies and good choice of restaurants serving tasty fare.

GETTING THERE Follow the motorways towards Quimper, from where you take the D34 then the D45 south to Fouesnant. Continue through Fouesnant on the D45 to Beg-Meil. On the road to Beg-Meil, take a left with a small blue sign that says Lantecoste and Bot Conan beach.

OPEN May–October.

THE DAMAGE All prices per night, low–high season. 'Archipel' safari tent (sleeping 5) €99–€198. 'Archipel' safari tent (sleeping 4) €74–€148. 'Atoll' bell tent (sleeping 4) €59–€99.

camping la pointe

La Pointe, 29150 Saint Coulitz, France 0033 2 98 86 51 53 www.lapointesuperbecamping.com

La Pointe lies just outside the picturesque town of Châteaulin, close by a tree-lined bend of the canalised River Aulne. The site is British-owned – Marcus and Julie took over from another English couple in 2008 – but it attracts a loyal following of French *campeurs*, along with British and Dutch regulars, who appreciate the warm, considerate welcome. The site sits in a conifer-lined valley at the foot of a deciduous forest, which was recently incorporated within the borders of the Parc Naturel Régional d'Armorique.

The pitches are huge, separated by hedges and flowers, with terraces rising up the wooded hillside if you seek more shade and privacy. Experienced campers themselves, the owners know what their customers want – there's a spacious play area for the kids and a chill-out room; outdoor furniture for lounging and a handy fridge-freezer. If you fancy having a BBQ, you'll find them for hire here, and there's a daily *boulangerie* delivery as well as fresh eggs and vegetables from the kitchen garden. Along with the woodland, the canal path is ideal for walking, running, cycling or fishing (the canal is a grade two salmon stream), but adventure-sports junkies won't need to travel far either.

To get a bird's-eye view of the Breton countryside, take a trip 8 kilometres to the summit of Ménez-Hom, the highest peak in the Black Mountains. At just over 330 metres it's no Everest, and you can actually drive almost to the top, but it offers a panorama of Western Brittany and the Crozon Peninsula. The paragliders who use the peak get an even loftier view looking north towards Brest, south to Quimper and west, where the coastline curves around the sweep of the Baie de Douarnenez and on to the stunning views of cliffs at Pointe du Raz.

There are more thrills on the extravagantly long, level stretches of sand near Douarnenez. The *char voile* (sand-yachting) world championships were held at Pentrez beach and there are plenty of them lined up for hire if you fancy a spot of eye-watering, seat-of-your-pants speed. There are smaller coves beyond, such as Trez Bellec, where you won't be sandblasted by sea breezes. Surfers who want to catch the Atlantic swell can head for Pen Hir Point, but slower-motion adrenaline junkies will find pleasure here, too – Marcus and Julie are keen bird-watchers, who recommend the rugged cliffs around Pointe du Raz, and local marshland sites near Le Faou, to fellow twitchers.

Another essential excursion is to the remarkable medieval town of Locronan, a perfectly preserved, cobbled, car-free haven that became famous in the 14th century for making sailcloth. The sand-coloured granite houses and 15th-century church have made it a favourite location for film-makers, and it's so reminiscent of Hardy's Wessex that Roman Polanski's version of *Tess of the d'Urbervilles* was filmed there. The town feels quite touristy in the afternoon, so it's probably best to go on a Thursday evening, when there's an atmospheric 'starlit' market.

In short, there's plenty to do around La Pointe. The visitors' book is full of comments like 'I only meant to stay one night and I'm still here a week later'. Which says it all, really.

COOL FACTOR A warm welcome that comes with cool, shady pitches in the forest, even in high season.

WHO'S IN Tents, campervans, caravans, well-behaved dogs, large groups by arrangement – yes.

ON SITE Campfires are allowed (but not in the forest) – please ask first. 60 pitches, almost all with electric hook-ups. A fully equipped, 2 bedroom, canvas tent lodge available for hire. A large wash-block with plenty of sinks and showers, plus laundry washrooms. There is an information room and book exchange, plus free Wi-Fi. The communal room isn't fancy, but has table tennis and space enough to relax on a rainy day. Kayaks and pedalos are available for hire nearby for use on the calm waters of the River Aulne, which forms part of the 315km of the Brest–Nantes canal.

OFF SITE Châteaulin, a stroll along the river from the site, is a lovely riverside town, with shops and a weekly market, restaurants, tennis and heated indoor swimming pool. Beaches, water sports and sand-yachting are 16km away. Quimper, the medieval capital of Finistère, is a 20-minute drive.

FOOD & DRINK Fresh bread is available each morning, along with eggs and vegetables. Thursdays in high season is crêpe night on site, but otherwise there are special ways to enjoy Breton crêpes close by. The Crêperie St Côme (02 98 26 55 86; creperie-stcome.com), on an old farm at St Côme, near Pentrez beach, has 580 different crêpes to choose from; and Marcus and Julie recommend Crêperie de l'Enclos in Pleyben (02 98 26 38 68), where they may add truffles, foie gras, peach and other exotic gastronomic flavours. In Châteaulin, Le Minuscule (02 98 86 28 66) is an easy-going, friendly pizza and seafood restaurant.

GETTING THERE Coming from Rennes, take the N12 and then the N164, signposted Quimper. Once you get to Châteaulin, drive down to the river in the centre, cross the bridge, turn left and follow signs to Quimper on the D770. After 1km turn left, signposted St-Coulitz, and the campsite is on your right.

OPEN Mid March–mid October.

THE DAMAGE Camping, car, and 2 adults €15.50–€18 (€12–€13.50 on bikes). Extra adult €4. Child €2. Electricity €4.

le ferme de croas men

Croas Men 29610, Plouigneau, France 0033 2 98 79 11 50 www.ferme-de-croasmen.com

Brittany and Cornwall share a Celtic–British history and a similar geography. Each is a westernmost promontory buffeted by Atlantic waves, with rugged capes and cliffs sheltering fishing villages and sandy beaches, while inland lie moors and neolithic menhir monuments. Brittany, though, is almost 10 times the size of Cornwall and retains its own language and distinctive cultural traditions.

In a part of northern Brittany that is blessed with place names like Plouezoc'h, Trudujo and Beg ar C'hra, you'll find La Ferme de Croas Men, nestled in the rolling countryside. The flowery signs by the roadside were painted by Monsieur Cotty, who started the campsite 20 years ago and created the many sculptures that you'll find around the site. It's also a working dairy farm shared by four generations of the Cotty family, who raise and grow food for 45 cows is also home to donkeys, goats, sheep, ducks, rabbits, chickens and Max the pig among 30 or so breeds. Such a menagerie makes coming to this site a great opportunity to introduce children to all sorts of animals but this is much more than a glorified petting zoo. There is a museum of farm machinery next to Ty Coz, the original family cottage, which looks just as it might have done in 1900, complete with a beaten-earth floor, massive table and benches, four-poster bed, vintage dresser and grandfather clock opposite photos of the great grandparents. Rather than being a dusty, hands-off rural museum, though, this room can be booked for a special breakfast – a stack of pancakes, fresh bread and homemade jams

just waiting to be devoured with tea, coffee, or hot chocolate.

The Cottys, of whom Raphael speaks excellent English, allow small visitors to watch the milking, feed the animals and witness the farm in action throughout the day, asking only that adults are present to ensure safety and that animals are allowed to rest between 11am and 4pm. There are tractor rides and donkey-cart rides around the farm in July and August, and plenty to see along the beautiful sunken-road walks starting from the farm itself.

As for location, the site is just 32km down the coast from the port of Roscoff, and the historic port of Morlaix is just 10 minutes' drive away, while the closest beaches and coves on Brittany's heather-covered northern coast, the wonderfully named 'Armorican Corniche', are 15 minutes away. Morlaix is famous for its colossal viaduct, the remarkable 16th-century house of Queen Anne of Brittany, and for beating off an attack by an English fleet in 1522.

Fortunately, there are no worries about overstaying your welcome at the campsite, which has spacious pitches, cabins and pre-pitched tents, and indeed is used to visitors year-round as the farm is often visited by school groups. One of its most prominent features is 'Oscar', a building Monsieur Cotty constructed from boulders and stone blocks that Obélix would have been proud to lift. Inside this wonder is an equally massive table for campers and farm visitors to socialise and feast around, whatever the weather.

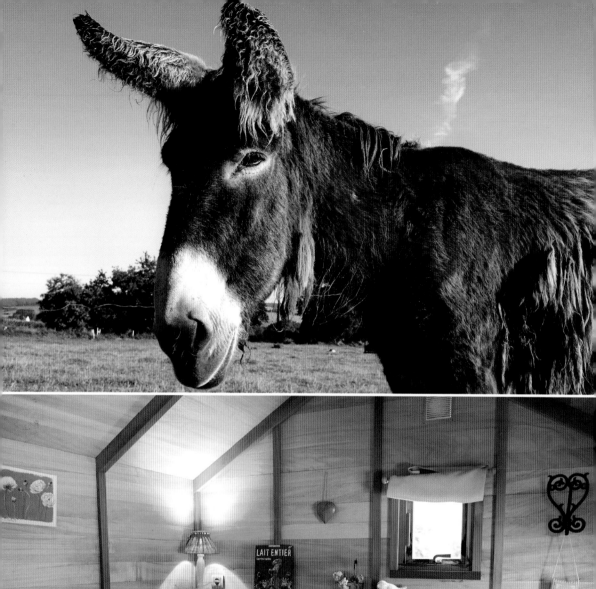

COOL FACTOR Proper camping on a proper farm, but with every creature comfort.

WHO'S IN Tents, campervans, caravans, and dogs (on leads), large groups, young groups by arrangement (there's plenty of room) – yes.

ON SITE 50 large pitches, all with electric hook-ups. There are 2 wooden roulottes (gypsy caravans), chalets, cabins and wood-and-canvas tents to hire, too. There are 2 wash-blocks, best of which is the newer one in the middle of the site, which is bright and airy with efficient warm showers, laundry sinks, disabled access, a parent-and-baby room, washing machine and chemical disposal point. Next door is a reception room with walking routes and tourist information, toys, books and games. Campfires are allowed.

OFF SITE Family fun can be had right here on the farm, feeding the animals. Offsite, Morlaix hosts one of the local markets, which take place every day of the week. Only one of them is further than a 15-minute drive from the site, so fans of *produits régioneux* can get a daily fix if they fancy, and discover lovely Breton towns and villages in the process. There's a big indoor pool with slide and jacuzzi at Plouigneau, but otherwise there are lots beaches and coves to explore nearby – we like Locquirec. Beyond lies the medieval town of Lannion and the pink-and-orange rock formations of the enticingly named Côte de Granit Rose (Pink Granite Coast) are just 40km away.

FOOD & DRINK Whether you choose to breakfast in the atmospheric old farm cottage or *chez vous*, it's a meal to savour on a farm where milk, eggs, butter, yogurt, preserves, honey, cider and apple juice are either made on the spot or locally produced and bought at reception. Factor in local markets and this is a real foodie treat. The Crêperie L'Hermine (2 98 88 10 91; restaurantmorlaix.com) on the quiet rue Ange de Guernisac, in the heart of Morlaix, makes a good traditional Breton pit-stop after the Saturday morning market.

GETTING THERE Plouigneau is close to Morlaix, just off N12 between Brest and Rennes. Take the Plouigneau exit off the N12, but don't go into Plouigneau; head for Lanmeur on the D64. Drive for 150m and you should see the first of the pale-blue signs for the farm, 6km away.

OPEN April–October. (all year for cabins, chalets, gypsy caravans, etc).

THE DAMAGE Camping with a vehicle plus tent or caravan and 2 adults €14.44. Extra people over 7 years €3.50; children €2–€2.80. Electricity (6 amp) €3.50. Pre-pitched tents €250–€395 a week; gypsy caravan from €60 a night/€350–€500 a week; chalet from €50 a night/€350–€500 a week; cabin from €45 a night/€415 a week.

camping milin kerhé

Rue du Moulin, 22200 Pabu, France 0033 2 96 44 05 79 www.milin-kerhe.com

On and around the Brittany coastline are no shortage of cool camping destinations. But Camping Milin Kerhé stands out from the pack. Not many campsites can boast such an idyllic setting. With pristine terraced fields hugged lovingly by enchanting woodland with a majestic, salmon-rich river meandering languidly through, Camping Milin Kerhé is the very picture of tranquillity. The general laid-back air of the place is mirrored in the camping options on offer. Want to pitch up your tent? No problem. Fancy rocking up in a VW relic-on-wheels? Go ahead. Too lazy for all those pegs and guy ropes? Rent one of the spacious and quirky hanging tents slung up in the woodland! Moreover, there's more than enough onsite fun to please everyone, from kayaking and nature trails to volleyball and boules. It's easy to take it all for granted once you've been here for more than a few moments. The setting simply lends itself to the kind of campsite this is – laid back, relaxed and wonderfully natural; simply thinking of a rowdy holiday park should be a criminal offence. Instead, the beautiful River Trieux slides calmly past, sparkling in the French sunlight and catching your eye as you try to peacefully work through the new book you've been reading. It couldn't be further than the swarming Euro-camp parks that have popped up in recent years – and that's just the way we like it.

The Trieux shouldn't hold back tiny campers either. For those worried about the river, there is a fence separating the pitches from the water and for most of the summer it's families that form the bulk of the customers here. The resulting atmosphere is wonderfully social, with little ones quick to breach any language barriers with a lively game of volleyball or a bit of hide and seek among the trees.

The all-round bonhomie of the place is largely down to your amazingly welcoming hosts Jonathan and Margareth Low. Their hospitality knows no bounds and their midweek evening barbecue are the stuff of legends! Breathe it in folks, breathe it in...

COOL FACTOR Tranquil, idyllic waterside camping in the heart of Brittany.

WHO'S IN Tents, campervans, dogs (in low season) – yes. Motorhomes and dogs (in high season) – no.

ON SITE The 3.8 hectare site is spread out over 3 terraces. It encompasses 50 pitches for tents and a designated area for caravans and campervans. There are also firepits, caravans, trailer tents and tree tents for hire. A spacious sanitary block contains 6 showers, 8 toilets, a washing machine and separate men's and women's wash area. There are also electric hook-ups. There is plenty of wildlife on site, including kingfishers, owls, deer, coypu, otters and a huge bat colony. Guided bat and nature walks are held in high season. Kids will love playing with the dwarf goats and ducks. Campers have free use of the canoes, kayaks, stand-up paddle boards and rowing boat. There is a volleyball pitch, boules pitch, table tennis, children's play area, cliff with 3 climbing routes and a swimming-hole in the river above the weir. At the reception you'll find information and permits for river fishing for salmon/trout/coarse species.

OFF SITE Beyond the neighbouring mountain biking trails and hiking routes are the historic Breton towns of Guingamp, Pontrieux and Tréguier. The beautiful island of Bréhat is worth a day-trip, not least for its charming harbour and Paon Lighthouse. Other beauty spots worth visiting are the pink granite coast and La Roche Jagu, a wonderfully preserved medieval fortress.

FOOD & DRINK There's a small shop in reception from which guests can buy beautiful Breton produce. The nearest bar is 5 minutes' walk and the nearest supermarket is 5 minutes by car. During the high season, the Low family put on a delicious weekly evening BBQ – which is great way to meet your fellow campers.

GETTING THERE By car the site is an hour from Roscoff ferry port and 1½ hours from Saint Malo. Take the N12 to Guingamp and, from the centre, follow signs for Pabu (3km). Once in Pabu, continue along rue de la Poterie for 800m and turn left at the restaurant into rue du Moulin. The campsite is at the end of the road.

PUBLIC TRANSPORT Trains run from the ports of both Roscoff and Saint Malo to Guingamp, from where the number 2 bus will take you to Pabu.

OPEN Mid May–mid September.

THE DAMAGE Pitches €6/€4.50 (high season/low season). Adults €5/€4.50, children €3/€2,50), Dogs €1 (low season only), electricity €3. There is also a caravan that you can rent for €20 a night, trailer tents for €18, and a suspended tree tent for €40 – all plus the above prices per person.

le bois coudrais

35270 Cuguen, France 0033 2 99 73 27 45 www.leboiscoudrais.com

'Turn left at the crossroads and then look out for the drapeau Britannique on your left,' grinned a helpful couple. There's a French flag flying outside the site, too, but it's mostly British and Dutch campers who appreciate the friendly, family-run, traditional camping here. At night the peace and quiet is only disturbed by leaves rustling in the poplars, although the myriad birds hereabouts deliver a memorable dawn chorus, so if this kind of twittering disturbs you, then you had best drive by.

The reward for getting up early is the sweet smell of fresh croissants delivered before 8am, and perhaps a chance to visit the goats, chickens and ducks that live on the site. Children so enjoy petting and feeding them that the animals need to be put on a diet come summer's end. In high season the owners bake cakes, hot food and a selection of salads, so campers can eat outside the bijou café-bar next to the excellent pool. Inspiration and activities are on a map showing Mont St-Michel 20 minutes in one direction and the fairy-tale feudal castle at Fougères, with towers and turrets in all the right places, a 35-minute drive in the other.

It's not big , it's not clever, but it's a great, very friendly campsite in a beautiful Breton location that's perfect for cool campers. And If you don't fancy bothering with your own tent, you can rent a pre-pitched one, plus they have four gîtes available too.

COOL FACTOR Traditional family-run camping in beautiful northern Brittany.

WHO'S IN Tents, campervans, caravans, dogs (on leads) – yes. Large groups – by arrangement.

ON SITE 25 large pitches spread over 3 areas. Shady or sunny pitches. The top pitches all have electric hook-ups and are near to the facilities, ideal for caravans or vans. The middle camping area is under shady trees, while the lower field has plenty of space for ball games in the evenings. Bright wash-block with free hot showers and good laundry. Washing-up facilities. Kids' play and animal-petting areas. Heated swimming pool. Free Wi-Fi. Equipped pre-erected tent for hire plus 4 gîtes. No campfires, BBQs okay.

OFF SITE Head to the local tourist office in Combourg for a coffee, shop, play area, and starting point for walks, strolls and off-road cycling.

FOOD & DRINK The Auberge de la Cour Verte in Dol-de-Bretagne (02 99 48 41 41) is a welcoming mid-range auberge. Or treat yourself to the best seafood at Côté Mer in Cancale, which has menus from €27 (02 99 89 66 08; restaurant-cotemer.fr) and lovely views over the harbour.

GETTING THERE From Combourg follow the signs to Mont St-Michel on the D796 and then to Cuguen on the D83. The site is signposted left about 2km after Cuguen. From Pontorson take the D90 to Trans-la-Forêt, then the D83 towards Cuguen. The site is signposted right before the village.

OPEN Start of May–mid September.

THE DAMAGE Camping, car, 2 adults €20. Extra adults €4. Children (up to age 14) €3. Electricity (10 amp) €3.

castel camping le brévedent

Route du Pin, 14130 Le Brévedent, France 0033 2 31 64 72 88 www.campinglebrevedent.com

In the heart of Calvados country, near the idyllic village of Blangy, is the friendliest château-camping experience you can find. Camping at Le Brévedent was first set up to pay for repairs to the Louis XVI hunting lodge after the Second World War. Fortunately for us, it was the only way that the Marquis de Chabannes La Palice could afford to stay on the land, which had been in his family for 350 years. Now his great-grandson, Raphael Bony, heads up the operation, and every night opens the bar in the main house so that guests can drink local cider and calvados, wander through the ground floor looking at paintings of his ancestors and shoot pool. Twice a week he hosts music sessions with his friend, Léon, who plays the accordeon. The duo are into traditional French folk music but they invite guests to play what they like. This year a Belgian family treated the residents of Le Brévedent to Mozart and Rachmaninov on the violin and piano. They were followed by a guy on the bagpipes. Assumption Day on August 15th, is celebrated here, as in many places in France, with fireworks. At Le Brévedent they host a spectacular display over the lake, a barbecue and an impromptu jam session. Any excuse for a party, Raphael now winds up the season with an official music festival. It might be smaller than the Big Chill, but the line-up is just as eclectic.

Plastic bags have been outlawed on site and each guest is given a reusable green Le Brévedent sac to carry their morning croissants home from the shop. Living in sync with nature extends to the free kids' club in July and August, when they take full advantage of the apple season. In the morning the children gather windfalls in the orchard and compete in apple-and-spoon races before pressing them into juice after lunch. The delicious results are distributed among passing campers at the end of the day.

In Cool Camping terms, Le Brévedent is a big site, but its canny design results in a beautifully chilled atmosphere. The play areas are handily situated by adult distractions such as the restaurant, café terrace (with free Wi-Fi), and lake, where huge carp can be caught. The heated swimming pool and paddling pool have been tastefully cut into the slope in front of the main house, from where there's a spectacular view of the lake, which is where most people choose to camp. Behind the lake is a stream, the banks of which are populated by a community of guinea pigs. Elsewhere ducks and chickens meander about among the apple trees and herbaceous borders. On Sunday evenings, in the salon, Madame Gurrey (Raphael's granny) recounts tales of aristocratic eccentricities. She maintains that Raphael has inherited the relaxed charm of his great-grandfather, who often failed to charge campers. Today you can hire a canoe for a scenic paddle across the lake; there's a small hourly fee but Raphael is laid-back about counting the minutes. After all, there's no reason to rush here. No reason at all.

COOL FACTOR Lakeside lounging in the grounds of a Calvados château.

WHO'S IN Tents, campervans, caravans, large groups, young groups – yes. Dogs – no.

ON SITE Campfires allowed off the ground. 140 pitches with hook-ups. Several brand new 24m² lodge tents. 3 modern washrooms. Baby-changing and disabled facilities. 3 playgrounds, heated swimming and paddling pool, games room in the lodge, fishing on the lake, boules, volleyball, badminton, football, mini-golf. The games room in the house is open all day and has a pool table. Tennis €5 per hour; canoe hire €3 per hour; bike hire €4 per hour. Onsite restaurant and café with sun terrace and free Wi-Fi. The well-stocked shop sells local produce.

OFF SITE What could be better than a ramble or cycle through gentle, rolling fields full of sturdy cattle and traditional, timbered Normandy farmhouses? Each camper is given a map detailing 3 local walks. There's a horseriding centre 1km away, or, for wilder animal thrills, go on safari at Parc Zoologique Cerza (02 31 62 17 22; cerza.com), that has tigers, alligators and a rare Indian rhinoceros.

FOOD & DRINK Thursday is foodies' day, starting with the morning market in Blangy-le-Château. It might be small, but it's charming and has a fine fish van selling oysters and mussels. On Thursday afternoons the campsite organises a trip to Les Bruyères Carrées, a small distillery that produces top-notch Calvados and cider.

GETTING THERE From Rouen take the A13 to Pont-l'Evêque. Head 1km south on the D579 towards Lisieux before joining D51 to Blangy-le-Château. From Blangy take the D98 south 2km; the site is located on your left before you reach the hamlet of Le Brévedent.

OPEN Late April–mid September.

THE DAMAGE Low season: tent plus 2 adults €17.50, electric hook-up €4.70, children under 7 years €3.40, children 7–12 years €4.50. High season: tent plus 2 adults €29.30, electric hook-up €4.70, children under 7 years €5, children 7–12 years €6.10.

camping val d'or

Um Gaertchen 2, L-9747 Enscherange, G.D.-Luxembourg 00 352 920 691 www.valdor.lu

Think of Luxembourg and you think of, well, not much really. To most people it's one of those anonymous places with little to boast about – no famous sports stars or A-list celebs in rehab and not even a laughably poor record in the Eurovision Song Contest to spice up their image. (They've won it five times.) Perhaps the most interesting fact about the country is that its area is 999 square miles. However, out into the countryside of the Ardennes, tucked away in the trees in the valley of the Clerve River, you'll find one of the finest spots in that entire 999 square miles – the little gold mine of Val d'Or in Enscherange.

The friendly Dutch owners who took over the site in 1991 have turned it into an enchanting little oasis of greenery; a perfect family campsite. There's room to pitch by the river and, over a wooden footbridge, there are more spacious pitches hidden away behind high hedges if you fancy a little peace and quiet.

Not that the place is a riot at the busiest of times. The village has a population of 140 and the old bar that once tickled locals into a lively evening sing-along has long since closed its doors. But it's only a five-minute drive to neighbouring Drauffelt, where a pleasant *pâtisserie* and a Chinese restaurant have taken up the challenge. If you're willing to travel a little further, the little town of Clervaux has a cluster of shops and eateries presided over by an old, whitewashed castle that's home to a world-famous photo exhibition 'The Family of Man'.

COOL FACTOR Peaceful riverside camping in the green heart of the Grand Duchy.

WHO'S IN Tents, campervans, caravans, pets – yes.

ON SITE The facilities are good, although you need a digital gizmo from reception (€25 refundable deposit) in order to get any hot water. Charge it up with cash and watch the balance on it decrease at a rate of €0.03 every 10 seconds. There's everything you need on site for a bit of family fun: the river, for a start, and loads of play areas with various swings and so on. The real star is a wooden and metal water feature that will keep the kids quiet for hours. A railway line runs right by the campsite but it's not that busy and trains don't run at night.

OFF SITE Grab a train from Wilwerwiltz main station and enjoy the scenic journey into the country's capital, Luxembourg City (a day return only costs €4). It's a small and compact place, with a wonderfully walkable centre. Be sure to visit the Grand Duke's Palace (47 22 28 09; monarchie.lu), the monarch's official residence, smack-bang in the middle of town and open for tours in summer.

FOOD & DRINK The nearest supermarkets are in Marnach, so it's best to stock up there and self-cater. Eating out, the Koener hotel restaurant in Clervaux (92 10 02; hotelkoener.lu) serves both light snacks and full meals.

GETTING THERE The site is about an hour's drive from the city of Luxembourg. Head up the A7 through Ettelbruck and on to Hosingen. Follow the signs for Enscherange and, as you reach the village, the entrance to the site is on the right over the railway line.

PUBLIC TRANSPORT The train station is 1.5km from the site and there are half-hourly trains to/from Luxembourg city (45 mins). The owners can pick you up if arranged in advance.

OPEN April–Early November.

THE DAMAGE €16–€24 for a pitch, electricity and 2 people.

camping de roos

Beerzerweg 10, 7736 PJ Beerze-Ommen, Netherlands 0031 523 251 234 www.campingderoos.nl

A *zwembroek* (if you're a guy) or a *badpak* (if you're a girl) is an absolute must for a stay at Camping De Roos. Also known as swimsuits, trunks or cozzies, these items are (unless you fancy a skinny-dip) wardrobe essentials for a refreshing dunk in the River Vecht, which meanders through this sprawling campsite. So be sure you pack at least one or two.

Located within an area of outstanding natural beauty, between the towns of Ommen and Beerze, the campsite occupies an expanse of sloping clearings surrounded by dense woodland, boasting friendly neighbours such as roe deer, nightingales and woodpeckers. Despite the site's capacity of 280 pitches the careful layout means that it rarely feels overcrowded. The pitches are extremely roomy, and the undulating land, scattered with trees, bushes and winding paths, creates the illusion of a much smaller site, with more than enough room to go round. But if you'd rather a complete slice of countryside peace and quiet, two designated *trekkersvelden* are on hand to provide just the sanctuary you might need. Tucked away amid the ground's chunkier trees, they are reserved for anyone who has come by bike or on foot. The site's sensible 'no-car' policy, with vehicles only allowed on site for unloading and loading, helps maintain that natural feel.

In fact, preserving the natural beauty of the site is a priority at Camping De Roos, as it's a rare honour to be granted permission to run a campsite in a protected area. Timed showers and recycling bins, plus gentle requests not to pick the flowers, ensure the site is as kind to its environment as possible. There's also an onsite shop chock-full of healthy foods, planet-friendly cleaning unguents and the most local of local produce, of which one – ice cream made at a nearby farm – is worth several return trips.

The merry tinkle of children's laughter is a constant backdrop here, with the owners taking the term 'child friendly' to a whole new level, with a volleyball court, football pitch, kite-flying field, boules ground and dinghies dotted along the river bank – as well as a kiosk where kiddywinks (along with sweet-toothed mums and dads) can get their fill of tasty treats. And on rainy days there's plenty of indoor fun to be had. But the firm favourite has got to be the jumping into the water and splashing around. The river's tributary forms the ideal spot for a children's pool – even boasting its own mini-beach – and when the weather's fine the kids jump, dive and bomb from its little pier. The surrounding area is criss-crossed with cycle routes. You can hire bikes from the site, and a short pedal will find you plunged deep into wonderfully quiet woodland. Or if you'd like to dispense with wheels completely, the long-distance Vecht Valley footpath passes right through the campsite.

This site's enviable location means that, even with numerous amenities and kids' activities on offer, it still exudes a tranquillity that can be hard to find at other European sites. And if it takes you a while to tune in to the country vibes, try floating along the cool river, with blue skies and fluffy clouds above and grassy banks on either side, to enjoy a bit of Mother Nature at her finest.

COOL FACTOR A stunning woodland location alongside the River Vecht – relaxing, environmentally friendly and heaven for kids.

WHO'S IN Tents, caravans – yes. Dogs – no.

ON SITE 280 spacious pitches for tents and caravans. Cars are only allowed on site for loading/unloading. An onsite shop stocks organic and local produce as well as hot pizzas and vegetable pies, and there's a tea room and kiosk on a terrace near the river. There's also an onsite launderette complete with iron and board. Handy cooling elements and freezer packs are available. There's also a payphone and free internet. The loo blocks are heated, with each shower doling out 5 minutes of hot water.

OFF SITE Take the kids on the Wolf Trail adventure walk through the woods. Games are played throughout the 2.5km route, and each child gets a rucksack full of descriptions, assignments and a magic sweet that will apparently turn them into a wolf (sounds like fun). Info and rucksacks (€5.95) available at Ommen's Tourist Info Centre (529 451 737). Take a canoe trip (529 451 924) along the River Vecht to experience the valley's beautiful scenery. A bus will take you to the starting point and from there you travel at your own pace back to Ommen.

FOOD & DRINK For mouth-watering pancakes try the De Gloepe (523 251 231; degloepe.nl) farm restaurant which is located in Diffelen.

GETTING THERE Leave Amsterdam on the A1 towards Almere/Amersfoort. Take exit 14 for A28 towards Zwolle. Just past Zwolle, take exit 21 for the N340 to Ommen. In Ommen, turn right on to the bridge and turn left on to Zeesserweg, which becomes Beerzerweg. The campsite is approximately 6.5km along the road on the left.

PUBLIC TRANSPORT The closest you'll get is Ommen if you come by train, which is 7km from the site. The Regio taxi (900 8412) has cheap rates on routes where there is no public transport. Flag-down rate €2.61 plus €0.42 for each kilometre.

OPEN Mid April–late September.

THE DAMAGE The basic rate per pitch per night is €16.50–€19.50 for 2 adults (including a tent/caravan/camper and parking space). Extra person (over 3 yrs) €3.90. Tourist tax €1 per person per night. Electricity €3.20. There are also special packages available.

thyencamp

Laaghalerveen 23 9414VH Hooghalen, Netherlands   0031 593 592 330   www.thyencamp.nl

Paul and Marjo Tienkamp's son makes no bones about calling his parents 'hippies'. A city lawyer himself, he's watched them hang up their suits in favour of beads, shorts and sandals to join various environmental groups and run an art gallery and campsite in the grassy flatlands of Drenthe.

The campsite offers 38 pitches spread over a lawn interspersed with fruit trees, shady oaks and berry-laden hedges. It's the only carbon-neutral camping site in the Netherlands and the owners have a passion for all things environmental. Luckily they refrain from hopping on soapboxes and lecturing anybody about their carbon footprint. Their approach is more about how to take care of the planet by taking small, simple steps that don't cost the earth – a quiet conviction that suits perfectly the calm, unspoilt nature of this camping retreat.

As well as generating electricity with solar panels, Paul and Marjo implemented the more wallet-friendly step of using low-watt LED bulbs, one of which was purchased a whopping 25 years ago and is still glowing strong. They have also planted 12 walnut trees in both the sheep paddock and the garden. A true symbol of sustainability, walnut trees live for 250 years or more, sucking in oodles of CO_2, producing tasty nuts and providing shiny, durable furniture along the way.

Running the campsite and gallery may now be a far cry from his former life as an ICT project manager, but the hippified life is definitely for Paul, and many campers return year after year to enjoy his campsite's serenity, its philosophy and the simple views of green and ochre fields. A dyke playing home to ducks separates the camping lawn from next-door's field, with its lazy grazing Friesian cattle. When the sun comes out campers sunbathe on the clover-carpeted grass and enjoy snoozes beneath shady boughs. All you can hear are the sounds of the breeze rustling through the leaves or the spluttery coughs of a nearby tractor, so your city stresses evaporate as quickly as the morning dew.

A small children's play area keeps kids happy when they're not off on family days cycling, fruit-picking and sightseeing around the pleasant countryside. And there's a computer for anyone in need of a cyber fix. If you are an art-lover, you'll enjoy the art of all kinds that is on show everywhere, both indoors and out. Funky sculptures keep you company on the picnic tables while you munch your lunch and bird statues in the garden are an eccentric but graceful presence. Inside, gorgeous paintings adorn corridor walls and special exhibitions brighten up both the attic space and recreation hall. What better place to retreat from the evening chill and enjoy a glass of organic beer? And in the mornings the air is thick with the delicious aroma of freshly baked bread from the local bakery. All you do is place an order in the evening and Paul collects the precious cargo in his hybrid car the next day.

In the midst of the slow-pace of Drenthe, where cyclists outnumber motorists, this is the ultimate laid-back Dutch eco-campsite. You'd be mad not to try it.

COOL FACTOR Scenic, peaceful, guilt-free camping with the added bonus of lovely owners.

WHO'S IN Tents, trailer tents, caravans, campervans – yes. Dogs – by prior arrangement and on leads at all times.

ON SITE 38 pitches spread across a tree-festooned lawn, plus wooden eco-lodges. Lovely, pristine, bathrooms (well stocked with loo rolls and soap), comprising 2 toilets and 2 showers each for men and women, inside the main house. Washing (€3) and drying (€2) machines available. Fair-trade eco drinks and locally produced eco ice creams are sold at reception. There are also 2 recreation rooms and a small children's playing area. The eco-lodges are solar panelled, well insulated and lit with LED lamps throughout and come complete with kitchenette, dining area, porch and canopy.

OFF SITE Hire bikes or get into your walking boots to enjoy Drenthe's flat, beautiful scenery. Near to the campsite you can explore Hijkerveld, the old Celtic fields in the region. The walks vary from 5km to 15km.

FOOD & DRINK Hooghalen's bakery, Fledderus, is a goldmine of tasty treats and a must for all campers; a cosy place with fresh bread, rolls, pastries, cakes and scrummy ice creams, and a sunny outdoor terrace.

GETTING THERE From Amsterdam, take the A1 towards Almere/Amersfoort. Take the A28 to Zwolle at exit 14. Keep on the A28 towards Assen, passing Hoogeveen until you see signs for Smilde and Hooghalen. Turn off the highway and drive through Hooghalen for 2.5km and you'll see a sign for Thyencamp to the right.

PUBLIC TRANSPORT The best bet is to take a train to Assen. Paul or Marjo will kindly collect you from the train station if you organise it in advance.

OPEN Mid April–September.

THE DAMAGE Caravans and trailers €4.50, campervans €5.50; tents €4 and hikers' tents €3. Charges per person are €3.50 (children under 3 go free). Pets €1. Tourist tax per person is €1 and environmental tax per person is €0.25. Anyone arriving by bicycle gets a 10% discount. Electricity costs €2.50. Onsite eco-lodges €25 a night (minimum 3 night stay).

watersportcamping heeg

De Burd 25a, 8621 JX Heeg, Netherlands 0031 515 442 328 www.watersportcampingheeg.nl

Situated in the far north of the Netherlands, the province of Friesland is known for its lakes. Lots and lots of them. A bit like England's Norfolk Broads, when the Frisian peasants dug these boggy wetlands for peat, the scars left on this flat landscape caused countless rivers and waterways to form. Well the farmer's loss is the holidaymaker's gain, as today Friesland is the centre for Dutch water sports. Surprisingly little-known outside of the Netherlands, the Dutch lake district attracts scores of aquatic adventurers from the rest of the country, keen to savour this blissfully tranquil region. The area's many charming towns and villages are interlinked by canals, and it is on the outskirts of one such lovely lakeside settlement, Heeg, that we find this water sports oasis.

While Watersportcamping Heeg won't be winning any prizes in the imaginative naming

stakes, the site can't be bettered for location. Right on the shores of a vast, sparkling lake, the site accommodates around 150 touring pitches on nearly 25 acres of pristine grass. Take a few steps to the shore and you have your choice of water-based pursuits to enjoy, from sailboat hire and kite surfing to sloop lessons or just a good old-fashioned swim. There's a chilled-out beach party vibe throughout, helped in no small measure by the buzzy beach bar and the 'Dutchtubs' for hire. And then there is Heeg itself. Just a leisurely five-minute stroll from the site, this is a quintessentially Dutch village, and quite idyllic. Why not enjoy a traditional treat of smoked eel on the banks of the Heegermeer lake? Or visit nearby Ijlst, the home of the singularly Frisian sport of *fierljeppen* – that's... er... canal-vaulting to you and me – an annual summer celebration that is not to be missed.

COOL FACTOR A water sports mecca right on the shore in the Netherlands' beautiful lake district.

WHO'S IN Pretty much everyone! Tents, campervans, mobile homes, families, large groups, dogs – yes.

ON SITE 150 touring pitches, 25 seasonal pitches, 8 rental chalets, 1 willow cabin. There are 18 showers, 18 toilets, 45 electrical hook-ups and a laundry facility.

OFF SITE Why not hire an electric scooter on site to zip around to the charming leafy canal cities of Ijlst and Sneek. The Museum Belvédère (513 644 999; museumbelvedere. nl) in Heerenveen exhibits many interesting classic and contemporary art pieces from the Friesland region. Visit also Lemmer's 'Cathedral of Steam', the Woudagemaal (514 561 814; woudagemaal.nl) – the world's largest still-operational steam-powered pumping station.

FOOD & DRINK The 'Zimpel' beach bar is a quirky old shipping container that serves sandwiches, coffee and other delicacies. On a sunny day, the riverside terrace at Hotel Café Restaurant De Watersport (515 442 229; dewatersportheeg.

nl) is the place to go, not least for their hearty pub-grub-style meals. Heeg is famous for its eel fishing and the campsite can arrange for you to take a fishing trip with the last remaining eel fisherman in a traditional *palingaak*. No visit to the region would be complete without sampling the potent Frisian tipple, *Beerenburg*, which you can do at the Weduwe Joustra distillery and shop in Sneek (515 412 912; weduwejoustra.nl).

GETTING THERE Take the road to Bolsward/Sneek, and the Woudsend/Hommerts exit, then the first exit on the roundabout in Hommerts in the direction of Heeg. Follow this road and the 'Centrum' signs. At the roundabout take the 2nd exit to Heeg Centrum. Pass a cul-de-sac, than take the first road to the right. Follow the road until you arrive at a T-junction. Turn right to 'Gaastmeer'.

PUBLIC TRANSPORT Take the train to Sneek, then the 46 bus to Heeg.

OPEN April–October.

THE DAMAGE Tents €5.30, plus €5.70 per person (kids €3.10). Cars €3.60, electricity €3.50.

camping lauwerszee

Hoofdstraat 49, 9975 VR Vierhuizen, Netherlands 0031 595 401 657 www.camping-lauwerszee.nl

Cycling in the UK often feels like taking your life into your own hands. Big, boisterous buses, few cycling lanes and angry motorists can make it a bit of an ordeal. Happily, such scenarios are rare in the Netherlands, where cyclists have priority over everyone else. Whether you're four or 84, the preferred method of transport here is a bit of sedate pedalling.

One of the country's top locations for enjoying a bit of biking is around Lake Lauwersmeer and its surrounding national park. Twitchers will delight to hear that this area is home to over 140 species, to be spotted flapping and wheeling overhead or paddling in the lake. An easy pedal away is tiny Vierhuizen, watched over by its large wooden windmill. At the other end you'll find Camping Lauwerszee, tucked behind its owners' cosy restaurant, where local diners (just the men, thankfully) boast the kind of bushy moustaches that would have the likes of Ned Flanders burning with tache-envy. The campsite resembles a landscaped garden, with brightly coloured hedgerows and huddles of trees providing tent privacy, while sprinkles of flowers, host to butterflies, adorn the spacious lawns. Its laid-back ambience makes it the perfect place to relax after a good day's exploration in the saddle.

As for other things to do nearby, why not try a spot of *wadlopen* – that's 'mud-walking' – across the mudflats to the nearby islands at low tide. You'll need a guide – but there are several local outfits that organise trips.

COOL FACTOR Peaceful, spacious camping with a lake within cycling distance.

WHO'S IN Tents, campervans, caravans, dogs – yes.

ON SITE There's a new toilet and shower block, a play area for kids, and bikes are available to hire.

OFF SITE Go to nearby Anjum to visit the tiny mustard museum and candle-making factory (where you can make your own candles). Try a ghostly Full Moon Excursion around the mudlands of the lake. The walk begins at 11pm and finishes at 2am. For *wadlopen*, try the trips run to the island of Schiemonnikoog (wadlopen-pieterburen.nl).

FOOD & DRINK The Herberg Restaurant on the site is well known in the area for its tasty treats. The menu is entirely in Dutch, so you could be adventurous and go for something completely unpronounceable.

GETTING THERE From Amsterdam, take the A1 towards Almere/Amersfoort. After a short while, turn on to the A6 past Lelystad towards Groningen (at Heerenveen it changes into the A7). Leave at exit 33 (marked Zuidhorn/Boerakker) and turn left, following the N388 through Boerakker, Grijpskerk and Zoutkamp; 3km past Zoutkamp, turn left on to the Hoofdstraat and the campsite is located 1km down the road on the right.

PUBLIC TRANSPORT Take the train to Groningen and then hop on the QBUSS towards Zoutkamp for the 90-minute journey. The bus stops outside the church at Vierhuizen.

OPEN April–October.

THE DAMAGE One night for 2 people with a tent or caravan and car costs around €16.50, plus €3.95 per extra adult. Children under 12 cost €2, dogs €2.50. Electricity costs €3.75.

uhlenköper

Uhlenköper-Camp Uelzen Festplatzweg 11 29525 Uelzen, Germany 0049 5817 3044 www.uhlenkoeper-camp.de

'The hiiills are aliiive with... the sight of heather?' Yes, from August until September, Germany's Lüneburger Heide region hits its purple patch. Its heathlands are transformed into oceans of mauve so expansive that Prince could write songs about them. There are heather festivals and annual crownings of heather queens, and tourists overwhelm local towns and villages.

Amid this violet fury lies Uhlenköper, a tranquil German eco-site ensconced in the itsy-bitsy village of Westerweyhe, near Uelzen in the northern part of the country. Run by two families, the Kördings and the Pauls, this three-acre site has been carved up into areas for 'dauercampers' (permanent residents), caravans and larger tents, tenters and cyclists. In between lie the site's public areas – a solar-powered reception (with shower block, restaurant and bio-shop), modest playground and – the pièce de résistance – a brand-spanking new swimming pool with sections for swimmers and paddlers.

Offsite fun can be had cycling, kayaking on the Ilmenau river or checking out Natur Park Südheide, where you can glimpse the black-haired rams with white bodies that resemble woolly pints of Guinness. If nothing else, they make a change from all that purple.

COOL FACTOR Relaxed eco-site with good access to the Lüneburger Heide region.

WHO'S IN Tents, motorhomes, groups, dogs – yes.

ON SITE Uhlenköper Camp has won awards for its eco-commitments and the facilities reflect this – no chemicals in the pool, organic food in the shop, free herbs and solar power where possible. There are 85 pitches in total, the shower block is clean and modern and the restaurant offers good food. The pool has a shallow section for younger children.

OFF SITE The site owners are qualified canoe guides and can take you for a family trip along the river – or you can hire your own canoes and bikes on site and do your own thing. Hotel Kenners Landlust (5855 979300; kenners-landlust.de) in Dübbekold offers organic food, shiatsu massage and a pool and sauna for total relaxation.

FOOD & DRINK Apart from the onsite restaurant, you can grab a tasty schnitzel at the village restaurant, Dorfkrug (a 2-minute stroll); otherwise the nearest spots are in Uelzen. For local produce, Bauckhof Farm shop (58 190 160) sells everything from free-range eggs to sausages and cheese.

GETTING THERE From Hamburg take the B4 and continue along the A255, following signs for A1/Bremen, then continue along the A1. Take exit 39-Maschener Kreuz and merge on to the A250 towards Lüneburg/Maschen. Continue on the B4 (signposted Uelzen and Lüneburg). Take a right at K40/Westerweyhe Strasse, follow the K40, turn left at Am Waterbusch, then a right at Festplatzweg.

PUBLIC TRANSPORT Train to Uelzen, then the 1973 bus towards Weinbergstrasse/Ebstorf, getting off at Westerweyhe train station. Follow the footpath, taking a left then straight on into Altes Dorfstrasse, keeping the school to your right.

OPEN All year.

THE DAMAGE For 2 people and tent plus car the cost is €22, with 2 kids €29.

naturcamping vulkaneifel

Feriendorf Moritz, 54531 Manderscheid, Germany 0049 6572 92110 www.naturcamping-vulkaneifel.de

The Vulkan region may sound like the kind of interplanetary place Dr Spock might hang out in, but it's not. It's Germany's only volcanic region, a low mountain range in a southwestern section of the Rhineland-Pfalz (known as the Eifel), which lures tourists with its water-filled craters (the so-called 'eyes' of the Eifel) and tantalising landscapes.

Naturcamping Vulkaneifel lies in the centre of the region, 1km outside the village of Manderscheid in Bernkastel-Wittlich. Owner Wolfgang Moritz has been in charge for 30 years, starting it initially as a children's summer camp and gradually expanding it into a campsite for all. Moritz is a keen advocate of the ideas of Rudolf Steiner but those not sold on Steiner need not worry. Apart from an emphasis on organic products in the children's canteen, the use of natural materials around the site and a 'free' environment for children to be themselves, you wouldn't notice.

The centre of the campsite is given over to the Jugendferiendorf, or children's village, a collection of multi-coloured huts set around a landscaped area. The camping pitches are situated along a series of quiet, green terraces shaded by fruit trees, slightly away from the site's centre. The pitches are categorised as A, B or C, according to their size. The north side has the biggest and quietest pitches and is the most popular with campers, although the southern pitches are perfectly pleasant, too. The facilities are clean and modern, with separate shower blocks for men and women, outdoor sinks and a small kitchen. In keeping with the child-friendly ethos, there's also plenty of green space to relax or run around in, plus a badminton court and playground, BBQ area and a field brimming with red poppies.

Nearby Manderscheid is a comely spa town with 1,300 or so inhabitants. Though it's generally coy on the sightseeing front, it does offer some convenient facilities for campers – a couple of supermarkets, some restaurants, and an enthusiastic tourist office – as well as a truly stunning castle, some sections of which are said to date right back to the 10th century.

The real draw, though, is the volcanic region of the Eifel itself which, since 2004 has been part of the UNESCO Global Geoparks. Most of the area is easily accessible from the campsite and is interlaced with a web of walking and cycling trails, some of them literally starting at the site's front door. The Geo-Route Manderscheid, for instance, is a 140-km walk that takes in a lot of the region's highlights. Cyclists will marvel at the Maare-Mosel-Radweg path, which runs from Manderscheid along an old railway line and takes you either to the lovely town of Daun or to the beautiful Mosel River, a great place to check out some local wines. Towns like Koblenz make a wonderful stopover, as does the ancient city of Trier. As luck would have it, there's even a road that joins the two together – the Mosel Wine Road – how totally logical! Even Spock couldn't fail to enjoy himself here.

COOL FACTOR Great family-friendly site with a natural vibe and great access to the fascinating Vulkaniefel region.

WHO'S IN Tents, kids, dogs – yes. Caravans – no.

ON SITE 90-odd pitches, varying in size, shade and quietness. Facilities are good and include a large shower block, washing machine and dryer, a small kitchen for campers, a kiosk in reception, badminton net, BBQ area and playground.

OFF SITE The site is geared towards children and families so finding entertaining stuff to do here is not a problem. The Manderscheid Tourist Board (6572 932665) run regular geological excursions around the area, and the site works with a range of independent companies to arrange everything from raft-building and orienteering courses to climbing, hiking and cycling. There's also a wildlife park at Daun (6592 3154; wildpark-daun.de). You could also try a volcano safari by Landrover (6592 95130) or take a plane ride to see the 'eyes' of the Eifel' from above (6592 2976).

FOOD & DRINK The canteen serves tasty organic meals, but only at specific times (breakfast 8–9am; lunch at noon; dinner at 6pm). You can also cook in the dedicated BBQ area. For farmyard delicacies head to the Vulkanhof in Gillenfeld (65 73 9148; vulkanhof.de), which has a nice selection of mustards, jams, goats' cheese and the like.

GETTING THERE From Koblenz follow the signs to Trier and exit at Manderscheid on the A48/A1. From Belgium on the A60, head towards Wittlich, again following signs to Koblenz and exiting at Manderscheid on the A48/A1.

PUBLIC TRANSPORT You can catch a train from Köln (Cologne), Trier or Koblenz to Wittlich, then take a bus from there to within 500m of the site – ask for Manderscheid-Dauner Strasse.

OPEN April–October.

THE DAMAGE €7 per adult; teenagers (14–15 years) €4; ages 8–13 €1; children under 8 free.

müllerwiese

Hirschtalstrasse 3, D-75337 Enzklösterle, Germany 0049 7085 7485 www.muellerwiese.de

Alchemists and apparitions, ghosts and goblins, nefarious kings and needy water nymphs – these are just some of the characters that have tramped through the Black Forest over the centuries. Not your usual tourist demographic, granted, but then Germany's source of myths and legends is not the kind of forest you'd bring home to meet your mother. Or at least it wasn't a couple of hundred years ago.

These days, the most dangerous thing about the forest is the amount of famous gateau it serves up. And the only thing that is dark or mysterious about the award-winning campsite Müllerwiese is the brooding bulk of its 1970s shower block at night. No, Müllerwiese is a family-run, family-friendly oasis, a small but perfectly formed operation that's been running since 1972, headed up by the laid-back but efficient team of Friedrich Erhard, his wife Susanne and his father, Hans. In the last 30-odd years they've perfected the art of running a campsite with the vital two Ps: professionalism and passion.

The site can be found at the edge of the picturesque village of Enzklösterle. Most of the 75 pitches are past the house and beyond the main gate, along the border of a burbling mountain brook (actually the River Enz). This section of Müllerwiese is devoted to caravans and large tents, but campers needn't go that far. You can just turn left and pitch in a grassy, car-free area that's purely for tenters. There are also two holiday apartments and log cabins nearby. The area resembles nothing so much as a pretty – and pretty spacious – garden. The Enz gurgles

its way past here too, and fir trees provide shelter and scenery. Though the site isn't huge, it's large enough to accommodate around 30 tents without it feeling like the Big Chill on a Sunday morning. The facilities are modest but adequate. A playground is built into the garden and includes table tennis, a swing and various bouncy things for kids. The brook makes for a nice, clean, natural distraction, and you get your own bathroom, shower (and washing-up sink), in a brand-new block. You can also use the main shower block – it looks a lot less menacing in the daytime – which is older but better equipped.

Enzklösterle, situated between 600 and 900 metres above sea level, contains just 1,200 souls. But like many small German towns it has lots of facilities: local butchers selling tasty Schwarzwälder Schinken, cafés hawking the eponymous gateaux, restaurants, a chemist and a tourist office opposite the campsite. Beyond the town lies the Black Forest 'proper': a shimmering universe of proud firs, rustling woodlands, crystal-clear water, tinkling brooks, expansive lakes and untouched moorland, criss-crossed by 3,000km of hiking trails and 800km of cycling tracks, all very well signposted. Black Forest towns such as Bad Wildbad (11km) and Freudenstadt (27km) make for pleasant stopovers and are accessible for free by bus for those staying on the site. The brand-new free-to-enter Black Forest National Park is also reachable within 30–45 minutes by car (90 minutes by bus). You may not see any ghouls or goblins en route, but there's a slice of cake around almost every corner just waiting to get you.

COOL FACTOR Charming, rural site on the doorstep of Germany's Black Forest.

WHO'S IN Tents, campervans, caravans, dogs – yes.

ON SITE 75 pitches, including a car-free, tents-only field that also hosts 2 apartments and 2 log cabins (for a couple or family of 3–4). There is a third cabin in the caravan area. Good clean shower block in the main camping section and brand-new facilities for campers near the main house. Onsite playground and a (shallow) stream for splashing around in. Wi-Fi available throughout the site (€6 for 24 hours).

OFF SITE 500m away there is a tree-climbing garden with a 'free fall' jump and a 400m-long high-wire over the valley; 5km away in Poppeltal is one of the longest mountain slides in Germany (7085 7812; riesenrutschbahn.de), a ride guaranteed to make the surliest child beam.

FOOD & DRINK There's nothing on site, but Enzklösterle has a bakery and a butcher's as well as cafés, beer gardens and restaurants. A short drive away, Kaltenbronn's Hotel Sarbacher (7224 9339; hotel-sarbacher.de) offers a wide range of regional dishes, often involving local game. There are also farmers' markets that take place in Altensteig and Bad Wildbad on Saturday mornings.

GETTING THERE From the north take the A8, exiting at Pforzheim-West and then following the B294 to Calmbach. There you turn right and drive through Bad Wildbad. If you take the A5 from Basel or Frankfurt, take the Rastatt exit, along the Black Forest Valley Road through Freudenstadt – or the mountain pass Gernsbach–Reichental–Kaltenbronn. From Munich take the A99 towards Stuttgart/Augsburg/Dachau and follow the A8, then follow the directions as from the north.

PUBLIC TRANSPORT Take a train to Bad Wildbad, 11km from Enzklösterle, from where 10 buses a day run to a stop just 300m from the campsite.

OPEN Mid March–mid November and over the Christmas holidays.

THE DAMAGE Adults €6.50; children (2–14 years) €3.50; dog €2; caravan/campervan/tent €4.50–€7.

hirzberg camping

Kartäuserstrasse 99, D-79104, Freiburg, Germany 0049 7613 5054 www.freiburg-camping.de

As you pull into Hirzberg, surrounded by an endless trail of motorhomes and eager campers intent on finding their perfect pitch, that anxious, pessimistic notion of never being able to find a secluded spot creeps over you. You soldier on, only to be greeted by the sight of an ugly string barrier. Like an oversized index finger that rises and lowers, this white and red boundary is not the finest of first impressions. But then you meet Georg Ziegler; Hirzberg's approachable owner who shows you to your shady pitch, surrounded by lush woodlands and open fields. Georg has certainly done his hosting homework. In the morning there's a small breakfast buffet available with cereals, bread and jams to take away. Indeed, clasping a hot cup of coffee while taking in those serene countryside views is a wonderful way to start your Deutschland day.

The facilities here are modern and well maintained, but they can get overcrowded in the summer months. A short walk from the tents is the new sanitary block, with free hot showers, toilets and a launderette (with washing machine and tumble dryer.) Take the short walk across the meadow and you'll discover Hirzberg's secluded reading room, complete with a small library, and games to keep you busy whatever the weather.

There's plenty of fun to be had in the local surroundings, too. Whether it be a rewarding stroll around the centre of Freiburg (only 20 minutes away on foot), or a traffic-free bike ride through the enchanting woodlands of the neighbouring Black Forest. While some parts of the forest (named after its dark canopy of evergreens – not the gateau!) burst with crowds, a modest walk from even the most populous spot will place you in the tranquil countryside, dotted with traditional farmhouses, slow-paced villages and grape-bearing vineyards.

With the snake of motorhomes and string barriers forgotten, you can relax with a beer and take in the site's warm, good-natured atmosphere – a unique and indescribable characteristic that makes Hirzberg a truly special place to camp. You may even ponder that the barrier isn't about discipline or forbidden fun, but more to separate the busy city below from this Shangri-La of a campsite. If this thought does cross your mind, put that beer down – you've clearly had one too many.

Review and photos taken from Cool Camping Deutschland. See p.320 for more information.

COOL FACTOR Nestled among sleepy green hills, yet only 1.2km from the cheerful university town of Freiburg.

WHO'S IN Tents, caravans, campervans, kids and dogs – yes.

ON SITE Room for 65 pitches with electric hook-ups. A modern heated sanitary building features hot showers (free), a, kitchen, dish-washing, launderette) and a small play/common room. The reception has plenty of brochures and maps with suggested hiking and biking routes. There's also a small onsite shop selling essentials.

OFF SITE Situated at the foot of the Black Forest's woodlands is Freiburg, a cheerful city with an alluring array of cobblestone streets, charming townhouses and café-packed plazas. Freiburg's 11th-century Münster (7612 02790) is a red sandstone colossus that's one of the oldest and most impressive churches in Europe.

FOOD & DRINK Every morning but Sunday there's an open-air farmers' market on the square adjacent to the church in Freiburg. There's a buzzing atmosphere at Drexlers (7615 957 203; drexlers-restaurant.de), a sleek-style brasserie. Or try the Mediterranean food at Enoteca (7613 899 130; enoteca-freiburg.de).

GETTING THERE From the A5 motorway, take the 'Freiburg-Mitte' exit towards 'Freiburg-Titisee', then follow the signs for 'Freiburg Ebnet – Stadien'; take the left lane (don't enter the tunnel!) and turn left at 'Sandfangweg (Sport Kiefer)' and follow the signs to the site. Arriving via the Black Forest (B31), after Kirchzarten take the exit 'Kappel/Littenweiler' (before the tunnel) and continue in the direction of Freiburg and follow the camping signs.

PUBLIC TRANSPORT From Freiburg train station, take tram 1 (buy your ticket on the tram) towards Littenweiler and, after 10 minutes, get off at Musikhochschule. The site is a 5 minute walk from here.

OPEN All year round.

THE DAMAGE Adults €7–€7.80, children (up to 13) €2.50–€3 and kids (up to 6) €2–€2.50. Small tents €3.50–€4, large tents €4.50–€5, caravans €4–€4.80, campervans €4–€4.80, cars €2–€2.50.

adventure camp schnitzmühle

Schnitzmühle 1 94234 Viechtach / Bayerischer Wald, Germany 0049 9942 94810 www.schnitzmuehle.com

If the Black Forest is Germany's dark secret, a place of goblins and ghosts and the occasional slice of devilish gateau, its easterly cousin, the Bavarian Forest, is all easy-going charm and woody innocence. It comprises a seamless landscape of undulating hills, winsome spa towns and dense woodlands, criss-crossed with comely copses and titillating trails for bikers, hikers and cyclists.

Located slap-bang in the centre of this leafy nirvana is Camping Schnitzmühle, arguably the first really cool campsite in the country. Unlike most German sites, this one is run by young people determined to make the tenting experience a memorable one. The owners in question are Sebastian and Kristian Nielsen, who adopted their parents, hotel business a few years back and have lovingly transformed it into a funky one-stop-shop for all things outdoorsy. Not only did they give the hotel's interior a modernist makeover, they also overhauled the restaurant, added the capacious camping area, constructed an expansive spa and built a beach area around the site's natural lake.

The Nielsen brothers' rejuvenating spirit haunts the whole place, and in a good way. The site, located right next to a pretty section of the Schwarzer Regen River, is green and airy, peppered with trees, bushes and flowers. Even without the funky extras it would be nice, but when you discover the delights of the Bongo Bar

(a thatch-roofed drinks bar surrounded by sand and deckchairs), Stonehenge (a cheeky replica of the great British landmark that doubles as an open fire and grill place) and the Group Camping section (that has adventure facilities and experienced instructors leading rope-climbing, canoeing and mountain-biking escapades), well, it's hard not to be impressed.

Being blessed with two rivers – the Regen and the Schwarzer Regen – means waterbabies are going to feel totally at home here. Stroll around for a minute or two and you'll find a lovely natural swimming spot, while you can easily arrange canoe trips on the site. A shuttle bus whisks you to a starting point and you make your own way back to Schnitzmühle.

The surrounding area isn't short of charming countryside or traditional towns and villages. Arnbruck is world famous for its superior glass production and is a perfect place to pick up some quality wine glasses at decent prices to take home. Nearby Viechtach has some good cafés and gives insight into small-town Bavarian life.

Back at the site, the nearby beach and lake, located on the other side of the hotel, is the perfect place to cool off and sunbathe, and if you're feeling indulgent, the spa is just a short pumice stone's throw away. Bliss on tap, in other words.

COOL FACTOR Authentic cool camping in the heart of the Bavarian forest.

WHO'S IN Tents, caravans, campervans, dogs, groups – yes.

ON SITE 100 pitches, with a separate camping area for groups. The facilities here are superb, including a clean (and colourful) shower block, well-stocked kiosk selling everything from lovely local *Weizenbeir* to freshly baked bread, onsite bar, a place for campfires and BBQs, a playground, internet – plus a hotel, spa, restaurant and lake right next door.

OFF SITE The site can organise everything from canoeing and hiking, mountain biking, cycling and tree-climbing tours. Canoes costs €45 each for 2 adults/2 adults + child. There's a playground on site with table tennis tables, and you can swim in the lake. Another great option is the bobsleigh ride at the theme park Rodel Paradies (9965 1203; sommerrodeln.de), a 20-minute drive away. For a truly relaxing experience, try one of the many massages at Schnitzmühle's spa – maybe the Yanomami (with banana leaves), the Hot Stones (€75 for 60 minutes) or Aloa Massage (€48 for 50 minutes).

FOOD & DRINK The kiosk sells fresh bread in the mornings and general camping essentials. The hotel-restaurant serves up a funky fusion of Bavarian and Thai food (the mixed tapas is especially good – neither Thai nor Bavarian but who cares?), and has a generous breakfast buffet each morning for €8, as well as salads and sandwiches for lunch.

GETTING THERE Leave the B85 on the St2139 travelling north, signposted Viechtach, and continue on Bahnhofstrasse/St2326. Take a right towards Blosserberg, right at Schönauer Strasse and right at Leuthenmühle. Then it's a left towards Rothenbühl, left at Rothenbühl and left at Gmeinholz.

OPEN All year.

THE DAMAGE Tent plus 2 adults is €22.90 (including tent, car and tax).

camping zellersee

Reiner Müller, Zellerseeweg 3, 83259 Schleching-Mettenham, Germany 0049 8649 986719 www.camping-zellersee.de

As its name suggests, Zellersee is all about its lake. It's not a huge lake, but what it lacks in size it makes up for in sheer convenience. You can literally slide out of your sleeping bag, forward-roll through your tent flaps and slip straight into the lake's watery embrace: the perfect way to wake up. This tranquil waterhole lies in the breathtaking Chiemgau valley in the Geigelstein nature reserve next to the Alps. Enough said.

Afterwards, treat yourself to a nice hot coffee and fresh bread from reception while you decide what to do with your day. A bike ride to the Chiemsee (15km away) where you can swim some more? A paddleboat cruise to the Herrenchiemsee – a collection of Versailles-like palaces? Or perhaps you fancy some more watery action at Lake Taubensee – just a 1,138-metre hike up the hill?

For those preferring a flight of fancy, there's the world-famous gliding school in nearby Unterwössen, offering gliding and paragliding. This is the place to catch the most amazing thermals – the kind that can apparently keep you afloat for up to 900km, so make sure you know how to get down before you take off.

In the evening, unwind with a beer from reception and reflect on how everyone around seems to be so happy. Is it the community-minded ambience that fills every camper with a warm glow? Or could it be that you forgot to get dressed after your morning dip? Whichever it is, Zellersee is an open-minded place, so just keep smiling.

COOL FACTOR Intimate site located on a natural lake, with superb access to both Germany and Austria.

WHO'S IN Tents, campervans, caravans, groups – yes. Dogs – no.

ON SITE 90 pitches open all year round. There's a kiosk/reception, a decent shower block (toilets, showers, washing machine, dryer) and a small kitchen for general use. There is Wi-Fi available all over the site.

OFF SITE There's a playground, tennis courts and a lake to keep kids and adults occupied, plus a climbing wall (training is available once or twice a week during summer). There is also a children's park in Marquartstein. If you're into aerial pursuits, try a gliding trip with the world-renowned DASSU school (8641 698 787; dassu.de). It costs €20 for 10 minutes and €1.50 for each additional minute.

FOOD & DRINK On site you can buy snacks and drinks, and there's a small kitchen. The Gasthof Zellerwand (8649 217; gasthof-zellerwand.de is about a kilometre away and sells traditional German/Austrian food. Head to Grassau's market 7km away on Saturday mornings) and pick up sausage, cheese and fruit.

GETTING THERE From Munich or Salzburg, take the A8. Exit at 106 Bernau, towards Reit im Winkl. In Marquartstein drive towards Schleching. Exit 109 Übersee, looking out for the Zellerseeweg sign on the road between Schleching and Raiten.

PUBLIC TRANSPORT You can catch a train to Übersee and a bus from there to Schleching, getting off at Zellerwand/Mettenham. From there it's a 5-minute walk to the site.

OPEN All year round.

THE DAMAGE A tent, car plus 2 people costs €17 (plus €2 tax). Children aged 4–6 cost €2 and those aged 7–16 cost €4 plus €0.50 tax.

park grubhof

St. Martin, nr. 39, 5092 St. Martin, Lofer, Land Salzburg, Austria 0043 6588 82370 www.grubhof.com

In general we prefer smaller campsites at Cool Camping. We like their intimate feel, and are usually happy to forgo a few facilities for the sake of a bit of character, so well-equipped Park Grubhof is not the sort of place we would normally choose. However, located in the Salzburgerland region of Austria, set in the former gardens of an ancient castle, this beautiful site is very much an exception to our rule. It covers over 10 acres and is centred around a huge meadow full of alpine flowers during summer, creating a natural feel that's echoed through the chestnut trees lining the Saalach River.

When you arrive and see the broad boulevards lined with caravans and mobile homes, you may wonder why on earth you've come at all. The reason is the capacious field set apart from the motorhome area, which runs right down to the river and is dedicated solely to tenters. It offers spectacular views over the mountains, and you can listen to the gentle splashing of the river or watch the sun going down between the Breithorn and the Loferer Alm.

But that's not the only reason for coming here. Despite being one of the 'big boys' of Austrian camping, Park Grubhof does not rest on its laurels. It's excellently managed by Robert Stainer and his staff, who work tirelessly to create a communal atmosphere and look after the needs of their guests. The facilities are superb, especially the shower blocks. The latest block is spectacular: a light-filled, loo-lover's dream featuring brushed aluminium and pine interiors, glass-walled showers, a baby-changing room, hairdryers and even a dry room for wet canoeists. While most campers head for the aforementioned meadow, you can pitch in most of the site's other sections too. Apart from the main boulevards there are pitches along the riverside, subtly divided into family- and dog-friendly/-free areas. From these riverside spots you can really get a back-to-nature vibe – especially when you lie back and admire the fantastic mountain scenery surrounding the site.

If you're feeling energetic you can just jump into the Saalach with your kayak. Or do a spot of hiking in the nearby mountains, though be warned that the walking there can be steep and is not for the faint-hearted. Slightly easier to explore are the region's villages and towns. St. Martin (about 1km away) and Lofer (just over 2km) are both quintessentially quiet Salzburgerland towns; further afield you can cycle the 325km Tauernradweg, which runs from Krimml, site of a famous waterfall, to Passau. Salzburg itself is only 40km away and the fabulous Grossglockner road can be reached in an hour. Just over the German border is Bad Reichenhall, a friendly spa town that serves as an entry point to the Berchtesgadener Land – one of the most beautiful areas in Germany and home to Hitler's notorious Eagle's Nest retreat.

Grubhof may be one of Austria's larger places to camp, but it has the intimacy and charm of a much smaller site and, of course, a fabulous location.

COOL FACTOR Large site with a separate camping area on the banks of the Saalach in Austria's Salzburgerland.

WHO'S IN Tents, campervans, caravans, dogs – yes.

ON SITE Unmarked pitches in a large meadow with electricity or marked hard-standings with hook-ups. Facilities are generally excellent, with ultra-modern shower blocks and a new central building with an info-packed reception, sauna, spa facilities and a gym. There's an onsite restaurant and minimarket, playground/teenager lounge (with table tennis and TV), baby room and Wi-Fi access.

OFF SITE Visit one of the massive gorges nearby, climb the mountains (by foot or by cable car) or head to the outdoor Lofer swimming pool in July and August, the use of which is included in the camping price. You could also take your family for some canyoning or rafting. The Motion Team (6588 7524; www.motion.co.at) organises both activities (and many more besides), and their base is just 1km downstream from the campsite.

FOOD & DRINK You can get tasty and reasonably priced Austrian food in the onsite restaurant or in the beer garden at the pond, but there are also many other cafés and inns in the vicinity where you can gorge yourself on regional specialities like apfelstrudel and schnitzel. If you want some great views and food, drive to Loferer Alm and visit Schönblick (6588 82780) run by Vanya, a friendly Yorkshire lass.

GETTING THERE From Munich take the A8 towards Salzburg, exit Traunstein/Siegsdorf (Germany), and follow the signs to Lofer. In Lofer take direction Zell-am-See from the roundabout and follow the signs to Grubhof. From Innsbruck take the A12, direction Salzburg, exit Wörgl West, then follow signs to Lofer; at the roundabout take the direction Zell-am-See and follow the signs to Park Grubhof.

PUBLIC TRANSPORT There are direct buses to Lofer from St Johann in Tirol, Saalfelden, Zell am See, Kitzbühel and Salzburg. Trains will only take you from Salzburg to Zell am See and Saalfelden.

OPEN All year except November.

THE DAMAGE €28.70 per night for 2 adults, car and tent, €23.60 in low season (tax included). €40.30 per night for 2 adults, 2 children, car and tent, €32.80 in the low season (tax included). There are also camping huts, costing €43/€53 per night.

panorama camping sonnenberg

Hinteroferst 12, 6714 Nüziders nr. Bludenz Vorarlberg, Austria 0043 5552 64035 www.camping-sonnenberg.com

Every Sunday at Sonnenberg the site's owners (and friends) graciously bedeck themselves in their traditional mountain livery and put on a performance with the alphorn – a long, wooden wind instrument used to summon cattle and serenade tourists. Now, this may seem a bit of a cliché, but it's a perfect introduction if you've just arrived here; the pure alpine drone accompanied by the thrusting peaks and curves of the mountains. As the sombre sounds echo around the site and the last rays of sun daub the summits of the surrounding mountains, it's impossible not to get that 'I'm in Austria' feeling.

At 600 metres above sea level, Sonnenberg – 'sunny mountain' – is run by the Dünser family (Matthias and Beate) and has an air of tradition and meticulousness that is often lacking in other campsites. Tents and small caravans mingle on the site's kempt terraces; a well-equipped reception takes care of all enquiries and a nearby bakery sells fresh bread each morning. The spotless facilities block has baby-changing, spacious washing and drying rooms plus Wi-Fi and a library. But the best thing about Sonnenberg is the views. The site is ringed by glorious peaks and no matter where you pitch you'll be greeted each morning by the Silvretta in the southeast, the Rätikon to the south, the Lechtaler Alpen in the north… even the Swiss Alps are visible in the distance on a clear day.

The surrounding Vorarlberg region is easy to explore. Each valley has its own character, and every town its points of interest. Nearby Nüziders offers campers handy shops and eateries; Feldkirch (20km away) is a medieval town full of young hipsters; Bludenz (just 3km away), where the five valleys meet, is the outdoors hub of the region, a base for hiking, biking and winter sports activities. Chocoholics may be happy to hear that Suchard are based here too. The local valleys include the Klostertal, Montafon, Walgau, Brandnertal and the nearby Grosses Walsertal, a UNESCO Biosphere Reserve. Highlights include a hike up the 'Matterhorn of Vorarlberg', the Zimba Massif – a one- or two-day hike, depending how fast and how fit you are – and the must-see Lünersee, a crater lake 1,970 metres up. If you're not fond of walking, a cable car from Brand will get you most of the way there. And if you don't wish to walk alone, the site also organises regular group hikes. You can also drive down to the region's picturesque capital, Bregenz (50km), at the foot of enormous Lake Constance (Bodensee). On the lake you can hire boats and bikes, or hike up to the Pfänder (1,064m) for peerless views. You can also explore the Bregenzerwald, a gorgeous region that's all alpine dairies and chocolate-box villages.

Meanwhile, back at the site, you'll find it easy to unwind on the grassy terraces and enjoy the quiet as night descends on the mountains like a velvet duvet. If it's Sunday, you already know what to do – sit back with a beer and enjoy the alphorn dirge resounding through the evening air.

COOL FACTOR An atmospheric campsite ringed by the peaks of Vorarlberg's mountains.

WHO'S IN Tents, campervans, caravans, dogs – yes.

ON SITE 115 terraced pitches, some hard-standings. Facilities consist of a 2-storey building containing everything from WCs, hot showers and a baby room, to a drying room, laundry room, internet and dish-washing facilities. The reception building has a cinema room on the upper floor and a sleeping loft for campers if the weather gets bad. There's also a shop selling basics, a playground, indoor games room, table tennis and Wi-Fi and there are regular programmes of activities for youngsters. You can hire bikes onsite, and down on Lake Constance you can also hire bikes as well as boats.

OFF SITE Why not have a night in the Frassen Hut (6991 705 1089; frassenhuette.at), a cosy Alpine hut (with restaurant) that lies on the hike to the Hoher Frassen? You can hike all the way or take the cable car for part of the distance. High-flyers should head to the paragliding school in Schnifis (5556 767 17; tandemgliding.at) and take a tandem flight over the Montafon valley.

FOOD & DRINK Basics are available on site, but restaurant/café Daneu (300m away) serves Austrian and international food; Angelo – a tiny Italian restaurant just over 2km away, serves tailor-made meals (closed Sunday) and in Braz (8km) is lovely Rössle (5552 281 050; roesslebraz.at).

GETTING THERE From Munich, take the A96 towards Lindau/18/Stuttgart, following it across the border into Austria. Continue on to the A14, taking exit 57-Nüziders. Follow the signs to Nüziders, then to Sonnenberg. From Innsbruck, take the A12/E533/E60 road, following the signs to Bregenz/Garmisch/E60. Continue on to the S16 and the A14, taking exit 57-Nüziders. Follow the signs to Nüziders, then to Sonnenberg.

PUBLIC TRANSPORT There are train stations in Bludenz and Nüziders, from where you can take a bus to close to the site. Pick-ups are possible.

OPEN May–September.

THE DAMAGE In low season it costs €22 for 2 adults and €28 for 2 adults plus 2 children; in high season it's €31.50 for 2 adults and €39.50 for 2 adults plus 2 children.

camping arolla

Route de Tsallion 1986 Arolla, Switzerland 0041 2728 32295 www.camping-arolla.com

Switzerland is, of course, a little odd. It's no coincidence that Einstein developed his theory of curved space-time while working as a patent clerk in Bern, nor that the giant CERN particle accelerator buried in the Swiss soil has men with wild hair and perspex goggles poring over pesky little particles that may or may not exist. Yes, there's certainly something different about a place that seems to lend itself to wacky scientists, discombobulated theories and strange coincidences. Take Camping Arolla, for instance. Back when Cool Camping first visited the place we were struck by the inspiring views – surroundings that ached for activity and mountains that longed to be climbed. Yet while we were penning our first reviews and snapping away with the camera, current owners Laurence and Georges were still scaling the local slopes and enjoying the undeniable beauty of this Swiss gem. Indeed as we pitched our tent and pushed our pegs into the fertile mountain soil, they too might just have been claiming their patch of paradise beside us. Didn't someone help us with the guy-ropes? Who was that man that pointed out the quiet local walk?

The only thing we could be sure of when we returned to one of our favourite European campsites was that these affable owners had fallen in love with Camping Arolla just as much as we had – and had come back and taken over the place in 2014. But was it a coincidence that they discovered the place just as we did? Is there a reason they have been blessed with just the right attitude to run this alpine campsite? Is there a science behind the

perfect camping experience? Who knows? Who cares? Just take a look at the views and you can forget all about the local desire for quirky theories.

Just shy of 2,000 metres high in the Swiss Alps, Arolla is a spacious site of grassy terraced pitches. Some spots provide sweeping vistas back over the valley through which you arrived. But if you pitch your tent on the shoulder of the hill you can enjoy the best views up towards the 4,000-metre summit of the north face of Mont Collon and the Pigne d'Arolla. Apart from the challenging climbing, there's fine walking to be had in these parts and one of the best routes is the one up to Lac Bleu, a relatively short walk that meanders gently through forest and meadow before climbing, admittedly pretty steeply, up to the lake. When you reach the top, you'll certainly need to give yourself a reward. This comes in the form of an absolutely crystal-clear lake – watch the waters cascading over rocks into a series of pools trickling down the hill. Even more good news is that there's a pleasant little café down at the start of the walk, with the chilled beer you'll probably be in need of after your exertions.

If that sounds like too much effort, there's always the luxuriant green grass of the site itself. Blame the altitude and all that wonderful pure mountain air for getting you so giddy that you find yourself in urgent need of a quiet, relaxing lie-down. Either that or blame the weird goings-on at CERN, which no less than Stephen Hawking has warned that could create an enormous black hole to swallow us all up. All the more reason to get up to Arolla while it's still there.

COOL FACTOR The highest campsite in Europe, with head-clearing air and great views.

WHO'S IN Tents, caravans, campervans, dogs – yes.

ON SITE The campsite has no designated pitches. Pitches are on perfectly flat terraces with alpine grass and all have excellent views. There is a spacious new facilities block with all the trimmings and a CHF1 charge to operate the showers. Pitches are flat, some with electric hook-ups. The reception has a surprisingly well-stocked shop, given you're up in the mountains, with gas, maps, drinks and fresh bread delivered each morning. In the village you'll also find two groceries, a sports shop, a post office and a tourist office. Free washing machines for use. Wi-Fi available across the site.

OFF SITE The reason you come to Arolla is for the hiking, and you're spoilt for choice when it comes to routes. Luckily the site and its owners have lots of suggestions for both gentle day hikes and longer affairs.

FOOD & DRINK There's a small *épicerie* at the site for basic provisions (you can order bread for the morning). Up the hill in the village of Arolla there's the Café du Pigne (2728 37100), with a sunny terrace looking up the glacier. It sells Belgian fruit beer and is a fantastic little place to relax. If you've ever seen The Shining you'll enjoy a visit to the Hotel Kurhaus (2728 37000; hotel-kurhaus.arolla.com). It's been there since 1896, plenty of time for strange goings-on in its wood-panelled rooms, and has a bar/restaurant if you can't face staying the night.

GETTING THERE From the main east–west E62 road take the road signed Route d'Hérens towards Vex. Carry on all the way through Evolène and Les Haudères until just before Arolla. There's a sign to the campsite on the left, just by Hotel La Tsa. Follow the dirt track over the river and back up the hill.

PUBLIC TRANSPORT Public buses run 7 times a day between Sion and Arolla. Ask the driver to drop you at the campsite. From the bus stop it's a 5-minute walk.

OPEN June–September. Exact dates depend on the weather conditions. Please consult their website.

THE DAMAGE CHF7 per adult and CHF4 per child. Tents are between CHF7 and CHF12, depending on size; cars CHF3.

camping des glaciers

Route de Tsamodet 36 – CH-1944 La Fouly, Switzerland 0041 2778 31826 www.camping-glaciers.ch

The Swiss don't do clichés – but if they did they'd probably be the best clichés in the world. Sure, there are a few images that pop immediately into your head when you think of Switzerland – Heidi in flaxen pigtails, yodellers in tight leather shorts, triangular chocolate bars and cuckoo clocks. That sort of thing. And here at Camping des Glaciers you certainly get all the standard features – Alpine meadow, forest glade, mountain glacier, gushing river, crystal air, wildflowers underfoot, puffy white clouds overhead. But, somehow, it all resists cliché because it's just so refreshingly... refreshing.

The site is spread out like a giant green picnic blanket on the side of the hill, and you can take your pick from three types of pitch – in among the grassy rocks thrown down the mountain by the action of ice and gravity, with views up to the mountain tops; on the open meadow looking back down the valley; or in among the pine trees and wildflowers, where you can't see the wood for the trees (and the bees).

Since Cool Camping's first visit in 2008 the owners of the site have passed it along to the next generation, keeping it in the family now for over 40 years. They seem to have intimate knowledge of every blade of grass and flower in the place. Alain will show you the seven different types of wild orchid that grow on the site and can even occasionally point you in the direction of a rarer mountain flower, such as *Campanula thyrsoides*, growing wild somewhere about the place. It helps

enormously that he speaks excellent English along with a number of other languages. His mother, Agathe, can sometimes be seen bustling about the place, popping in for a quick drink with some guests who are back for at least the 30th year in a row. The regulars also remember Alain's father, Michel, who has passed away since founding the site. His spirit, though, lives on in mountain folklore, most notably as the first man to scale the north face of the Eiger solo – a feat he achieved in 1963.

The campsite is a 10-minute stroll from the hamlet of La Fouly, a modest ski resort in winter, with a black run and a couple of reds and blues. But it's probably even more popular in the summer, when the meadows are laced with a profusion of wild flowers and the melon-green river comes crashing down from the glacier. There's an intricate maze of walks and climbs from the village, or from Ferret a couple of miles up the valley. While the mountains around La Fouly are not quite in the Eiger league, the twin peaks above the site and the mountain pass that leads over to France are sufficient for most serious walkers; and you'd need to do more than strap a pair of crampons to your Gucci loafers if you wanted to have lunch in Chamonix. It's only 16km away as the crow flies, but it will take you an hour and a half by road over the Col des Montets.

Not that you need to go all that way when everything you need is here – all those boringly bog-standard Alpine sorts of things anyway.

COOL FACTOR Mountains, meadows, glaciers, wildflowers – everything you associate with summer in the Swiss Alps.

WHO'S IN Tents, campervans, caravans, and well-behaved dogs – yes.

ON SITE The newer 2 facilities blocks are great, the older 2 (beneath the reception area) are a little tired, but perfectly serviceable. There's also a handy day-hut with a TV.

OFF SITE Take a trip to the breathtaking Gorges du Durnand (gorgesdudurnand.ch), a collection of 14 waterfalls with wooden walkways connecting them. The walkways are built into the rocks and you might find some of them pretty hair-raising, but it's worth it for the spectacular views. In June and July there's an open-air cinema at Martigny (open-air-kino.ch). Check what films are on and which are dubbed into French, otherwise you'll end up watching Indiana Jones et le Royaume du Crâne Cristal and not knowing what's what.

FOOD & DRINK There's a supermarket in the village, about 10 minutes' walk from the campsite. Just above it is the Restaurant des Glaciers, (2778 31171; aubergedesglaciers. ch), which has recently been taken over by a new chef who's introduced a bit of flair to the menus, which start at CHF22 for a set 3-course lunch. Hôtel Edelweiss (2778 32621) is also in the village and has an excellent restaurant serving traditional meals.

GETTING THERE From Martigny head for Champex-Lac and the Grand-Saint-Bernard Tunnel. Turn right at the town of Orsières (where there's also a railway station) and follow the road up to La Fouly. Drive through the village and, opposite the chair lift, veer down to the right, cross the river and you're there.

PUBLIC TRANSPORT Buses and trains run from Martigny to Orsières and there's a bus from there to La Fouly. It takes about 20 minutes and runs from 06:45 to 18:05.

OPEN Mid May–end September.

THE DAMAGE Adults CHF6.40–CHF8; children CHF3.20–CHF4; dogs CHF2.40–CHF3. A pitch costs CHF10–CHF16.

lo stambecco

Frazione Valnontey 6, 11012 Cogne, Val d'Aosta, Italy 0039 016 574 152 www.campeggiolostambecco.it

Big Paradise Park is quite a name to live up to. Luckily the Parco Nazionale del Gran Paradiso in the Italian Alps is more than up to the challenge. On the Italian side of the Mont Blanc Massif, the park ticks so many Alpine boxes that even a meticulous Brussels bureaucrat would have trouble in finding fault with its paperwork.

First there are the views up the valley towards the summit of Testa della Tribolazione, whose southeast wall is a favourite with climbers, despite its rather daunting name (something about the peak of tribulation). Across from the site is a steep shoulder of mountain, behind which the sun settles for the evening. And rumbling through the valley below the site is one of those high mountain rivers that is three parts glacier-melt and one part crushed rock, giving it the distinctive grey green mineral colour of a river of Margaritas. Dips are not recommended, however; it's fast-flowing and your extremities would not thank you for the exposure.

Lo Stambecco is in the tiny village of Valnontey, a stopover on one of the great summer Alpine walks – the Alta Via from Champorcher to Courmayeur. With an average altitude of over 2,000 metres and the pass of the Col Loson measuring up at 3,300 metres, the Alta Via (a literal 'highway') is a fairly serious multi-day walk but, thankfully, you can sample the atmosphere of it by doing nothing more strenuous than waving at passing walkers from the comfort of the grassy slopes of Lo Stambecco, which are perfect for a prolonged lounge. The thick grass is so soft and comfy that carpet slippers seem more appropriate footwear than clumpy walking boots.

There is a variety of pitches, some on the grassy slopes, some venturing into the pine cover that sneaks down the hill. The further up the hill you go, the thicker the trees. Like Hansel and Gretel you might want to leave a trail of breadcrumbs from your tent to the facilities block at night, just in case you get lost.

If you are itching for a hike, there are walking maps on sale from the campsite's reception, so you can tackle anything from a half-hour stroll to a day's hard slog up the valley in search of the elusive ibex (*stambecchi* in Italian) – those hairy things with horns that look like upturned stacks of ice-cream cones. There's actually an old hunting lodge called the Rifugio Vittorio Sella on the walk, originally owned by King Victor Emmanuel II who became the first king of a united Italy in 1861, and who used to come up here to hunt stambecchi. It's about two-and-a-half hours' steady climb from Valnontey and there's a restaurant nearby to help prepare you for the descent. Much easier is the downhill, 3-km walk to the bright lights of Cogne, a typically gorgeous Alpine village, which, with nearly 1,500 inhabitants, feels like downtown Manhattan after a few days up at Lo Stambecco. It's true that the return walk is back up the hill but, with the prospect of your carpet slippers waiting for you back at the campsite, it will seem like a breeze.

COOL FACTOR Box-ticking Alpine camping – views, air, walks and trees.

WHO'S IN Tents, campervans, caravans – yes. Dogs – no.

ON SITE 140 spaces for tents and caravans. Facilities are okay. The showers are fine, but the squat loos will test those with dodgy knees (though there are a few more orthodox ones too). Laundry facilities are available for use and there are hairdriers. There is a very nice bar and reading area with a selection of board games and an open fire if the weather is particularly cold. There is also a decent selection of postcards, so you can sit at the tables outside and pencil a gloating 'wish you were here' to your friends back home.

OFF SITE Take the kids to La Ferme du Grande Paradis (165 749 361; lafermedugrandparadis.it), just across the river from the campsite, for a little family fun. There are cows, pigs, mountain goats and more, and you can treat yourself to some of their excellent collection of homemade cheeses too; it is a working farm, after all. Everything is locally produced and predictably delicious – though some of it is pretty strong, so be prepared!

FOOD & DRINK There's a miniature bar/restaurant onsite with a few tables outside for admiring the mountain view. In Valnontey itself there are several restaurants, the best-situated being the Hotel Paradisia (016 574 158; hotelparadisia.it), which offers a range of standard mains such as pasta and steaks for €7–€17.

GETTING THERE From Aosta, take the SR47 towards Cogne. Turn right in the town up the cobbled street signposted for Valnontey. After 3km there is a sign for Lo Stambecco on your right-hand side, just before the village.

PUBLIC TRANSPORT Buses run regularly from Aosta to Valnontey.

OPEN Late May–late September.

THE DAMAGE €7 per adult and €5 per child (extra between 20 July and 26 August). A tent and caravan are €5 each, a campervan €7. Electricity is an extra €2.

camping seiser alm

Saint Konstantin 16, 39050 Völs am Schlern, Italy 0039 471 706 459 www.camping-seiseralm.com

If you're not the world's greatest linguist, you can be forgiven for getting tongue-tied here. It's not the altitude, which can surely make you dizzy, but the language. You're in Italy, but they speak German, and there's more than a hint of a Swiss-Austrian-German twist to everything. The cute peak-roofed doll's houses are enough to make you start yodelling, while the clanging cow bells make you wonder if Julie Andrews is about to come skipping over the nearest hillock.

Seiser Alm (its German name) or the Alpe di Siusi, as it's known in Italian, is in the very heart of the Dolomites. This Italian region of the Alps is a sprawl of massive Triassic rock formations, rising like doomsday monoliths from a soft bed of pine trees and Alpine fauna. The area has three main towns: Castelrotto, Siusi and Fiè. Between them, in the foothills, are many smaller villages, and here the long shadow of the 2,500-metre Sciliar Massif falls across Camping Seiser Alm. Not too far from the base of this carbonate marvel, tiny tents are pitched randomly on a couple of grassy knolls. Despite the minor irritation of somewhat unsightly serried ranks of caravans and statics, the unhindered front-row Dolomite view is sublime – gorgeous enough to take your breath away. In winter the valley is covered in thick unyielding snow, and the mountain peaks – the highest over 3,000 metres – are like fins of chocolate mud cake dusted in icing sugar. Meals are served on a long terrace at the site's Zur Quelle restaurant, with truly spectacular views of the Dolomites on one side and the valley on the other. Food is hearty and typically German: perfect

for building up energy for the main event at this site, which is hiking.

In summer cagouled-and-booted walkers arrive en masse to discover the sublime landscape. Flower-covered pastures erupt from colossal mountains of rock, the peaks, columns and crags set off against the big blue sky. Hiking has been a big thing here since the 19th century and it plods along today on over 350 kilometers of marked tracks – take your pick from the different grades on offer. The Seiser Alm cable car – the world's longest – and connecting chair lifts are an alternative if you'd really rather do the whole thing sitting down. You'll have to get up off your backside, though, if you want to have a little sit-down in the Rifugio Bolzano. This is one of the oldest mountain huts in the Alps and nestles just below the 2,300-metre Monte Pez on the backbone of the Sciliar Massif. Another clever idea is to take the easy stroll to the Punto Panoramico at the top of Chairlift Three. This has a big wow-factor, with its views to the Marmolada or Punta Di Penia, the highest peak in the Dolomites. If serious hiking isn't really your thing, you may enjoy rubbernecking around the area's fortresses, ruins, castles and pint-sized villages instead. The beautiful Laghetto di Fiè, a natural lake known for its intact ecosystem and excellent water quality, is a must for a refreshing little dip when the weather warms up. If you're a mountain biker or a road cyclist, the region's rocky slopes and undulating roads can provide heart-pumping scenic adventures, whatever your ability.

COOL FACTOR The front-row Dolomite view and the sublime hiking make this a must for Alpine adventurers.

WHO'S IN Tents, campervans, caravans, dogs – yes.

ON SITE Restaurant, excellent bathroom and toilet facilities plus a mini market, Wi-Fi and the morning newspapers.

OFF SITE Take a cable car to the Seiser Alm plateau (alpedisiusi-seiseralm.com). Grab a chairlift to head further afield once at the top, or treat yourself to a 15-minute tandem paraglide down the valley (338 604 19 79). If you'd prefer something more sedate, enjoy a famed Tyrolean 'hay bath' at the Hotel Heubad (471 725 020; hotelheubad.com), an age-old peasant practice whereby relaxing in the herbs and oils of freshly-cut hay has strangely rejuvenating effects.

FOOD & DRINK The campsite's own Zur Quelle restaurant has a large outdoor patio with a view of the Dolomites. The little town of Siusi has a couple of bars and a decent pizzeria, the Hauenstein (471 704 302; hauenstein.it). Ristorante Bullaccia (471 727 822), at the top of Chairlift, 3 is the perfect top-of-the-world spot for a beer. There are markets on Friday at Castelrotto and every Saturday at Fie.

GETTING THERE The campsite is signposted along the SS24 between Fie and Siusi at Saint Konstantin (or San Costantino).

OPEN December–November.

THE DAMAGE €7.80–€11.50 per adult and €4.40–€8.80 per child per night, depending on season and age.

bellavista

Via Gardesana 31, 38062 Arco, Italy 0039 464 505 644 www.camping-bellavista.it

Come and make a splash at Camping Bellavista. The site sits on a bay at the northern end of Lake Garda, arguably Italy's most magnificent lake, and is in prime position for all campers who love to get wet – really wet.

It is a simple and welcoming campsite, very well equipped, with generous grassy plots neatly spaced under rows of shady olive trees. All have hook-ups and, given the boutique size of the site, you're never too far from any thing you need. From the front of the property you can step on to a picturesque waterfront with blue water so clear (and cold) that you can see your tootsies sinking into the white sand. On each side of the lake, imposing limestone mountains retreat into the distant horizon, framing the 180-degree view. The landscape is a perfect playground if you are keen on hiking, canyoning, rock climbing or mountain biking. But given the site's location, your first priority should really be all about getting wet. Windsurfing and sailing are the most popular ways of doing this and you can hire everything you need.

When you've had enough and towelled off, you could head down the lake to the holiday town of Riva del Garda, or just hang out in the nearby town of Arco, surrounded by a green valley of orchards and vineyards and with an old centre with a busy main square and streets flanked by classically quaint shuttered houses. Its ruined castle is something of a symbol for the town, teetering above the houses on a sheer rock face. Just don't try high-diving off the top.

COOL FACTOR A quintessentially Italian campsite just a hop, skip and a jump from Lake Garda.

WHO'S IN Tents, caravans, campervans, dogs – yes.

ON SITE There are 4 bathroom blocks, 2 of which are heated, with showers, laundry facilities, disabled access, baby-changing, private bathrooms (€8 extra) and dish-washing areas. There are recycling facilities, chemical disposal point, a minimarket, reception bar and play area. Wi-Fi is available around the main communal areas.

OFF SITE Take a guided tour of nearby Arco Castle (464 532 255) or head into the atmopsheric old resort town of Riva del Garda for an ice cream on the promenade. As for adventure, you could try canyoning in the beautiful mountain crevices of the Upper Garda (canyonadv.com; 464 505 406), or paragliding off the mountains behind nearby Malcesine (347 967 0730; paraglidingmalcesine.com) – just two among a host of possible activities, including sailing, windsurfing, walking, mountain-biking and climbing. Grab a bunch of leaflets from reception and take your pick. More sedate but equally spectacular is the Parco Grotta Cascata (464 521 421; cascata-varone.com), a gorge and waterfall you can view on a series of walkways.

FOOD & DRINK The campsite bar and café has al fresco seating and excellent coffee. For dinner, try Ristorante Alla Lega (464 516 205; ristorantealalega.com), where Italian fare is served on a vine-covered patio.

GETTING THERE The campsite is on the waterfront at Nargo-Torbole on the SS-240 between Arco and Riva del Garda.

PUBLIC TRANSPORT Bus S202m runs regularly form Brescia and up the west side of the lake to Arco via Riva del Garda.

OPEN Late April–early October.

THE DAMAGE Pitch €11.50–€12.50; adults €10–€10.50; child (3–12 yrs) €7–€7.50; dogs €3–€3.50.

san biagio

Via Cavalle 19, 25080 Manerba del Garda, Brescia, Italy 0039 365 551 549 www.campingsanbiagio.net

DH Lawrence may be best known for writing about naughty ladies and randy gamekeepers, but he was a dab hand when it came to Italy, too. The original beard-and-sandals Brit abroad, Lawrence came to Lake Garda just before the First World War and marvelled, with arty-farty lyricism, at 'cypress trees poised like flames of forgotten darkness' and 'the green-silver smoke of olive trees' – enough to make your mouth water.

Lake Garda, Italy's largest and grandest lake, might have lost some of the innocence of Lawrence's time since tourists started turning up in droves, but the cypress and olive trees still grow amid the terracotta-roofed houses, and they now have citrus orchards and vineyards to add extra charm. The campsite at San Biagio is on the western side of the lake, in the lushly green region of Brescia, near Salò. It occupies its very own private peninsula, which juts northeasterly into the water. It has 161 pitches, all power-connected, which extend along the narrow stretch of land, cleverly creating the intimate ambience of a much smaller campsite. Most pitches are either shimmied up against the water's edge (for a small extra fee) or not too far from it. Others are slightly elevated so that you peer through the boughs of enormous blossoming magnolia trees to the blue water beyond, a vista enhanced by the soft, floral waft of magnolias in the fresh air.

But, wherever you end up pitching, you're never far from a bit of water-based activity. In most cases the beaches allow easy access, but where sharp boulders nudge the edge of the lake, there are handy steps into the water – just the job for launching your inflatable mattress when you go for a relaxing drift around the lake.

If you can drag yourself away from the crystal-blue lake water lapping languidly on three sides of you, there's plenty in the surrounding countryside to keep you amused. Towards the east there's the Rocca di Manerba, a 222-acre natural archeological park, where a re-discovered fortress dominates the skyline. At the northeastern tip of the peninsula, where six of the best pitches hide among the reedy waterfront, you can also see the Isola San Biagio, known locally as Isola dei Conigli, or 'Rabbit Island'. When the water is particularly low you can reach the island by picking your way along a narrow strip of sand and shingle. When it is high, wading knee-deep with a towel around your neck and a bucket and spade in your hand makes for a perfect little adventure. Once across, you can pull up a seat at the island kiosk and relax with a cool drink as the hours tick by.

If you're feeling a bit more energetic, there is a smattering of small towns a short drive away; and further afield still is Salò, the capital of Mussolini's Nazi-backed state and, these days, a beautiful town with a waterfront that will make you feel as though you've just stepped right into a Venetian painting. Its little lanes are full of the kinds of tempting shops and cafés that even DH Lawrence might still recognise.

COOL FACTOR A small campsite in a prime location.

WHO'S IN Tents, campervans, caravans, dogs (on a lead at all times) – yes.

ON SITE 161 pitches, all with electricity and free Wi-Fi access. A large, clean, central block has male and female toilets, hot showers with separate changing areas, washing machines, a dryer and basins. There is a fridge for freezing cooler blocks and ice packs. There's also a small playground and an onsite shop. The campsite has its own restaurant, overlooking the water, and there is a slipway for campers to launch boats from.

OFF SITE Water and swimming options are endless here. In July and August the nearby village of Manerba plays host to an evening market each Tuesday night. Further afield there is Salò, without question one of Garda's most elegant towns, and Gardone Riviera, a sprawling but appealing resort town close to which Il Vittoriale (365 296 511; vittoriale.it) was the bizarre home of the Italian adventurer and Mussolini's favourite writer, Gabriel d'Annunzio, and is now open to the public for visits.

FOOD & DRINK The campsite's own waterside bar is a great spot for a cold beer, espresso or pizza. Those who wade across to Rabbit Island will find a handy kiosk waiting. Head into nearby Salò for a typically Italian evening at Cantina Santa Giustina (365 520 32), a rustic and cavernous eatery that offers cheese, charcuterie, wine – and, if Vasco, the owner, has anything to do with it, a hangover.

GETTING THERE From the north, turn off SS45bis near Salò on to the SS572 towards Desenzano. Exit at Manerba and follow the camping signs to Via Cavalle. From the south, turn off the A4 towards Desenzano on to SS572 north towards Salò. Exit at Manerba and continue as above.

PUBLIC TRANSPORT There are regular buses from Brescia and Desenzano to Manerba del Garda.

OPEN Easter–end September.

THE DAMAGE €15–€32 for tent and car/car and caravan/campervan depending on type of pitch and season, plus €8–€12 per adult and €5–€8 per child, depending on season.

internazionale firenze

Via San Cristofano 2, 50023 Bottai-Impruneta, Italy 0039 552 374 704 www.florencecamping.com

In imperial times it was said that all roads led to Rome and, thanks to Italy's idiosyncratic road signs, it can often still seem to be that way. Many a T-junction will tell you that Rome is to the left. And to the right. So if you're on your way to the forum and you see a sign that says 'Firenze', be sure to take it. No visit to Italy is complete without a couple of days in the company of Dante, Michelangelo et al, indeed if there is one city that sums up Italy in all its Renaissance glory, then the little city by the Arno is it.

Camping Internazionale Firenze is as 'internazionale' as the name suggests. There are more national flags aloft over the reception than in an Olympic athletes' village. This is Florence, after all, and in summer it's clogged with gaily clad camera-clicking culture vultures from all possible corners of the globe. But the site is a 20-minute, €1.20, bus-ride from the city centre, so in the height of a Tuscan summer you'll be able to relax a little way away from the hubbub that's happening in town.

The site is reasonably large and quite steep, but the good news is that the chalets are out of sight near reception and the camping area is on long, broad grassy terraces up the hill. Though you can't see central Florence from the site, you do have views of the illuminated convent of San Paulo on one hill or the church of Certosa from another. As night falls, you'll see bats on the wing, flitting between the trees with their built-in sat-navs picking out bugs and moths in the air, and you'll be winked at by the fireflies that are

lurking in the grass. You'd be hard-pushed to find that sort of thing in a two-star pensione back in town.

Down the hill there is a fairly lively bar, frequented by a youngish crowd whose attire is usually as loud as their voices. Luckily for all campers in need of a peaceful time, it's all well out of earshot of the camping area. There's also a modest restaurant (no awards, as yet, and don't hold your breath) and a reasonably well-stocked little shop, where the basics of breakfast can be found in the morning and a cold beer in the evening if you want to take one back, sit on the grass and Bluetooth the bats.

And when it's time to hit the tourist trail you just won't know where to start. Michelangelo at the Academia or Donatello at the Bargello? A caffè macchiato or a glass of Chianti? Prosciutto or formaggio? Ponte Vecchio or Ponti's ice cream? You need to take a deep breath, lace up your most sensible walking shoes and prepare yourself for culture, Italian-style. Luckily, Florence is one of those cities in which the main attractions are all within handy walking distance of each other. But unfortunately there are so many to choose from that you can easily cover an Olympic marathon distance getting from one to the other, and on to the next. At least the centre's streets are largely pedestrianised so you're in more danger of tripping on the ancient cobblestones than anything else.

Just pick up a map and don't pay too much attention to the road signs. They'll just point you in the direction of Rome.

COOL FACTOR On the doorstep of the finest collection of Renaissance art and architecture in the world.

WHO'S IN Tents, campervans, caravans, dogs – yes.

ON SITE Terraced, grassy pitches mostly in the shade of trees (olives, acacias, oaks, pines, poplars). Ample showers and WCs and plenty of washing facilities (clothes and dishes) in a central block. The reception has leaflets and boards with local information, a small shop selling essentials (including postcards and stamps). There's a bar and pizzeria. There is an internet point, Wi-Fi and a TV room. An outdoor swimming pool is free for campers to use. There's a large electricity pylon slap-bang in the middle of the site and there is a bit of noise from the motorway.

OFF SITE Three sights to start you off. Climb the dome of Brunelleschi's Duomo, a twin-skinned structure built without scaffolding, and then regain your breath by enjoying the views from the top. See Donatello's über-camp statue of David – a far cry from Michelangelo's massive muscular marble version – at the Bargello. And check out the paintings and sculptures at the Uffizi.

FOOD & DRINK The campsite has its own small bar, pizzeria and restaurant serving a few local Tuscan dishes, with a shaded area for outside dining. Eat on the hoof when you're in town. Just by the Duomo there's a great little enoteca called Alessi (055 214 966; enotecaalessi.it), which serves delicious bruschetta and quality wines by the glass. For something near the Uffizi, try Giulliano Centro, a small café with local grub – spiced and herbed chicken, local sausage, rosti and a dollop of spinach and broccoli mashed up with garlic and olive oil. Just opposite is a great stand-up place serving Tuscan nibbles like artichoke and truffle on bread and help-yourself chianti at €2 a go.

GETTING THERE Come off the A1 Roma road at the Certosa exit. As you pass through Bottai, the campsite is signposted to your left. Follow the road back under the motorway and the campsite is on your right.

PUBLIC TRANSPORT A number 37 or 68 bus (depending on the day) runs from Florence's train station to Bottai. It's a 10-minute walk to the site from the bus stop.

OPEN All year.

THE DAMAGE €7–€12 for adults, €5–€6 for children aged 3–11 years (but free in low season). A pitch is €12–€13.50 with a tent, €12–€14.50 with a campervan or caravan.

agricampeggio madonna di pogi

Via della Madonna 52, Pogi AR, Italy 0039 340 490 2643 www.madonnadipogi.it

Tuscany has long been the holiday destination of choice for Brits seeking that quintessential slice of the rural Italian 'dolce vita', as portrayed in *Under the Tuscan Sun*. But as anyone who has experienced Pisa at the height of the season will tell you – deluged with scores of sharp-elbowed, snap-happy holidaymakers brandishing their selfie-sticks like swords – a summer break here can be far from relaxing. However, there's another corner of Tuscany that seems to have evaded the tide of tourism; in short, a Tuscany the Brits haven't found... but, we're happy to report, a certain Italian-German man has.

Towards the top of the boot, where Tuscany's eastern fringe converges with neighbouring Emilia-Romagna, Le Marche and Umbria, Agricampeggio Madonna Di Pogi lies nestled in the heart of the Val d'Ambra. Lush, green hills stretch for miles around in every direction, while tranquil inland lagoons puddle the valley floor. This lush land of plenty is famed for its farming. Little wonder, then, that Stefano Loew Cadonna chose this as the spot for his *agricampeggio*, which opened in spring 2014. As Stefano puts it, 'Our main idea... was to provide our guests with the opportunity to freely experience the Tuscan countryside, its nature, and, above all, its tranquillity'. And how. There's over 120,000m² of unspoilt forest and farmland to explore here, with organic gardens offering a bounty of GM-free fruit and veg. When the weather's nice, the private lake is perfect for a cooling dip or a spot of lazy fishing in the shade of the cypress grove.

Accommodation-wise, guests have a choice of two kinds of wooden wigwam-like structures that Stefano has christened 'tent houses' and 'wooden caravans'. These ingenious, cosy abodes are scattered among the woods and come in a range of sizes. The caravans are furnished with a kitchenette, double beds, tables and chairs, while the tent houses have a bed inside and a table with benches outside. There are proper flush facilities and hot water showers, while the communal firepit barbecue area is at your disposal to cook up some of the wonderful local produce.

As far as location goes, the site's position in the heart of Tuscany takes some topping. From the idyllic village of Pogi, some of Italy's most iconic Renaissance sights are easily reachable, with both Arezzo and Siena just a short drive away. You can also explore two countries for the price of one with a hop across to the landlocked micro-state of San Marino, which boasts spectacular views of the coast and mountains from its fortress atop Mount Titano. Get your passport stamped at the tourist office for the ultimate memento. Then retire back to camp with a glass of local Chianti and count yourself lucky that you picked a piece of Tuscany the tourists haven't found... yet.

COOL FACTOR Discover the side of Tuscany the tourists don't yet know about.

WHO'S IN Glampers, couples, groups (by request) – yes.

ON SITE 8 'wooden caravans' sleeping 2–4 people, plus 5 wooden 'tent houses' for couples. Washing area, internal showers, toilets and washbasins with hot water and external sinks for dish-washing and laundry. BBQ area. Private lake with swimming and sunbathing areas and fishing facilities. Also a small swimming pool for children. Mountain bike hire available. Complimentary holistic massage service. Outdoor games equipment. Free Wi-Fi. There is a common area with gas stoves for those staying in the tent houses.

OFF SITE The various forest trails emanating from the farm are ideal for hiking and cycling. Siena is less than an hour away to the southwest, Arezzo slightly closer to the southeast, and Florence is only an hour away to the north.

FOOD & DRINK The farm's organic garden offers a bounty of free fruit and veg, while the chicken coop offers freshly laid eggs. You can also buy the local products, including olive oil and wine from local vineyards. Chianti is the famous regional tipple – enjoy a glass or two on a tour at Val delle Corti (057 773 8215; valdellecorti.it). There's also a local market at Bucine (2.7km away) every Wednesday. Eating out, Osteria Cassia Vetus (055 917 2116; osteriacassiavetus.com) in Loro Ciuffenna serves delicious rustic 'slow food' cuisine that won't blow the budget.

GETTING THERE In the heart of Val d'Ambra, the site is just a few kilometres from the town of Bucine. Coming from Rome or Florence, it can be easily reached via the Valdarno exit on the A1 motorway, following the signs for Bucine.

PUBLIC TRANSPORT The site is easy to reach by train, alighting at nearby Bucine station, on the Florence-Arezzo line, just 10 minutes from the campsite.

OPEN Opened spring 2015 – see website for full details.

THE DAMAGE Tent house for 2 people: €25 per day (cleaning charge of €14; linen included). Caravan tent from €35 per day for 2 people, €50 for 4 (cleaning from €20–€25; linen, crockery, electricity, refrigerator included).

stella mare

Lacona, Isola d'Elba, Italy 0039 565 964 007 www.stellamare.it

Not a man to twiddle his thumbs, Napoleon Bonaparte spent his year-long exile on the island of Elba compiling crossword clues and planning a range of branded luxury goods. Of the former the only memorable example is the rather neat palindrome 'Able I was ere I saw Elba', and of the latter all that survives is the modish logo that adorns the gates of his villa. Sadly, the range of high heels and handbags for the WAGs of his favourite generals never made it to the production line because, after a year on the island, the little general decided to escape and go for one last fling at Waterloo.

Italy's third-largest island, Elba is a craggy volcanic outcrop off the Tuscan coast, covered in lush, almost tropical, vegetation. It's a little like the Caribbean but without the banana palms, and is a perfect getaway from the hustle of the mainland. The Emperor's villa on Elba is now a museum, and you can't help wondering, as you walk up the impressive cobbled drive, past bamboo stands, sprigs of wildflowers and the odd eucalyptus, quite why he wasn't happy just to put his feet up and settle down here. A more modest man would almost certainly have stayed put. Napoleon wasn't the first wanderer to land on Elba. Legend has it that Jason and the Argonauts stopped off for a bit of shore leave back in the mists of time. And you'll be quite happy to have made landfall here, too.

From the picturesque town of Portoferraio you can head up west into the volcanic highlands, east towards the hilltop town of Capoliveri or south over the shoulder of the hills towards Lacona, where you'll come across the quiet little bay that Camping Stella Mare overlooks.

The bay's water is only knee-deep (waist-deep if you happen to be as short as Napoleon) and perfect for kids to splash about in while you keep an eye on them from the narrow strip of beach. There's a host of bars and restaurants right by the water and, around the back of the site, there is also what is effectively a private beach (and one where it seems occasionally people 'forget' their swimming cozzies). This can be reached by some steep steps from the campsite.

When you're done sunning yourself, it's only a short stroll up to the campsite, where the pitches are alphabetised; the further you go beyond ABC, the higher you climb up the cliff. The 'A's are down near the beach, if you don't want to have to walk too far, and can't be bothered with the climb. By the time you get to the far reaches of the alphabet – particularly the 'S's and the 'U's – the pitches are raked into steep terraces overlooking the water and dotted with dinner-plate-sized cactus plants and all manner of different trees. Most of these pitches are inaccessible to caravans and campervans; you have to park your car up top and carry your gear down the steps to your pitch. But it's worth it.

And so if you were Napoleon, surely you'd be quite happy to retire from all that gallivanting about. You'd lie back, let Josephine feed you sculpted melon balls for breakfast on the sun terrace of your lavish villa, and think to yourself, 'yep, Elba will suit me just fine'.

COOL FACTOR Crumbly clifftop camping overlooking a quiet bay on a wonderful little island.

WHO'S IN Tents, campervans, caravans, dogs – yes.

ON SITE Terraced camping pitches overlooking the sea, all with electricity. Chalets available to rent. 3 shower blocks, which are fine and the showers hot. Limited dish-washing capacity. Bicycles for rent and walking excursions organised by the campsite in low season. A swimming pool and children's playground keep the little ones busy. There is a bar, restaurant-pizzeria and a shop selling essential groceries. Wi-Fi available.

OFF SITE There's a funky glass-bottomed boat run by Aquavision (3287 095 470; aquavision.it) with an underwater viewing gallery, which sails from either Portoferraio or Marciana Marina on 2-hour marine-life spotting trips. It's €15 for adults and €8 for kids under 12.

FOOD & DRINK Apart from a restaurant and snack bar on the site (and the restaurants by the beach), the best option is to head to Capoliveri, where Le Piccole Ore (335 126 7316) is an atmospheric bar with decent brunch items before 2.30pm. Most of the locals seem to eat at Ristorante Pizzeria da Michele (565 935 197), a standard pasta/pizza joint where you'll catch all the local gossip.

GETTING THERE Ferries to Elba run from Piombino up to 16 times each day and take an hour to reach Portoferraio. From there, follow the dual carriageway out of town towards Porto Azzurro. Turn right at the traffic lights, where the road heads for the hills and to Lacona. Once over the hills, turn right at Lacona and just past Camping Lacona you will find the turn-off for Stella Mare on the left.

OPEN End April–end October.

THE DAMAGE Depending on the season it's €9.50–€15 per adult, €5–€10 per child (2–9 years) and €9.50–€19 for a tent and €11–€26 for a campervan.

il falcone

Vallonganino 2/A, 050203 Civitella del Lago Baschi, Italy 0039 744 950 249 www.campingilfalcone.com

Some people think that Umbria hasn't got the same good looks or popularity as its flashier Tuscan cousin, but its rolling hills and scattered lakes do have one clear advantage over what's rightly known as Chiantishire – you won't find hordes of braying toffs unloading hampers of champers from the boots of their Chelsea tractors out here. You're more likely to find some crumple-faced old farmer humping crates of olive oil out of the back of a battered Fiat, while the silence is broken only by the chirrup of birds, the gentle stir of olive leaves and poppies nodding their heads in the breeze.

At Camping Il Falcone you get the olives and poppies, but it would be simply unfair to describe owner Carlo Valeri as a crumple-faced old farmer. He's far too young and chipper. Mind you, he does harvest the olives from the trees that are planted along the terraced rows of the campsite, though he claims there's only enough of the resulting oil for 'family'.

The site at Il Falcone is a lasso-shaped slice of hill, terraced between youngish olive trees and dotted with crimson poppies. Caravans and campervans are mainly confined to the outer reaches of the site, leaving the steep terraces for the canvas crew. You have to ditch your wheels at the top and clamber down the hill with your gear to pick a pitch on grass as thick as sprigs of spring onion. If you choose the left-hand side of the site, there are sumptuous views down to the lake and across to the village of Civitella del Lago; one of those ancient shadowy villages

populated by nothing but old folk and kittens.

If you wander over to the village and look west over the Lago di Corbara you can just make out, through the heat haze, the outline of another hilltop community – Orvieto. It's a larger version of Civitella del Lago, but houses one of the most visually stunning of Italy's many cathedrals. In candy stripes of grey and white stone, the massive duomo and its ornate mosaic front look good enough to eat. Inside is that marvellous church smell of old pew and cold stone mingling with centuries of burnt incense and evaporated candle wax.

Back at Il Falcone, you might – as you sip your olive-garnished martini – wonder about the name. The image of the falcon adorns the walls of the village and there's a weather-washed old stone falcon at one of the village's viewing points over the surrounding countryside. What does it all mean? Well, this mountainous region was once a medieval hunting ground. While our Norman ancestors were busy breeding racing pigeons and stick-thin whippets, the Italians were pulling on long leather gloves and feeding bits of minced-up field mouse to beaky birds of prey. You're unlikely to see any now, though, as the locals have taken to the more sedate pursuits of growing olives and raising kittens. As evening falls and the suns sets directly behind the village, sinking through the smoke from barbecue fires, you'll just spot little geckos darting around your feet, looking for a warm rock for the night, and thanking their lucky stars that all the hungry falcons have gone.

COOL FACTOR Pitches in among poppies and olive trees, with views of the lake and a medieval hilltop village.

WHO'S IN Tents, campervan, caravans, dogs (on a lead) – yes.

ON SITE Smaller tent-only terraced pitches near reception, large tent-only pitches higher up on the left-hand side with spectacular views. The flat pitches near the bottom are for caravans and campers (though lacking in views). Olive trees and some oaks see to it that there is a variety of shady and sunny spots, though motorhomes might have trouble to find a suitable spot among the low olive trees. There is one well-maintained block with good showers (3 each in the men's and women's), plus separate clothes- and dish-washing areas. The site has a kidney-bean-shaped, non-chloride swimming pool. There are several stone BBQ pits available to use. Wi-Fi available but not at every pitch.

OFF SITE Just 30 miles down the A1 at Bomarzo is the Parco dei Mostri (Monster Park; parcodeimostri.com), a weird 16th-century collection of stone monsters and woody groves set in a 'sacred wood', aka the grounds of an old estate. For a little luxury, brush off your plummiest wine-tasting phrases by sampling some bottles of Orvieto Classico, the local tipple, which dates back to the time of the Etruscans. It's available in most places, especially Orvieto itself. Quaff a glass or 2, and practise saying 'Mmmm, it's as lively as a wet spaniel'.

FOOD & DRINK There's a tiny onsite bar (but with really cold beer), along with a small shop where you can buy wine grown by the campsite's neighbour, Barberani – a real treat. Last year Carlo also bought a small pizza oven

so you can order fresh pizza for lunch served directly to your pitch, provided you remember to order the night before. In Civitella, Mangia e Bevi (744 950 432) does great pizza too, and – in the same street and run by the same people – the renowned local restaurant Trippini's (744 95 0316; trippini.net) serves up excellent local cuisine. In Montecchio you will find La Locanda (744 951 017; lalocandadacrispinomontecchio.it) – for top food and fair prices – or head to Orvieto to indulge at Maurizio's (763 341 114; ristorante-maurizio.com), just by the Duomo, which serves a great 'taster' menu for €30 – Umbrian cured meats and entrecôte steak cooked with Sagrantino wine. For coffee and snacks try Café Barrique (763 340 455).

GETTING THERE Come off the A1 between Florence and Rome and, just past Orvieto, take the SS448 towards Todi. After approximately 5km turn right up the SP90 towards Civitella del Lago. As you approach the village, veer right and follow the road round the hill (towards Melezolle). The site is signposted to your right.

PUBLIC TRANSPORT A bus from Orvieto makes it here once a day, but the owners will pick you up from Montecchio if you're staying longer than 3 days.

OPEN Early April–late September.

THE DAMAGE Adults and children from 10 years upwards are €5.40–€8, children 3–10 years €4.40–€6.60. A medium tent is €6.20–€9.50 and a car is €2.40–€3.10. Higher prices apply in July and August. Free hot showers plus free electricity and running water at every pitch.

il collaccio

06047 Preci, Perugia, Italy 0039 743 939 005 www.ilcollaccio.com

Hidden deep in the valleys of the Umbrian hills, where the villages are so out of the way and ancient that you half expect a Roman legionnaire to come marching up the road and hail you in the name of Caesar, this agriturismo site lies across the hills from the pointy little village of Preci and keeps a wary eye up the valley for the distant approach of Caesar's renegade legions.

Like a number of Italian agriturismi, this is a complex combining a small family-owned truffle farm with a modest hotel, a pool, some basic chalets and cabins, and plenty of terraces for campers, caravans and tents. To be honest, the tents are in the minority. However, the site is so steep that, once you're settled into your little terraced bolthole, you can quite easily forget about everybody else and just enjoy the peace and quiet. The swimming pool is stunning and has fabulous views; there is a decent restaurant on site; and there are lots of activities too, ranging from tennis and volleyball to table tennis and pétanque. There's even a five-a-side football pitch if you can raise a team. And being the organized agriturismo it is, the folk at Il Collaccio can also organise guided hikes, painting classes and a shuttle bus to the major sights of the national park, among other things.

The site is right on the doorstep of the Parco Nazionale Monti Sibillini, which is slap-bang in the middle of Umbria's heavily wooded gorges and some fairly serious Appenine mountains. At just under 2,500 metres the highest of these, Monte Vettore, commands a bit of respect and certainly isn't something you should undertake wearing a pair of trainers and a mac that folds up into its own little pocket. You can get a sense of the scale of things by taking the road up from Visso beyond the tree line and on to a broad, shallow plateau of rocky meadow, at the end of which the town of Castelluccio pricks the skyline. Carry on over the ridge and there's a 1,500-metre-high mountain pass on Vettore's southern flank that eventually brings you back in a loop to Preci, via the comely town of Norcia. It's a great little taster menu of the à la carte delights that Umbria has to offer.

If it's Italian heritage that you're after, then you can always call in at the medieval town of Spoleto, whose cathedral is worth the trip alone, built around the 12th century and with a campanile constructed from Roman remains. It's a mishmash of styles, cool and white inside, with some wonderfully ornate little chapels. Spoleto itself is a more workaday place than some of the more touristy spots around and, other than the narrow, twisty cobbled streets leading up to the duomo, is not the prettiest place; but it has an authentic, lived-in air.

From the time of Caesar right through to the Allied campaign up the spine of Italy in 1944, the hilltowns of this part of Umbria have seen some action. Thankfully, the locals are far from defensive and you'll get a cheery wave from the Baldoni family at Il Collaccio when you arrive. And, if you're lucky, they might even treat you to a truffle.

COOL FACTOR Real off-the-beaten-track Umbrian camping with the Baldoni family.

WHO'S IN Tents, campervans, caravans – yes. Dogs – no.

ON SITE Around 100 pitches over 10 hectares of flat, green terraces with stunning mountain views. All have electrical hook-ups, some netted shade. Chalets also available to rent. The facilities are a little outdoorsy, but fairly good and well looked after. There is disabled access. The showers are fine and hot and there are washing machines at €4 a pop; 2 swimming pools are available for campers to use. They also run courses if you are so inclined; you can put your hand to anything, from cookery and painting to extreme sports or photography with award-winning photographer David Noton.

OFF SITE Try a spot of mule-riding with La Mulattiera (339 451 3189; lamulattiera.it). They're based in Norcia and run various trips in the Sibillini National Park, following ancient tracks and pathways.

FOOD & DRINK There's a decent restaurant, Al Porcello Felice ('The Happy Pig'), onsite, which serves good river-caught trout as well as pasta and wood-oven pizza, and a small shop with very basic provisions. The village of Preci is not much good for eateries. If you want to dine out, head up the road to Visso for a wider range of cafés and bars, of which you could try La Filanda (0737 972 027; lafilanda-visso.com).

GETTING THERE Heading south from Perugia on the SS3 road, take the SS685 just before Spoleto and then veer back north on the SS209 towards Visso. Just before Pontechiusita, turn right towards Preci. Just before the village, turn left up the hill and follow the signs for a mile or so (2km) over the undulating roads.

OPEN All year.

THE DAMAGE Depending on the season, rates are €6–€9.50 per adult and €3–€6 for children aged 3–12 years. A tent is €6–€9.50.

kokopelli camping

Contrada Garifoli, Serramonacesca, Pescara 65025, Abruzzo, Italy 0039 3334 636 075 www.kokopellicamping.co.uk

As far away from the rat race as you can get, the green mountain slopes of the Majella National Park, snow-clad during winter, rise and fall around their most central peak, the towering Monte Amaro. This natural adventure playground, webbed with 500 kilometres of hiking trails and boasting everything from enchanting waterfalls to mysterious caves, is a surprisingly unadulterated place. Here, in central Italy, tourists are too busy running to the coast or crowding into Rome to stop and wonder at the vast natural landscape of Majella, leaving a quiet and majestic wilderness, the perfect spot for a campsite.

Cue Jacqui and Kevin, adventure couple supreme, who have scaled the peaks, cycled the switchbacks and covered the ground of this area almost every day since they bought a plot of land on the park's northeasterly tip. Not content with exploring the Abruzzo, they have now put thought and attention into creating their ideal campsite so the countryside can be shared with the rest of us. The outcome of their hard work is magnificent; an authentic rural campsite in scenic Italian hills.

In keeping with the couple's self-sufficient, minimal-impact lifestyle, Kokopelli Camping is a simple and easy-going site with no designated pitches or electrical hook-ups. There's a distinctly laid-back feel to the place. Even their tents-only policy is suitably loose, with certain campervans – so long as they are small and cool enough – permitted. But the casual atmosphere masks the diligence and organisation that keeps the campsite in tip-top condition. Modern sanitary facilities, with showers, toilets, basins, hairdryers and power points, are clean and well-kept, while a communal barn area offers cooking and dining, as well as plenty of games to play on a rainy day. It is here that you can mingle with other campers or, on a fine summer's day, hang out on the sun-kissed tiles of the terrace, where barbecues provide the perfect excuse to kick back and enjoy some good food.

When it comes to sourcing the tasty local bounty you can grab some herbs and vegetables from the campsite's own patch or head to the butchers in Serramonacesca, a vibrant little village two kilometres from the site. Serramonacesca has a tiny cluster of shops, bars and restaurants, and a road leading out to a white stone abbey that dates back to 1080. From its centre, follow the winding road into the natural wilderness of Majella National Park, home to wolves, bears and birds of prey. Half an hour's drive the other way leads you to the pristine Adriatic Coast. Both provide a myriad of attractions and Kevin and Jacqui can provide plenty of local insight into where is good.

Kokopelli Camping is in a stunning location and is about encouraging people to explore the surrounding landscape. But it's the welcoming atmosphere of the site itself that sustains it year after year. Tucking yourself beneath the olive groves at Kokopelli offers plenty more than just a good base for resting your head.

COOL FACTOR Rural simplicity amid some of Italy's most stunning landscapes.

WHO'S IN Glamping and tents only – although they make the occasional exception for 'small, groovy campervans'.

ON SITE A tent-only site with a maximum of 40 people at any one time. Bell tents and a VW campervan are also available for hire. There are no marked pitches, intrusive lighting or electrical hook-ups. The campsite works on a shared communal basis whereby all equipment (pots, pans, crockery, cookers, BBQs – just about anything to do with camping life) is available for all to use. In a barn space there are fridge-freezers, a toaster, kettle, games and an extensive library of guidebooks and novels. A large sun terrace overlooks the mountains, with BBQs, parasols, pergolas and sun loungers – it's a fantastic place to relax. The campsite grows its own vegetables and herbs, which campers can pick as they wish, dropping a little money into the honesty box. They also supply their own organic olive oil and jams and have a local supplier of superb organic wines. Ablution facilities are clean and modern, with showers, basins, hairdryers and toilets. There are phone-charging points, dish-washing and laundry facilities. Mountain bikes can be hired to use.

OFF SITE The site is situated on the edge of Serramonacesca, a rustic village with an ancient abbey, and tucked away in a little valley within the foothills of the Majella National Park (0864 25701; parcomajella.it). Abruzzo is a relatively unknown region in south-central Italy that is well off the tourist trail, making it perfect for those wanting a little seclusion. The Abruzzo region stretches from the highest peaks of the Apennine Mountains (just under 3,000m) all the way to the Adriatic Sea (a 30-minute drive), and campers will find excellent hiking trails, mountain biking, road cycling, rock climbing, water sports and more. Jacqui and Kevin first moved to the area for the adventure activities and know the place extremely well, and they can offer plenty of guidance on how to get involved in outdoor sports; they also have a stack of maps and guides in the barn, along with their own homemade book.

FOOD & DRINK The local village of Serramonacesca, 2km away, has a butcher's and a couple of bars and restaurants. Ristorante Borgo Nuovo (085 859861) is in the centre of the village, while Villa Dei Monaci is just out of the main settlement next to the old abbey (085 859761).

GETTING THERE The site is about a 45-minute drive from Pescara. Follow the SS5 west, past Chieti and, at Ticchione, make a left into the mountains, following the road through Pozzo, then Manoppello, until you reach Serramonacesca.

PUBLIC TRANSPORT The closest train and coach stations are Chieti (a 20-minute drive from Kokopelli) and Pescara (40-minutes), both with excellent links to Rome.

OPEN All year.

THE DAMAGE Per person, per night: adults €10, children €6, under 4 yrs free; family of 4 €32 per night or €200 per week; couples €20 per night or €125 per week. Bell tents or Rosemary the Campervan €16 per person per night for adults.

riva di ugento

Litoranea Gallipoli, S.M. di Leuca 73059 Ugento, Lecce, Italy 0039 833 933 600 www.rivadiugento.it

Riva di Ugento is less of a campsite, more of a *gigantissimo* camping village. Nestled away from the peacock-blue Ionian sea in 79 acres of pine woods and Mediterranean scrub, it's so big you may feel the urge to pick up a map at reception and even perhaps make use of that boy scout's compass. But don't let that put you off; the fact that the site is so roomy means there's plenty of space for all, with many a cone-studded lane to jog down and dunes and woodland areas that are perfect for family treasure hunts. Visit the playground after a scrumptious breakfast in the yurt-style cafeteria, or hire bikes and go cruising along the lanes. Another idea is to hire a catamaran or kayak; the shallow water suits all ages and the powder-fine beach goes on forever.

The minimarket here spills over with fresh local farm produce, so there's no need to worry about finding good, healthy ingredients for picnics and campfire suppers. There's also handy internet access and Wi-Fi, and in the evening the restaurant is a cheerful chaos of bambinos and swiftly devoured pizzas.

Outside they show films for the kids every night, which is great for them and a boon for you if you want a little me-time at the end of a hard day's family holiday. In short, this wooded haven is the kind of place you can really kick back and breathe in the rugged air without worrying too much about anything – the site might be big enough for your kids to get a bit lost sometimes, but it's small enough for them to find their way back again.

COOL FACTOR With its twisting pine woods, beautiful rugged beach and dunes, there's endless scope for R&R.

WHO'S IN Tents, caravans, campervans, kids and beach lovers – yes. Dogs – no.

ON SITE Pitches are about 100m² each; those on the dunes (near the beach) are smaller. There are plenty of onsite facilities: a newsagent, first aid, supermarket, swimming pool, launderette, kids' playground, tennis courts, BBQ pits, internet and Wi-Fi, bikes for hire, restaurant, games room, outdoor cinema, water sports and boutique – and, of course, that long sandy beach.

OFF SITE The old town of Gallipoli is 25km away and is well worth a visit. If you're driving south you can't miss a visit to Lecce – a picturesque town crammed with wedding-cake-style Baroque buildings and moody, deserted piazzas – that seems to have leapt from the lens of a Merchant Ivory film. Wander down the narrow alleyways, passing mouth-watering *gelateries*, shadowy brasseries and fine-art shops, with children scampering here, there and everywhere in the shadows of shuttered townhouses.

FOOD & DRINK There's a nice restaurant on site, with a great selection of pizzas and pasta dishes, not to mention the supermarket, which encourages self-catering under the stars. But for more foodie options try Lecce or the neighbouring village of Ugento.

GETTING THERE If you're heading south, take the E55 to Lecce, then follow the signs to Gallipoli and Ugento. In Ugento just follow the signs to the site.

PUBLIC TRANSPORT There is a train station in Ugento with regular trains running from Lecce. The local bus route also runs from here.

OPEN Early May–end of October.

THE DAMAGE 2 people, a tent and child (optional) will cost €21–€47, depending on the season.

camp liza

Vodenca 4, 5230 Bovec, Slovenia 0038 653 896 370 www.camp-liza.com

If you're planning on pitching at Slovenia's Camp Liza it might pay to bring along your personal kayak. With so many others lying around, you might feel a bit left out without one. The site offers access to two rivers: the emerald-green Soča and the clear, wild Koritnica, making it a serious boon for all aqua aficionados.

Surrounded by the thrusting peaks and lush pastures of the Bovec valley, it is a large, laid-back site. Groups are usually directed to the lower terrace, next to the burbling Soča; families gather in the central area, while independent tenters head to the furthest field to strum guitars, sip cold beers and break out the barbie. The general atmopshere is one of live and let live, a place where the super active outdoorsmen are just as welcome as their nonchalant neighbours lazing idly in the sun.

Nearby Bovec is tiny, but it's 800 years old and one of the area's key centres for adventure sports. This means not just kayaking but mountain biking, canyoning, white-water rafting and even skiing in winter. Bovec also has an array of cafés, shops and restaurants, as well as a daily dairy market and a helpful tourist office. From here you can get up to the gorgeous Julian Alps (watch out for the windy roads!) and the attractive Triglav National Park.

Yep, Camp Liza, with its wonderful access to so much natural beauty and a fantastically relaxed ambience, is a truly inspiring place to be. Kayak or no kayak.

COOL FACTOR Attractive, friendly site on the banks of the Soča that's perfect for water babies.

WHO'S IN Tents, campervans, caravans, dogs and pets – yes.

ON SITE Facilities are a little bit lacking – there are toilets, hot showers and disabled facilities, but they're limited. There's a children's playground and a washing machine and dryer. There is also a decent onsite restaurant.

OFF SITE You can rent bikes for cycling tours around Bovec and you can organise white-water activities like canyoning, kayaking and rafting at reception. You can also play beach volleyball or tennis at Črna Ovca, a sporty hangout by day and top party spot by night. If you're still not tired, you can head off for a round of golf; there's a course 5km from the site.

FOOD & DRINK The onsite Liza restaurant offers a variety of typical dishes alongside more well-known global grub. However, it's only open during May–September. Offsite, the nearest eating spot is Martinov Hram (5388 6214; martinov-hram.si), on the way to Bovec, which serves traditional Slovenian fare. Bovec itself (just over 2km away) has several cafés and restaurants, including the central Kavarna 1920, a very popular coffee shop among locals and tourists alike, and the Gostilna pod Lipco grill (5389 6280).

GETTING THERE From Klagenfurt (Austria), take the A2/E55 towards Villach, then the 83, turning left past Hart on to the 109 towards Slovenia. Across the border, take the 201 to Kranjska Gora, turning right on to the 206. Follow the 206 to Bovec, then follow the signs to Camp Liza. From Ljubljana, take the E61/A2 north, past Bled, merging on to the 201 to Kranjska Gora. Take a right at Kranjska Gora on to the 206, which brings you past the town of Soča and directly to Bovec. Follow the signs for Camp Liza.

OPEN All year.

THE DAMAGE 2 adults plus a tent €19–€24; children 7-14 years €6.95–€9.35 per night; children 6–7 years €6–€7.20.

kamp koren

Ladra 1B, 5222 Kobarid, Slovenia 0038 653 891 311 www.kamp-koren.si

You can't go far in northwestern Slovenia without running into the Soča: this enchanting, 136-km-long aquamarine artery snakes from its source in the soaring Julian Alps, through the Triglav National Park and in northern Italy before finally splashing into the Adriatic. Situated along the Soča's banks, not far from the quaint historical town of Kobarid, lies Kamp Koren. Vast yet chilled, the site is overseen by the passionate Lidija Koren, whose penchant for responding to the needs of camping folk seems endless.

Lidija's 'baby' was born two decades ago. It was originally started in partnership with her family, though she has been running (and expanding) it solo for the last 10 years. Having developed step by step, the site is subtly divided into sections and is deceptively sprawling. Past the wooden reception, the main camping area caters chiefly for caravans and larger family tents, but skirt left up the bank and you'll find a charming wooded area made up of trees, fields, terraces and private camping pitches, all interconnected by natural walkways and wooden bridges. In similarly subtle fashion, the site has incorporated an impressive array of features and facilities: an 8-metre climbing wall (plus a smaller one for little kids), volleyball court, boules pitch and viewing benches (cheekily ensconced in the wooded river bank) and, last but not least, separate loo blocks for the camping area.

Once you've snuggled into one of Koren's cosy camping alcoves you can start getting to know the local area. The Soča valley, an important trading route for many centuries and the site of some significant World War I action, is today an outdoor enthusiast's dream. To get an early taste, hike to the Kozjak waterfall (half an hour away), tackle nearby peaks like Krasji Vrh or Krn (both solid three- to four-hour hikes) or hire a mountain bike and burn some rubber through the forest. Nearby Kobarid is famous for the decisive battle between the Central Powers and the fascists in 1917, a scene immortalised by Hemingway in *A Farewell To Arms*. Today it's a small but pleasant historic town with a smattering of shops and cafés and a world-class museum on Slovenia's role in the First World War as well as several places to arrange adventure sports. History buffs will enjoy the local history trail: a five-hour walk that takes in Roman archeological sites, waterfalls and World War I trenches. It's easy, too, to arrange trips via Kamp Koren, since the site offers tailored tours for small groups exploring off-the-beaten-track spots. The site can also arrange activities including mountaineering, climbing and paragliding plus, of course, river-based shenanigans, such as kayaking and rafting.

Proactive as you might be, however, be warned that you may not get past reception, which is a marvel of hospitality, with charming Slovenian women cheerfully handing out everything from great coffee and beer to local information and internet passwords. They can even order you a kebab from the local takeaway if you can't be bothered to cook – now that's Cool Camping.

COOL FACTOR A relaxed Soča valley site that arranges everything from sports activities to kebab delivery.

WHO'S IN Tents, campervans, caravans, dogs – yes.

ON SITE Hot, free, modern showers, spotless toilets, organic food and Wi-Fi at reception. The site also has play facilities for kids and arranges tours and trips. There are a couple of climbing walls on site (plus an instructor daily through summer), as well as volleyball, table tennis and boules. There is an adventure park next door. Bike hire and guided horse rides can also be arranged.

OFF SITE For family kayaking and rafting try Positive Sport in Kobarid (4065 44 75; positive-sport.com). For high-octane fun, the Adrenaline Club in Drežnica (5384 86 10; drustvo-adrenalin.si) can arrange tandem-paragliding for you. Visit the elaborate and world-renowned Postojna Caves 70km away (5700 01 00; postojnska-jama.si). An hour's drive from the site will bring you to one of Slovenia's best-known (red) wine regions, the Goriška Brda. The main town, Dobrovo, has a castle and a stone-walled enoteca selling samples, plus tasty regional meats and cheeses.

FOOD & DRINK The onsite shop has a good range of organic products and you'll also find several places to eat in the centre of Kobarid (a 15-minute walk), as well as above-average Italian 'slow food' at Hiša Franko (5389 41 20; hisafranko.com), in the village of Staro Selo, less than 5km from the campsite.

GETTING THERE From Ljubljana take the A1, turning off on to the 102 and following it through logatec, Idrija, Tolmin and Kobarid. From Kobarid, follow the signs for Kamp Koren. From Klagenfurt (Austria), take the A2/E55 towards Villach, then follow the 83, turning left past Hart on to the 109 towards the border. On the Slovenian side of the border take the 201 to Kranjska Gora, turning right on to the 206. Follow the 206 to Bovec (unless you are in a caravan or mobile home, in which case take the 203 directly), then merge on to the 203 to Kobarid. From here you will begin to see signs for Kamp Koren.

OPEN All year.

THE DAMAGE €11–€12.50 per adult, children aged 7–12 €5.50–€6.25, kids 0–7 are free. Dogs €2. Electricity €4.

camping menina

Varpolje 105, SI-3332, Rečica ob Savinji, Slovenia 0038 640 525 266 www.campingmenina.com

'Welcome', says the laminated sign pinned to the door of the wooden reception. 'If we're not present you can find us in bar… just find nice spot for you and see you later…'

The sign says a lot about Camping Menina. It tells you that the site is laid-back and it suggests that the owners – Jurij and Katja – are open-minded, trusting and probably very busy. And it reveals a beautiful truth – that this is a campsite with a bar.

Indeed, Menina buzzes in the way a campsite should. It's a wonderfully sprawling place that has developed slowly and organically in a section of natural forest within Slovenia's striking Upper Savinja Valley. Like the region, Menina has retained much of its sylvan charm. Branches flutter flirtatiously in the valley breezes, dapples of sunlight dance on the grassy floor and a silver brook tinkles merrily by. It's the kind of scene that makes you reach immediately for your acoustic guitar.

Though it's divided vaguely into sections – a tipi camp (complete with friendly ponies in an adjacent meadow) lies in one area, a row of comfortable wooden cabins in another – visitors generally do, as the sign says, find a spot. There are plenty of options too – with 180 spots in total, Menina tends to have room for everyone, though the site doesn't feel as big as that figure might suggest, due to the haphazard layout.

Menina prides itself on being a thoroughly sociable place. There's a nice, natural lake to gather around instead of a formal swimming pool; an extensive outdoor playground close to the bar/ restaurant so you can grab a coffee and chat while keeping an eye on the kids; and the staff take a spontaneous approach to organising everything, from discos and concerts to guided tours and excursions. In the evenings, people hang out at the bar/restaurant, taking advantage of the very decent food or just sipping a cold beer from the bar. This attitude engenders a broad demographic – everyone from kids and teens to young families and older folk feel comfortable here, which all makes for a friendly ambience.

As well as tents, you'll notice an abundance of canoes, kayaks, bicycles and climbing gear lying around. And indeed the site is perfectly placed to explore not only the gorgeous Upper Savinja Valley, but also the Kamnik-Savinja Alps and the nearby Logarska Dolina (Logarska Valley). The Upper Savinja Valley is in total over 35 kilometres long and, as well as the Savinja, boasts the Dreta river. Unsurprisingly, then, swimming and kayaking are popular here and, since it tends to rain at least once a week in the valley, rafting is, too. If you are an enthusiastic hiker you'll love the surrounding mountains, which offer a multitude of paths and mountain-biking treks, some including overnight stays in huts. The site can arrange tours and supply maps, and it also caters for more extreme interests, such as canyoning and paragliding.

All in all, though, the feel-good idyll of the site makes it a hard place to leave. You may just want to hang around and make the most of the location – and for that we wouldn't blame you at all.

COOL FACTOR Buzzing site set in a beautiful natural valley.

WHO'S IN Everyone! Campervans, caravans, tents, families, kids, dogs...

ON SITE There are 200 camping pitches (all with electricity) and a range of family huts and lodges. 4 new toilet blocks have been built in recent years, bringing the sanitary facilities up to date. The children's playground is comprehensive and an adrenaline park provides everything else you can imagine to wear them out – zip lines, climbing nets and tree-top walkways. The plethora of other activities includes rafting, canyoning and cycling, with bikes for hire at reception. The reception and bar serve cold beer and hot food. Campfires are permitted at some pitches.

OFF SITE Topolšica, 15km away (3896 3100; terme-topolsica. si) is a thermal resort with 5 pools (indoors and outdoors), toboggans and waterslides. The campsite can organise rafting, kayaking and canyoning in the Savinja valley with their local partner companies (4052 5266; savinjajezakon.com). An hour away, in Mežica, there's a mountain-bike park (2870 3060; mtbpark.com) with numerous trails and routes, including rides through mineral caves. Finally Slovenia's diminutive capital, Ljubljana, is just 80km away, and is a charming place, with a multitude of cool boutiques and hip coffee shops, and an array of historic sights.

FOOD & DRINK The onsite restaurant is open every night and serves meat, fish and vegetarian dishes. You can order fresh bread from reception and also buy salami, cheese, butter and jam. The nearest shop and bakery is just 300m from the site. For a culinary treat try Raduha (3838 40 00; raduha.com) 15km away in the village of Luče, which serves delightful local dishes under the 'slow food' banner.

GETTING THERE From Ljubljana take the road to Maribor. Around 55km from Ljubljana, turn left on to the Mozirje–Nazarje road. After about 3km take the road to Ljubno and follow the signs for Camping Menina.

OPEN Mid April–mid November.

THE DAMAGE Adults €9–€11; children €4–€7; pets €3; electricity €3–€6.

eco camping glavotok

Glavotok 4, 51500 Krk, Croatia 0038 551 867 880 www.kamp-glavotok.hr

When the lights are switched off at 11pm it can feel like you're in Dalmatian heaven at this campsite on the Croatian coast. All you can hear are the waves softly crashing against the grey stone sea walls of Krk island. All you can see are the twinkling lights on the island of Cres and the denser illuminations of Rijeka city on the Croatian mainland.

It hasn't always been so peaceful in Croatia. Various wars have affected the country's economy and, throughout history, numerous countries have jostled for a piece of this Adriatic jewel. Victims of the 1991–2001 Yugoslav Wars and the 1999 NATO bombing of Serbia are countrymen who have had to fight long and hard to reclaim their homeland.

Camp Glavotok's owner, Sanjin Barbalic, is one such man. It took him seven years, with the help of lawyers, to win back his campsite. Now back in the family, the restaurant is watched over by a portrait of great uncle Dr Anton Milohnic, who was accused of being a spy and shot on this spot back in 1945.

Sanjin's 18-year-old operation is a model Croatian campsite, and don't people know it? The best views, seen from pitches 263–280 and 327–334, are usually booked a year in advance. To bag one of these spots, aim for a June or late-August visit, or otherwise make do with one of the woodland pitches, a good way of shielding you from the growing number of mobile homes. Many of these seaside statics are actually set-up by the campsite itself, though, as completely furnished accommodation and family bungalows with the

appearance of traditional coastal houses. The main comfort, over and above the kitchen, sofas and TVs is surely the air conditioning – definitely a bonus in this neck of woods.

More like-minded souls who go for the pitch-up and peg-down option can cool off in other ways. Jump off the jetty, enroll in diving classes and swim your heart out. At night ask for extra ice in your cocktail while you laze at the beach-front bar, or head back into the trees for a quiet evening in. It's just you, your book and the softly crashing waves.

COOL FACTOR Croatian hospitality is generally welcoming and here it is as friendly as you could wish for.

WHO'S IN Tents, campervans, caravans, dogs – yes.

ON SITE Of the 333 pitches, 117 are used by permanent 'leaseholders'. There are also several new mobile homes (sleeping up to 5) for rent. Smart washing facilities. Hot showers, laundry/drying (24kn) and Wi-Fi (40kn per day). There is a playground, creative workshops, table tennis, basketball and beach volleyball, along with 'organised fun' such as zumba and aerobics, if that's your cup of tea. If you want to take it up a notch, try a diving course with the onsite dive school (51 869 289; correctdiving.com).

OFF SITE The Šotovento region on the island of Krk is made up of a cluster of small villages and hamlets linked with excellent walking and hiking trails that take in historic sights along the way – from the Franciscan monastery in Glavotok to the 9th-century Church of St. Krševan near the village of Milohnici. If walking is not your thing, the site takes in 500m of coastline with 3 crescent-shaped pebble beaches. All are safe for bathing and have a bustling local feel come lunchtime, when everyone arrives to take a dip.

FOOD & DRINK Pre-order the 3-hour slow-cooked octopus speciality from the onsite restaurant, which also offers pizza and has a TV showing football or films if it rains. In the evening enjoy cocktails in the beach bar. The bakery will supply you daily with freshly baked bread and cakes and a small shop has food (including vegetables) and newspapers.

GETTING THERE The island is connected to the mainland by a bridge, from which the road runs to the port of Rijeka, where it joins the main coast road. There are also daily ferries from the nearby islands of Rab and Cres.

PUBLIC TRANSPORT Regular buses travel from Trieste to Rijeka, and from Rijeka to Krk, then to Brzac, which is just over a 2km walk from the campsite. Expect to pay around 300kn for a taxi from Rijeka airport to Glavotok.

OPEN April–October.

THE DAMAGE 164kn–327kn per night for 2 adults with a car, depending on the time of year and the pitch. Dogs 19–31kn.

kamp straško

Zeleni put 7, 53291, Novalja, Pag, Croatia 0038 553 663 381 www.kampstrasko.com

Most of the year, the sheep on Pag Island outnumber the residents three to one. Until the summer, that is, when thousands of Croatians hit Novalja. Not called the Croatian Ibiza for nothing, Novalja's Zrce beach is home to three open-air dance venues, where the music never stops. Buses run regularly to and from the campsite, so dancing 24 hours a day, every day of the week, is a lure for many young campers.

This site isn't only great for party people however. The facilities for children are just as appealing and the vibe is surprisingly family focused. A kids' club will take yours off your hands whenever you need a siesta and there are numerous playgrounds and games rooms for kids to run amok in throughout the site. But if screaming children are the antithesis of your dream holiday, just decamp to the mile-long naturist section to skinny-dip in the silky seas in peace. New arrivals are driven around the site in a buggy so they can choose a spot. Front pitches under the pines offer great ocean views, but just be aware that they'll also amplify the early-morning clamour of beachside excitement. Anyone after greater privacy tends to park themselves near the entrance at the top left, under the ancient Dalmatian oaks.

The narrow sunbathing strip won't win this campsite any best-beach accolades, but you'll find you're not short of alternatives, since Pag boasts the longest coastline of all Croatia's Adriatic islands. The main thing is that you're guaranteed to find a truly varied clientele here – from frazzled ravers to frazzled parents and all the frazzled bits in between.

COOL FACTOR Something for all ages at this well-equipped, beachside campsite.

WHO'S IN Everyone! Tents, campervans, caravans, couples, families, nudists, pets – all welcome.

ON SITE Across the 140-acre site there are 400 pitches, each with electricity points, TV connections and Wi-Fi. There's also a bakery, supermarket, restaurants, bars, bike and scooter hire, souvenirs, camping gas, petrol, sports courts, mini-golf, 12 shower blocks and even a pet shower, plus everything you would expect of the ablution facilities, including baby-changing and disabled access. In tune with the Croatian penchant for naturism, there is also a dedicated nudist area.

OFF SITE The benefit of camping on an island is a host of beaches in every direction you go. A popular pastime for the tourist folk is to hire a banana boat or, for older kids, a jet-ski, but the best rewards come from finding the quieter spots. Head north along the finger-shaped island towards Lun and discover the sandy coves on the eastern, mainland-facing side. Its not a long journey, but leaves any crowds behind.

FOOD & DRINK Salty sheep's cheese is the local delicacy. For fish, spend an evening in a restaurant built like a boat at Straško's Starac i more ('The Old Man and the Sea'; Brac'e Radic'; 53 662 423).

GETTING THERE From Zadar drive over the Pag bridge 26km away from the motorway and keep going straight. Or, from the mainland, board a ferry at Prižna to connect to Žigljen on the island.

PUBLIC TRANSPORT From Zadar 3 buses run to the site every day (it's a 90-minute journey).

OPEN April–October.

THE DAMAGE Adults €4.50–€9.90; children (7–12 yrs) €4.10–€4.60 (but free in off season); pets €5–€9. Basic pitches €11–€35; premium pitches €10–€29.

pod maslinom

Na Komardi 23, 20234 Orašac, Croatia 0038 520 891 169 www.orasac.com

The Croatian word for 'sea' is *more*. Which seems apt when the sea is permanently glistening beside you on the 4,000-mile-long Dalmatian coast. The Adriatic Sea provides Croatia with its biggest income (from tourism, not from fishing). But before you imagine these shores to be a mecca of sandy beaches, a quick word in your ear: Croatia is a rather rocky, pebbly paradise.

Simply do as the natives do and throw down your beach towel on any spare bit of sea wall, concrete jetty or pebbly cove you can find. Such a free-for-all mentality means that everyone can get a spot at any time of day. If this sounds too far removed from your personal comfort zone, wait until you see the incredibly azure-crystal bays. Much of this coast epitomises the word 'picturesque', and sunning yourself under its craggy cliffs in the mid-30°C heat is a heavenly pastime that is hard to beat.

Just a little way north of the tourist honeypot of Dubrovnik is Autocamp Pod Maslinom, a hilltop campsite that has been a labour of love for the owner, Božo, who grew up in this village and could, by all accounts, have been a successful gardener. His conversion of an olive-tree jungle into an appealing landscaped, limestone-walled holiday ground is an enchanting find. Whatever size wheels you arrive on (bike, motorbike, car or bus) you can set up camp in the spacious privacy of the top, flat sections at Pod Maslinom. Down past the pristine washing blocks is a woody area that offers shade and sound-proofing from the traffic above. There's room for 250 guests here, but they usually only allow 30–35 tents or motorhomes in at any one time, so it never feels too crowded.

The limit on numbers means that the vibe feels inclusive and laid back. Inside a reception cabin, manned by the duty manager along with any number of village friends who happen to drop by, there are ice creams and drinks for sale. Follow the road until it ends at a viewing platform; it's a great spot to sit and idly watch the boats ferry people along their life paths in between the three small Elafiti islands opposite.

Most Croatian campsites are within a stone's throw of a beach. Here, that stone is falls almost vertically, with a steep hill to a cove accessed only along a stony ridge. Tiny tots will deem this hill to be nothing short of a mountain and pushing a pram up is not an option, unless you're super-fit. However, any efforts will be rewarded with a private beach and a bay to call your own. You can swim here knowing that, without any buildings nearby, the sea is as clean as clean can be.

Offsite, you'll want to check out Dubrovnik. It'll become glaringly obvious why it was once a vital port of call among the European glitterati and nobility. Modern campers on a budget will be equally fascinated by the city's Renaissance, Gothic and Baroque architectural mix, all framed by the shimmering ocean.

And, should you wish to see even more, then wend your way back to Split by ferry for a smashing view of Croatia's coastline.

COOL FACTOR The facilities, the view, the beach bar and the young owners win our vote.

WHO'S IN Tents, campervans, caravans, dogs – yes.

ON SITE 50 camping pitches beneath the olive trees. White-tiled constantly hot showers (8) and toilets (8) are regularly maintained by a resident cleaner. You won't find a cleaner loo anywhere else in Croatia. Plus, there's a washing machine (20kn), and they let you use the fridge, internet and cooking facilities for free.

OFF SITE A path through the pines leads you to 2 beaches and a small harbour. The campsite also arranges day-trips to the islands of Koloep, Lopud and Sipanfor a bargain 220kn per person including lunch and drinks. In the village, there is a food shop, doctor's surgery, post office and a school with a football/basketball court and playground that anyone can use. There is also a small but delightful botanical gardens.

FOOD & DRINK The great terraced beach bar, Hawaii, serves up grilled fish (50kn), sunset cocktails and the occasional weekend party. Its certainly the easiest place to go if you plan on having a drink or two a beach ball's throw from the main camping area. Treat yourself to a seafood dish in the small family-run restaurant Canosa in Trsteno (3km away); they even provide a free transfer for campsite guests.

GETTING THERE Dubrovnik is the nearest airport, an hour's drive away, but access is also easy from Split. Follow the scenic coastal road from Dubrovnik to Orašac; you'll see the campsite just next to the bus stop.

PUBLIC TRANSPORT From Dubrovnik airport catch 2 buses: one to the main bus station in Dubrovnik and, from there, the local bus to Orašac (lines number 12, 15, 22, 26, 35). The campsite is right by the bus stop in Orašac so you won't miss it once you arrive.

OPEN April–November.

THE DAMAGE Adults 31kn–40kn; teens (12–18 yrs) 20.50kn–31.50kn; children (3–12 yrs) 10kn–18kn; pets 2kn–12kn; tents 18kn–32kn; campervans 36kn–45kn, electricity 15kn–18kn.

dionysus camping

Dafnilas Bay Dassia, P.O. Box 185, Corfu, Greece 0030 2661 091 417 www.dionysuscamping.gr

In mythical days the final leg of Odysseus' journey found him shipwrecked on the peaceful island of the Phaeacians, where the kindly princess Nausicaa took him to her palace to hear his tale before letting him set sail on to the island of Ithaca. Nowadays, the island she took him to is commonly known as Corfu, but you can still find the same gentle hospitality there.

Later, Corfu became a major player in the region due to its handy location in the Mediterranean and, when you are ambling through the old town, you can feel the breath of history on your cheek. Corfu has seen a fair few tourists since the late sixties, but you can still catch a glimpse of the Greece of that era off the main drag, where all sorts of time-stands-still scenes greet you – from the crumbling, washing-strung piazza to octogenarians bedecked in black, clutching worry beads. Old-time Greece is never very far away.

Corfu means 'peaks' and Corfu's Old Town is sandwiched between two natural promontories, on which stand two mighty fortresses, strong enough to repel the aggression of five Ottoman sieges. If you get tired of drinking frappés in the stylish cafés or haggling over evil eyes and alabaster gods, there's a rich mix of options to take your interest. Whether it's water sports, hiking, museum-hopping or just basking on the beach, Corfu is a large island and you can easily lose yourself in the flower-filled meadows and secret, hidden coves, leaving the hustle and bustle of the resorts far behind you.

Around nine kilometres outside Corfu Town and a mere five minutes from chock-full Dassia beach is Dionysus Camping. If the name conjures up images of near-naked nymphs popping grapes into one another's mouths to the accompaniment of a lyre, you may perhaps be a little disappointed. But in every other sense, this serene spot, set in a tiered 400-year-old olive grove, more than justifies its evocative name.

The facilities at the campsite are excellent. There are two pristine shower blocks with hot water round the clock, a handsome bar overlooking a good-sized swimming pool, plus you have the choice of pitching your tent in the terraced meadows or – and these are terrific value for couples – taking one of Dionysus's 50 well-appointed Polynesian-style cabanas or tikis.

The site is run by Nikos, the warm and welcoming manager. A true Corfiot, he knows the island like the back of his hand. As well as having a wealth of printed info for your perusal, he can point you in the direction of the best beaches and charter a boat to take you up to the north of the island or pretty much anything else that your heart desires. During the busy months of July and August the site's bar and restaurant host traditional Greek dancers and are buzzing with a Babel of languages – a convivial atmosphere that is reminiscent of the Corfu hospitality of old.

But, unlike solo traveller Odysseus, be careful you don't find yourself on the back of a bike headed for a new life in Munich with a big bloke called Hans.

COOL FACTOR Warm hosts and a peaceful setting near lovely Corfu Old Town.

WHO'S IN Tents, campervans, caravans – yes.

ON SITE Facilities are good and include a communal cooking area, fridge, BBQ pits, internet and laundry facilities plus a mini-mart, bar/restaurant and Olympic-sized swimming pool. The beach nearby is a little on the rocky side but sandy Dassia beach is just a moped-ride away.

OFF SITE Experience your own odyssey on the Kalypso Star (266 104 6525), a glass-bottomed boat that runs tours each day and takes in the underwater delights of the island's diverse marine life.

FOOD & DRINK Restaurant Rouvas (266 103 1182) in Corfu's Old Town is a well-kept secret (the meatballs are life-affirming). The magical Starenio Bakery near the Town Hall Square is fab for afternoon coffee and croissants. For classic, romantic and al fresco dining, head to San Giacomo (266 103 0146) in Town Hall Square.

GETTING THERE From Corfu port follow the main coastal road (to the right) north; after 8km, at Tzavros junction, turn right. After just over 1km you'll find Dionysus.

PUBLIC TRANSPORT From Corfu airport take the city bus to San-Rocco square in town and change to the No7 blue bus.

OPEN Early April–late October.

THE DAMAGE Adult €5.60–€6.50; child (4–10 yrs) €3.10–€4; tent €4.10–€4.50, caravan €5–€5.90; campervan €7–€8; electricity €4.

tartaruga camping

Lithakiá, Zakynthos, Greece 0030 269 505 1967 www.tartaruga-camping.com

Zakynthos, or Zante as it's known locally, is one of the more emerald isles in the Ionian Sea. In times gone by it was called 'the Venice of the East' because of its buildings, which resemble something out of a Canaletto painting. Like many Greek islands its tenure has been mixed and colourful, running through Roman, Ottoman, Byzantine, Turkish and British rulers. The old town of Zante was reduced to rubble in the earthquake of 1953, but luckily the locals loved it enough to do a great restoration job, one that St Dionysios, the island's patron saint, would be justifiably proud of.

Every August the islanders hold a festival to celebrate their patron saint St Dionysios, a night-time event that sees the long-deceased, strangely preserved saint carried through the candle-lit streets snug in a glass cabinet — rather like an old-fashioned Popemobile. But, before you get stuck into Zakynthos' cultural highlights, you'll be needing to set up camp. If, on hearing Tartaruga Camping's pack of guard dogs heralding your arrival, you think Cerberus is at your heels, be reassured, you couldn't be further from Hades; in fact, you may have just happened upon the Elysian Fields.

Run by Veit and Anna Santner, Tartaruga boasts one of the best views of any campsite in Greece; you can gaze down from the giddy heights of their al fresco restaurant at the sea, unblemished but for the odd deserted island and occasional puttering fishing boat. Loggerhead turtles play their mating games in the turquoise waters beside the campsite. There's a floating platform to swim out to and wait on for the turtles to come, or use Veit's goggles and fins, which he leaves by the rocks for anyone to borrow. There are old diving shots from the seventies pasted on the walls of the basic eatery, which also doubles as a TV room. In summer, when the olive trees are crawling with children, there are weekly table-football tournaments, with ice cream for the lucky winners. Anna is a brilliant cook — if food is made with love, then Aphrodite has certainly taken up residence in her kitchen. The menu contains whatever Anna brings back from her daily visit to nearby butchers and fishermen and you can be sure there'll be plenty to get your taste buds going.

When it comes to putting up your tent, you have a considerable choice of pitches. You can try a spot in the shadow of pine trees, the light around you dappled like a Monet painting, or set up near the beach, where a fallen olive tree, bleached white by the sun, lies surrounded by sentinel rock sculptures that look as if they've been filched from the Tate Modern.

The mainland feels a long way away, even though you can see it just over the water. So, too, do over-harvested tourist traps like nearby Laganas. But here on the campsite, among the chattering of cicadas, the hypnotic scent of thyme and calm whispering of pine trees, you could easily have travelled back 30 years. Zakynthos or Zante, St Dionysios or St Dennis — whichever you prefer, Tartaruga Camping is a tenters' paradise. Come on in, the water's lovely.

COOL FACTOR Great food and arguably the best views of any campsite in Greece.

WHO'S IN Tents, campervans, caravans, dogs (by arrangement) – yes.

ON SITE Clean communal shower block, bakery, mini-mart, disabled toilet, al fresco restaurant, TV room, internet, laundry services, playground and, of course, the beach. You can play table football, go snorkelling, visit the peacocks or noodle about on the beach before you explore this idyllic island. You can see turtles in the spring/summer.

OFF SITE Let Golden Dolphin Tours (269 508 3248; goldendolphincruises.gr) take you to the Blue Caves and Shipwreck Beach, a heavenly strip of fine sand bordered by high cliffs and finished off with the wreck of an old boat.

FOOD & DRINK You may not want to leave Tartaruga after tasting Anna's cuisine, but the Village Inn, on the waterfront in Zakynthos Old Town, is good for traditional food.

GETTING THERE Zakynthos is the southernmost island in the Ionian Sea; head for Killini port to reach it by ferry. From Zakynthos town it's 13km to the site. Head for Keri – there's a sign for Tartaruga followed by a windy lane.

PUBLIC TRANSPORT There is a bus from Zakythos Town to the site twice a day. A taxi costs €15–€23.

OPEN April–end October; it is also possible to camp between November and March by arrangement.

THE DAMAGE Two adults sharing a tent can expect to pay €13.80–€16.50, depending on the season; children under 4 are free. Cars are charged €2.50–€3.

nicolas camping

Epidavros, Peloponnese, Greece 0030 2753 041 218 www.nicolasgikas.gr

Welcome to the Peloponnese, land of orange groves, myths and Heracles. If you need your fix of ruins and classic tales, this place has a higher concentration than anywhere else in Greece. It's spooky indeed going past the ruins of ancient Tiryns – the dreaded palace where Heracles had to return on completing each labour, only to be given another.

You'll see the sign for Tiryns as you head towards sleepy Epidavros. For most of the year, this water-lapped town is a somnolent tableau of old-timers flicking their worry beads at the end of the jetty. Then comes July and the population explodes with the fireworks of the annual festival of theatre, when culture vultures from across the globe come to witness the Aeschylus, Euripides and Sophocles performed Greek-style in the ancient theatre, which is among the best-preserved in Greece. Built in the 4th century BC, the theatre's acoustics are astonishing; actors can play to 15,000 people at a time and everyone can hear a pin drop, even from the very back.

A ten-minute wander from the town, through a shady grove, past a smaller theatre and along the beach, you'll find Nicolas Camping. Formerly an orange grove, its mulberry and orange trees provide plump natural arbours in a series of enchanting, sleepy hollows. And while the site might lack the sophistication of some campsites, Nicolas more than makes up for this with its luscious setting. How many campsites have you been to in which you can pluck a ripe orange from the leafy canopy then plop into a silk-calm bay a stone's throw away?

Nicolas is run by husband-and-wife team, Christina and Yiannis Gikas. Christina left the hubbub of Toronto to re-discover her Peloponnesian roots. Looking out through the palm-studded gardens, taking in the orange-scented air as you gaze at the nearby sea, it's easy to see why. She can organise visits to the theatre and diving trips for you.

If you fancy yourself as a bit of a Jacques Cousteau, there is plenty to explore scuba-style. Just down from the beach there are the remains of a sunken city, the victim of an earthquake and subsequent tsunami in AD 175. Follow the curve of the beach away from town, don your mask and weave past sea urchins lurking on the squat underwater ruins. You never know, you might just find something exciting; there are over 1,000 shipwrecks in the Aegean and Ionian waters, and potentially so much hidden treasure that most wrecks are off limits to commercial divers. If you need more than underwater entertainment, take yourself off to nearby Nafplio, a beautiful old town choking on Venetian architecture, bougainvillea and tamarind trees. Take your pick from half a dozen great restaurants, then work off the calories with a brisk walk up to the Palamidi fortress ruins and a refreshing dip in the sea on the other side of the hill. Nafplio has become something of a favourite with Athenian urbanites. If you spend an afternoon here you'll soon see why they like to keep it a secret from the package crowd.

COOL FACTOR The proximity to the beach (any closer and you'd be underwater).

WHO'S IN Tents, campervans, caravans, dogs (on a lead) – yes.

ON SITE There's a clean shower block, laundry facilities, chemical toilets, BBQ, mini-mart, Wi-Fi, 24-hour hot water, a small café and restaurant, fridge-freezers, a swimming pool and safe beach swimming. The campsite is 2.5km from the village centre and it's near to a bus stop.

OFF SITE Head for the theatre, the pretty harbour in town or drive to Nafplio for a taste of Aegean chic. The Epidive Center (275 304 1236; epidive.com) offers dives at all levels.

FOOD & DRINK The Mouria Restaurant (275 304 1218) next door is a favourite haunt of visiting actors, who sit beneath the mulberry tree practising lines between mouthfuls. The menu leans towards fresh seafood and dishes are delivered with a smile.

GETTING THERE If you're driving from Athens take the E94 motorway and drive via Argos and Nafplio. Then follow signs for Nea Epidavros.

PUBLIC TRANSPORT There are plenty of local buses to Epidavros from Nafplio and there is a stop 100m from the campsite entrance.

OPEN April–October.

THE DAMAGE Adults from €5.50; children (4–10 yrs) from €3.50. See website for full rates. A special Cool Camping discount is available for anyone who shows the owners a copy of this book!

camping areti

63081 Neos Marmaras, Sithonia, Chalkidiki, Greece 0030 2375 071 573 www.areti-campingandbungalows.gr

The charming little town of Neos Marmaras is kissed with blue waters and bobbing schooners. On Thursday mornings a market bubbles to life by the palm-studded wharf and it's easy to feel like one of the locals as you marvel doe-eyed at calamari and haggle over your pot of indigenous honey. It's interesting to think, as you gaze out at the distant wooded hills, that 2,500 years ago this was Alexander the Great country. Macedonian people are fiercely proud of this fact, too, so don't be surprised if their grasp of history is better than that of the average classics student. If your local hero once ruled half the world before he was 30, you'd probably be the same way.

Camping Areti, just 11km down the road, is sleepier than a drunken bouzouki player; the pace here is joyfully slow. Its spotless taverna is both welcoming and atmospheric, with locally caught fish sizzling away on the grill to the acoustic accompaniment of crickets and the Aegean waters lapping right near your table. On a clear morning the distant peak of Mount Olympus beckons you to breakfast with the gods. And if they could relocate, well they'd probably want to plant their trident in these pine-scented waters.

Areti sits among acres of mature eucalyptus trees and hibiscus-bordered pathways. You can throw up your tent in various locations. If you'd like to be near enough to the water to smell the salty air, then pitch up near the sea beside a sugar-sand beach, dramatically screened by gnarled olives. For the less watery inclined, head

to the back of the meadows for a little more privacy. If the heat becomes too much, try a night off in one of the Crusoe-style log cabins. There are about a dozen of them scattered across the site. Inside they're cosy and functional, with a kitchenette, separate double bedroom and WC, with an extra berth that could come in handy for a smaller person.

You'll find that Areti's minimarket is well provisioned, plus there's a wealth of amenities, including a kids' playground and tennis courts, as well as hidden recesses for cheeky romance and inviting lookout points with benches just begging to be sat on at sundown. If you are after a more physical challenge then why not swim to one of the three deserted islands across the cobalt turquoise-chequered bay. It's a fair old distance, but then it wouldn't be a challenge if it wasn't, would it?

Two and a half thousand years ago, a stubborn little collection of states known as Hellas were about to be disciplined by the Persian Empire. The attacking armada was stayed, albeit briefly, by the alleged sea monsters in the foaming reefs. These days it's a little safer to venture out into the sea. And, if you want to see more of the island life beloved of the locals, then talk to Giorgos, the softly spoken manager, about chartering an old schooner for the day to take you round the triple peninsulas.

Before you know it you'll be hailing everyone with a 'Yassas' and drinking ouzo like a local.

COOL FACTOR With its views, private beaches, distinct cuisine and charming, old-school management, you can't fault it.

WHO'S IN Tents, trailer tents, campervans, caravans and motorhomes – yes.

ON SITE The toilet block is kept immaculately clean. There's a minimarket, launderette, BBQ area, volleyball and tennis courts along with a decent kids' playground. Twin beaches are right on the doorstep and there is an onsite restaurant. Kayaks are available to borrow from the campsite free of charge.

OFF SITE Jet-ski, motorboat and windsurfing on demand at Lagomadra Beach, 15km from the campsite. The nearby Nireas Diving School (231 081 2813) can arrange local dives for the experienced or learning courses for those who want to take it up. Charter an old boat (it takes up to 30 people) plus a captain to take you on a trip around the triple peninsulas. It costs about €25 per person and food is included.

FOOD & DRINK Neos Marmaras has plenty of good places to eat. For freshly caught fish, head for the Bays Restaurant (237 507 1291; sithonian.gr) on the waterfront.

GETTING THERE From Thessaloniki head for the Sithonian Peninsula via Neo Modenia. Kassandra is the first peninsula; avoid this and push on to Sithonia, the second; 11km beyond the turn-off for Neo Marmaras you'll find the sign for Camping Areti. Follow the sign and you'll find the campsite nestled at the bottom of a pine-clad road.

PUBLIC TRANSPORT In Thessaloniki head for Chalkidiki bus station to catch a bus to the Sithonian Peninsula. Make sure you're headed for Sykia or Neo Marmaras and let the driver know where you're going so he can drop you off. If you end up in Neo Marmaras then you'll have to get a cab to the campsite (10 minutes).

OPEN Early May–early October.

THE DAMAGE €16.20–€18 per pitch per night, €8.10–€9 per adult, €4–€4.50 per child, electricity €4. Wooden family cottages (sleeping 4) will cost you €60–€80 and stone built bungalows (sleeping 4) cost from €100–€150.

camping antiparos

Antiparos, Cyclades Islands, Greece 00 30 2284 061 221 www.camping-antiparos.gr

Clambering off the boat in the whitewashed harbour of this diminutive Aegean jewel you can hardly believe your eyes. Everything you see is Greeker than Greek: old fishermen with crinkly faces and Charles Bronson eyes, cats stretching in the shadows, fruit spilling from colourful crates, plus an azure sky pure enough to melt the heart of a Mississippi lifer. Welcome to Antiparos, possibly Greece's best-kept secret.

It would be breaking a promise to Theo Kalygros, the son of the owner of Camping Antiparos, to disclose who's been quietly buying up land here in order to hide away from the paps. But let's just say that Antiparos has attracted its own pantheon of A-list deities.

The central, pedestrian-only street is a curious mix of tavernas, stylish cafés, homemade ice cream parlours and boutiques offering anything from jewellery made just for you to – curiously – fairies. There's no explaining it, but these now-you-see-them-now-you-don't little winged people pop up on every bougainvillea-clad corner.

Wandering the ruins of the old castle, which hug the town's backstreets, you get a chance to soak up the history of the island which, back in the 15th century, fell prey to pirates, who used it as a base. The locals built a near-impregnable squat castle to keep them out – yes, even Cap'n Jack Sparrow is banned. Defending themselves against a more contemporary nemesis during World War II, Antiparians were among the first Greeks to pledge themselves to the cause of the Resistance, and

there's still a sense of proud independence today.

No less enchanting is Camping Antiparos. Pitch up under a tangled canopy of cedars or find a secret spot in the site's bamboo field. Okay, so the facilities are a touch basic but, to be honest, that's part of the place's charm. Theo can show you grainy footage of music festivals and football matches that took place here back in the seventies; an endless summer of music and flares, afros and super-8 glare. Maybe the stoned ghosts of those hippies are still lurking somewhere or gazing up at the enormous 400-year-old giant cedar twisting its stairway to heaven, but music and free-spiritedness is still a feature, with Theo organising festivals and impromptu jam sessions for visiting troubadours.

There are three main beaches on Antiparos: the nearest is to be found through the dunes and vanilla-scented scrub. And if you like to don your nothing in particular for beachwear, then you're in luck – this first beach is of the naturist variety. But if people decked out in their birthday suits give you the willies, then head for the beach beyond the windmill, just past the edge of town. The site's restaurant is a honeypot of homemade indulgence, so a stay without a night or two sampling their fare would be remiss. Kindly Mrs Kalygros, when she's cooking, is well known for secretly pressing homemade biscuits into your hot, sticky palm, too; it would be rude to refuse, wouldn't it? It's also a tranquil place to sit and chat, or simply to sit and listen, like the Greeks do, to the melancholic chords of the bouzouki.

COOL FACTOR The campsite oozes 'escape' and the management couldn't be more friendly.

WHO'S IN Tents, campervans, caravans – yes. Pets – by arrangement.

ON SITE Myriad options for pitches: under the trees, in the reed fields. Bamboo huts also available to hire. Launderette, 24-hour hot water, mini-mart, bar, self-catering facilities, plus what must be some of the best home-cooking in Greece.

OFF SITE Check out the nightly open-air Cinema Oliaros (228 406 1717) up on Mr Pantelakis's rooftop; it's a wonderful way to watch your favourite films. Sea-kayaking is available through the aptly named Argonauts Blue Sea Kayaking (228 406 1364; .argonautsblue.com). Charter the old schooner, Alexandros, helmed by Captain Antonis (228 406 1273). The boat takes you around the neighbouring island and hidden bays and includes a BBQ lunch.

FOOD & DRINK If the wonderful squid stuffed with rice and raisins at the campsite restaurant isn't enough, then head off for some seafood that probably swam past you earlier in the day at Taverna Yorgis (228 406 1362) on the main street.

GETTING THERE Take the 4-hour ferry (€29) from Piraeus (Athens) to Paros (or a domestic flight from Athens to Paros), then catch the 5-minute shuttle boat to Antiparos at the tip of the island. The site is a 10-minute walk from the harbour.

OPEN May–end September.

THE DAMAGE Adults €6–€8; child (4–12 yrs) €3–€4; tent rental €2; car €2. Reservations not required.

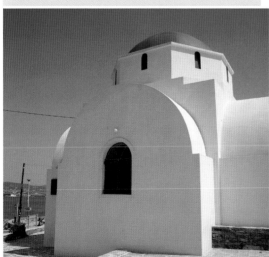

useful words and phrases

ENGLISH	PORTUGUESE	SPANISH	FRENCH	DUTCH
campsite	parque de campismo	un camping	un camping	camping
pitch	alvéolo	una parcela	un emplacement	kampeerplaats
large/small/family tent	tenda grande/pequena/familiar	una tienda grande/pequeña/familiar	une grande/petite tente/tente de famille	kleine/grote/familie tent
facilities	instalações/serviços	unas instalaciones	le bloc sanitaire	badkamers
toilets	casas-de-banho	unos aseos	les toilettes	toiletten
showers	duches	unas duchas	les douches	douches
washing-up/laundry sink	lavandaria/tanque	un fregadero/lavadero	un bac lave vaisselle/lave linge	afwas/wasplek
drinking water	água potável	agua potable	l'eau potable	drinkbare water
beer	cerveja	una cerveza	une bière	bier
wine	vinho	un vino	du vin	wijn
sleeping bag	saco-cama	un saco de dormir	un sac de couchage	slaapzak
campfire	lareira	una hoguera	un feu de camp	kampvuur
train	comboio	un tren	un train	trein
car	carro	un coche	une voiture	auto
petrol (unleaded)	gasolina (sem chumbo)	gasolina (sin plomo)	l'essence (sans plomb)	benzine (ongelood)
diesel	gasóleo	diesel	diesel	diesel
bicycle	bicicleta	una bici	un vélo	fiets
left	esquerda	izquierda	à gauche	links
right	direita	derecha	à droite	rechts
straight on	em frente/a direito	todo recto	tout droit	rechtdoor

GERMAN	ITALIAN	SLOVENIAN	CROAT	GREEK
Campingplatz	un campeggio	kamp	kamp	Κάμπινγκ (Camping)
Zeltplatz	una piazzola	postaviti	postaviti, razapeti	Θέση για σκηνή (Thési gia skiní)
ein kleines/grosses/ Familien-Zelt	una tenda grande/piccola/ familiare	velik/majhen/družinski šotor	veliki/mali/obiteljski šator	Μεγάλη/Μικρή/Οικογενειακή σκηνή (Megáli/mikrí ikogeniakí skiní)
Sanitärbereich	i servizi	ugodnosti, ponudba	sadržaji	Παροχές (Parochès)
Toiletten	i bagni/WC	WC, toaleta	WC, toaleti	Τουαλέτες (Toualètes)
Duschen	le doccie	tuši	tuševi	Ντούς (Doùs)
Abwaschwanne/ Wäschereiwanne	la lavanderia/il lavello	pomivanje/odtočni jašek pri pranju	Pranje/umivanje/Praonica rublja	Πλυντήριο/Σκάφη (Plintírio/skáfi)
Trinkwasser	acqua potabile	pitna vod	voda za piće	Πόσιμο Νερό (Pósimo neró)
Bier	la birra	pivo	pivo	Μπύρα (Bíra)
Wein	il vino	vino	vino	Κρασί (Krasí)
Schlafsack	un sacco a pelo	spalna vreča	vreća za spavanje	Σλίπινγκ μπαγκ (sleeping bag)
Lagerfeuer	il falò	taborni ogenj	logorska vatra	φωτιά (Fotià)
Zug	il treno	vlak	vlak	Τρένο (Tréno)
Auto	l'automobile	avto	auto	αυτοκίνητο (Aftokínito)
Benzin (bleifrei)	la benzina (verde)	bencin	bezolovno (gorivo)	Βενζίνη (αμόλυβδη) Venzíni (amólivdi)
Diesel	il gasolio	diesel	dizel	Πετρέλαιο (Petréleo)
Fahrrad	una bicicletta	kolo	bicikl	Ποδήλατο (Podílato)
links	a sinistra	leva	lijevo	Αριστερά (Aristerá)
rechts	a destra	desna	desno	Δεξιά (Deksiá)
geradeaus	avanti dritto	naravnost	ravno	Ευθεία (Efthía)

useful words and phrases

ENGLISH	PORTUGUESE	SPANISH	FRENCH	DUTCH
Hello	Olá	Hola	Bonjour	Hallo
How are you?	Como está?/Como estás? (formal/informal)	Cómo está?Cómo estas? (formal/informal)	Comment allez-vous?/ Comment ça-va? (formal/ informal)	Hoe gaat het?
Do you speak English?	Fala ingles?/Falas ingles? (formal/informal)	Habla inglés?/Hablas inglés? (formal/informal)	Est-ce-que vous parlez anglais?/Est-ce-que tu parles anglais? (formal/ informal)	Spreekt u Engels?/Spreek je Engels? (formal/informal)
Why not?	Porque não?	Por qué no?	Pourquoi pas?	Waarom niet?
Sorry, I don't speak [… whatever language].	Desculpe, não falo português.	Lo siento, no hablo español.	Désolé, je ne parle pas français.	Sorry, ik spreek geen Nederlands.
Some of my best friends are […nationality]	Alguns dos meus melhores amigos são portugueses.	Algunos de mis mejores amigos son españoles.	Quelques-uns de mes meilleurs amis sont français.	Sommige van mijn beste vrienden zijn Nederlanders.
What's the local tipple?	Qual é a bebida típica da região?	Quál es la bebida típica por aquí?	Qu'est-ce qu'on boît ici?	Wat drinken jullie hier graag?
Cheers!	Tchim-tchim (pron.: tcheen-tcheen)	Salud!	Santé!	Proost!
Mmm, that tastes lovely.	Humm, sabe muito bem.	Mm, es muy sabroso.	Mmm, c'est délicieux.	Hmm, dat smaakt heerlijk.
I am lost!	Estou perdido/perdida!	Me he perdido!	Je suis perdu!	Ik ben de weg kwijt!
Help!	Socorro!	Socorro!	Au secours!	Help!
The bill, please.	A conta, por favor.	La cuenta, por favor.	L'addition, s'il vous plaît.	De rekening alstublieft.
It's all Greek to me.	Isso para mim é chinês.	Me suena a chino.	C'est du chinois pour moi.	Ik versta er geen moer van.
Aren't you a little overdressed for beach volleyball?	Não estão demasiado vestidos para jogar voleibol de praia?	No vas demasiado vestido/a para jugar a vóley playa?	Est-ce-que tu n'es pas un peu trop couverte pour le beachvolley?	Ben je niet wat warm gekleed voor beach volleybal?

GERMAN	ITALIAN	SLOVENIAN	CROAT	GREEK
Hallo	Salve, ciao	Živjo	Zdravo	Γειά σου (Yá soo)
Wie geht es?	Come stai/state? (formal/informal)	Kako si?	Kako si?	Τι κάνεις? (Ti kánis?)
Sprechen Sie Englisch?/ Sprichst du Englisch? (formal/informal)	Parla inglese?	Govorite angleško?	Da li govoriš engleski?	Μιλάς Αγγλικά? (Milás aglika?)
Warum nicht?	Perché no?	Zakaj ne?	Zašto ne?	Γιατί όχι? (Ghiatí óchi?)
Ich spreche kein Deutsch.	Mi dispiace, non parlo italiano.	Oprostite, ne govorim slovensko.	Oprosti, ne govorim hrvatski jezik.	Λυπάμαι, δεν μιλάω Ελληνικά. (Lipáme, then miláo eliniká.)
Einige meiner besten Freunde sind deutsch.	Alcuni dei miei migliori amici sono italiani.	Nekaj mojih najboljših prijateljev je slovencev.	Neki od mojih najboljih prijatelja su Hrvati.	Μερικοί από τους καλύτερους φίλους μου είναι Έλληνες. (Merikí apó tous kalíterous fílous mou íne élines.)
Was trinkt man hier?	Cosa si beve da queste parti?	Katera je vaša lokalna alkoholna pijača?	Koje je lokalno alkoholno piće?	Ποιό είναι το τοπικό ποτό? (Pió íne to topikó potó?)
Prost!	Grazie, molto gentile!	Na zdravje!	Živjeli!	Γειά μας (Yá mas!)
Hmm, das ist lecker.	Mmm, è delizioso.	Mmm, to je zelo okusno.	Mmm, to je veoma ukusno.	Μμμ, είναι πολύ νόστιμο. (Mmm, íne polí nóstimo.)
Ich habe mich verlaufen!	Mi sono perso!	Sem zgubljen/a!	Izgubio/la sam se!	Έχω χαθεί (Ého hathí)
Hilfe!	Aiuto!	Na pomoč!	Pomoć!	Βοήθεια! (Voíthia!)
Die Rechnung bitte.	Il conto, per favore.	Račun, prosim.	Račun, molim.	Το λογαριασμό παρακαλώ. (To logariasmó parakaló.)
Ich verstehe nur Bahnhof.	Non capisco un acca.	To je zame španska vas.	To je sve špansko selo za mene.	Δεν καταλαβαίνω τίποτα.(Den katalavéno tipota.)
Bist du nicht zu warm angezogen für Beachvolley?	Non sei un tantino elegante per una partita di beach volley?	Ali nisi malo preveč oblečen za odbojko na mivki?	Nisli li malo previše obučen/a za odbojku na pijesku?	Δεν είσαι πολύ καλά ντυμένος για μπιτς βόλευ? (Den íse polí kalá ntiménos gia 'beach volley'?)

index

acknowledgements

Cool Camping: Europe (2nd edition)

Series Concept and Series Editor: Jonathan Knight

Editor: Martin Dunford

Researched, written, and photographed by:
Andrew Day, Sophie Dawson, Keith Didcock, David
Jones, Sam Pow, Paul Sullivan, James Warner Smith,
Richard Waters and Penny Watson.

Designers: Kenny Grant, Diana Jarvis

Proofreader: Leanne Bryan

Index: Helen Snaith

Editorial Assistants: Andrew Day, David Jones, James
Warner-Smith

Published by: Punk Publishing, 81 Rivington Street,
London, EC2A 3AY

UK Sales: Compass, Great West House, Great West
Road, Brentford TW8 9DF; 020 8326 5696;
sales@compass-ips.london

All photographs included in this book have been licensed
from the authors or from the campsite owners except
the following: Termas da Azenha (p.30–31) © Daniela
Meester; Yurt Holiday Portugal (p.32–35) © Hannah
McDonnell (www.lushplanet.com); Park Grubhof
(p.238–241) © Kerstin Joensson, Walter Schweinoester
and Robert Stainer. Further additional photographs kindly
supplied by Rui Teimao.

Front cover photo: Camping Domaine des Mathevies,
France © Michael Mann (michaelmannphotography.com)

No photographs may be reproduced without permission.
For all picture enquiries, please contact
enquiries@coolcamping.co.uk

Maps © MAPS IN MINUTES™
Reproduced with permission.

The publishers and authors have done their best to ensure
the accuracy of all information in Cool Camping: Europe,
however, they can accept no responsibility for any injury,
loss or inconvenience sustained by anyone as a result of
information contained in this book.
Punk Publishing takes its environmental responsibilities
seriously. This book has been printed on paper made from
renewable sources and we continue to work with our
printers to reduce our overall environmental impact.
A BIG THANK YOU! Thanks to everyone who has
emailed with feedback, comments and suggestions.
It's good to see so many people at one with the Cool
Camping ethos. Go forth and camp, one and all!

OTHER BOOKS YOU MAY LIKE:

Cool Camping France

Featuring 100 exceptional
campsites in France

Cool Camping Deutschland

60 sensational campsites
around Germany
(German language edition)

Available from www.coolcamping.co.uk